AFRICA'S DEADLIEST CONFLICT

AFRICA'S DEADLIEST CONFLICT

MEDIA COVERAGE
OF THE HUMANITARIAN
DISASTER IN THE CONGO
AND THE UNITED NATIONS
RESPONSE, 1997–2008

WALTER C. SODERLUND, E. DONALD BRIGGS,
TOM PIERRE NAJEM, BLAKE C. ROBERTS

WLU PRESS
WILFRID LAURIER
UNIVERSITY PRESS

This book has been published with the help of a grant from the Canadian Federation for the Humanities and Social Sciences, through the Aid to Scholarly Publications Program, using funds provided by the Social Sciences and Humanities Research Council of Canada. Wilfrid Laurier University Press acknowledges the financial support of the Government of Canada through the Canada Book Fund for its publishing activities.

Library and Archives Canada Cataloguing in Publication

Africa's deadliest conflict : media coverage of the humanitarian disaster in the Congo and the United Nations response, 1997–2008 / Walter C. Soderlund ... [et al.].

Includes bibliographical references and index.
Issued also in electronic formats.
ISBN 978-1-55458-835-0

1. Congo (Brazzaville)—History—Civil War, 1997—Press coverage—United States. 2. Congo (Brazzaville)—History—1997–. 3. War in mass media. 4. Press—Influence. 5. Humanitarian assistance—Congo (Brazzaville). 6. United Nations—Congo (Brazzaville). I. Soderlund, W.C. (Walter C.).

DT546.284.A37 2012   967.2405'4   C2012-904262-5

Electronic monograph.
Issued also in print format.
ISBN 978-1-55458-879-4 (EPUB).—ISBN 978-1-55458-878-7 (PDF)

1. Congo (Brazzaville)—History—Civil War, 1997—Press coverage—United States. 2. Congo (Brazzaville)—History—1997–. 3. War in mass media. 4. Press—Influence. 5. Humanitarian assistance—Congo (Brazzaville). 6. United Nations—Congo (Brazzaville). I. Soderlund, W.C. (Walter C.).

DT546.284.A37 2012   967.2405'4   C2012-904263-3

Cover design by Sandra Friesen. Front-cover image by Mikkel Ostergaard/Panos. Text design by James Leahy.

© 2012 Wilfrid Laurier University Press
Waterloo, Ontario, Canada
www.wlupress.wlu.ca

This book is printed on FSC recycled paper and is certified Ecologo. It is made from 100% post-consumer fibre, processed chlorine free, and manufactured using biogas energy.

Printed in Canada

Every reasonable effort has been made to acquire permission for copyright material used in this text, and to acknowledge all such indebtedness accurately. Any errors and omissions called to the publisher's attention will be corrected in future printings.

No part of this publication may be reproduced, stored in a retrieval system, or transmitted, in any form or by any means, without the prior written consent of the publisher or a licence from the Canadian Copyright Licensing Agency (Access Copyright). For an Access Copyright licence, visit http://www.accesscopyright.ca or call toll free to 1-800-893-5777.

RECYCLED
Paper made from recycled material
FSC   FSC® C103567

Contents

List of Tables and Maps vii
Acknowledgements ix
The Authors xi
Introduction xv

1. The Congo: Understanding the Conflict 1
2. The UN Response: From ONUC to MONUSCO 19
3. Mass Media, Public Awareness, and Television News Coverage of the Congo 41
4. *New York Times* Framing of the Second Congo War 65
5. *New York Times* Framing of the Third Congo War 91
6. Media Coverage of the Congo Wars: An Overall Assessment 121
7. Peacekeeping in the Age of R2P 141
Conclusion: The Impact of Mass Media on "The Will to Intervene" 159
Postscript: An Update on Events 165

Appendix: Descriptive Language 171
Notes 179
References 195
Index 227

List of Tables and Maps

Tables

Table 3.1a: Network TV Coverage of the Second Congo War, by Year   53
Table 3.1b: Network TV Coverage of the Third Congo War, by Year   54
Table 3.2: Number of Stories Containing Empathy- or Distance-Producing Visuals, 1997-2008   55
Table 3.3: Evaluation of European and UN Peacekeeping Operations in the Third Congo War, by Year   55
Table 3.4a: Major Sources and Number of Times Used during the Second Congo War, by Year   56
Table 3.4b: Major Sources and Number of Times Used during the Third Congo War, by Year   57
Table 3.5: Use of Positive and Negative Descriptors, 1997-2008   58
Table 6.1a: *New York Times* Coverage of the Second Congo War, by Type of Content, by Year   125
Table 6.1b: *New York Times* Coverage of the Third Congo War, by Type of Content, by Year   125
Table 6.2a: *New York Times* Coverage of the Second Congo War, by Dateline, by Year   126
Table 6.2b: *New York Times* Coverage of the Third Congo War, by Dateline, by Year   126
Table 6.3: Number and Percent of Intervention-Supporting and -Discouraging Items during the Third Congo War, by Year   128
Table 6.4: Percentage of *New York Times* Darfur and Congo Coverage, by Type of Content   129
Table 6.5: Percentage of *New York Times* Darfur and Congo Coverage, by Dateline   130
Table 6.6: Percentage of *New York Times* Darfur and Congo Coverage, by Source of Content   131

List of Tables and Maps

Maps

Africa   xiii
Democratic Republic of the Congo   xiv

Acknowledgements

Africa's Deadliest Conflict is the third in a series of books coming out of the Department of Political Science at the University of Windsor that deal with the complex intersection of humanitarian crisis and the role played by mass media in prodding the international community toward some form of meaningful action. The first of these, *Humanitarian Crises and Intervention* (2008), dealt with ten crises in the post-Cold War period of the 1990s, beginning with Liberia and ending with East Timor, and in between examining such humanitarian disasters as Somalia, Angola, Haiti, and Rwanda. The second, *The Responsibility to Protect in Darfur* (2010), assessed the early impact of the developing "Responsibility to Protect" (R2P) norm on the conflict-beset western region of Sudan. Two of the authors of this book, Professors Soderlund and Briggs, in addition to having focused on international intervention in their PhD dissertations written in the 1960s, were co-authors of both these books. In 2008 they enlisted two former students (one now the head of the department) to join them in the current undertaking on the Congo. The result was an interesting combination not only of young and old, but of varying approaches to research, and the process of researching and writing the book has been a rewarding learning experience for all involved.

In bringing this book to fruition, the Faculty of Arts and Social Sciences, under the leadership of Dean Cecil Houston, and the University of Windsor's research arm, under the leadership of Vice-President Ranjana Bird, have all provided valuable assistance to us along the way, as did students in a graduate course taught by Professors Briggs and Soderlund in the fall of 2009, and one taught by Professor Soderlund in 2011, upon whom were tested a number of our ideas regarding the Congo's woes. Likewise, commentators and audiences at two 2010 paper panel presentations of material dealing with television coverage of the Congo (the Midwest Political Science Association and the Association for Third World Studies) prompted us to sharpen our arguments on a number of

Acknowledgements

key points. Two perceptive reviews commissioned by the publisher led us to make some significant organizational changes which improved the manuscript significantly. James Leahy did a superb job of copy editing. And a special note of thanks to Ryan Chynces, the acquisitions editor at Wilfrid Laurier University Press, for his continued support throughout the project, and to managing editor Rob Kohlmeier who presided over a speedy publication. Thanks go as well to the Canadian Federation for the Humanities and Social Sciences' Aid to Scholarly Publications Program for its generous grant to Wilfrid Laurier University Press that made it all happen.

As with virtually all research we did not begin with a blank page. We are particularly indebted to Filip Reyntjens, who was interviewed in the summer of 2010 by Professor Najem. Insights gleaned from the interview, as well as his key work, *The Great African War*, are reflected in the following pages. We have also benefited immeasurably from the work of the numerous other scholars, journalists, and practitioners cited throughout the book, which has informed us on such diverse issues as the roots of societal conflict, the Congo's history, media effects, and the UN's and the international community's responsibility to respond to humanitarian crises. In turn, we hope that our efforts will in some way broaden the understanding of an urgent and complex problem and will prompt others to continue in the search for solutions. Please note that all of the views expressed in this book, including any omissions, errors, or oversights, are the responsibility of the authors.

Walter C. Soderlund, E. Donald Briggs, Tom Pierre Najem,
Blake C. Roberts

Windsor, Ontario
March 2012

The Authors

Walter C. Soderlund (PhD, University of Michigan, 1970) is Professor Emeritus in the Department of Political Science at the University of Windsor. He has a long-standing interest in intervention, beginning in the late 1960s with research for his PhD dissertation, "The Functional Roles of Intervention in International Politics." He has also worked extensively in the area of international communication, where his focus has been on the Caribbean, especially the way in which events in Cuba and Haiti have been portrayed in North American media and the possible impact of this coverage on US foreign policy. He is the author of *Media Definitions of Cold War Reality* (2001) and *Mass Media and Foreign Policy* (2003) and co-author of *Humanitarian Crises and Intervention: Reassessing the Role of Mass Media* (2008), *The Responsibility to Protect in Darfur: The Role of Mass Media* (2010), and *Cross-Media Ownership and Democratic Practice in Canada* (2012).

E. Donald Briggs (PhD, University of London, 1961) is Professor Emeritus of Political Science at the University of Windsor, where he taught international relations and African politics from 1963 until his retirement in 1999. His interest in intervention and mass media dates back to his PhD dissertation, "The Anglo-French Incursion into Suez, 1956," which analyzed press opinion regarding the legality of the 1956 Suez invasion. Among his publications are *Media and Elections in Canada* (1984), *The Zapitista Rebellion in Chiapas, 1994* (2003), *Humanitarian Crises and International Intervention: Reassessing the Role of Mass Media* (2008), and *The Responsibility to Protect in Darfur: The Role of Mass Media* (2010). For many years he was the coordinator of the WUSC (World University Service Canada) program at the University of Windsor, in which capacity he was responsible for sponsoring fifteen refugee students from conflict-ridden countries in Africa to come to Canada.

The Authors

Tom Pierre Najem (PhD, University of Durham, 1997) is the Department Head of Political Science at the University of Windsor and an Associate Professor specializing in International Relations, Comparative Politics of the Developing World, and Middle East Politics. His most recent research interests have been in the field of conflict resolution, and he is the project manager of the Jerusalem Old City Initiative, a major international track-two diplomatic proposal. His publications include *Lebanon's Renaissance: The Political Economy of Reconstruction* (2000); *Good Governance in the Middle East Oil Monarchies* (2003) (co-editor with M. Hetherington); and *Lebanon: The Politics of a Penetrated Society* (2011). He has previously held academic posts at the University of Durham (UK) and Al Akhawayn University (Morocco).

Blake C. Roberts worked in journalism for thirteen years, eight of them with the Canadian Broadcasting Corporation. He has been an assignment editor, producer, reporter, videojournalist, and anchor. He holds a BA from the University of Western Ontario, an MA from the University of Windsor, and is completing his PhD at Wayne State, all in political science. He studies the role of the news media in political development and conflict, two areas he has examined first-hand in the Philippines and Egypt. He continues to work as a freelance journalist.

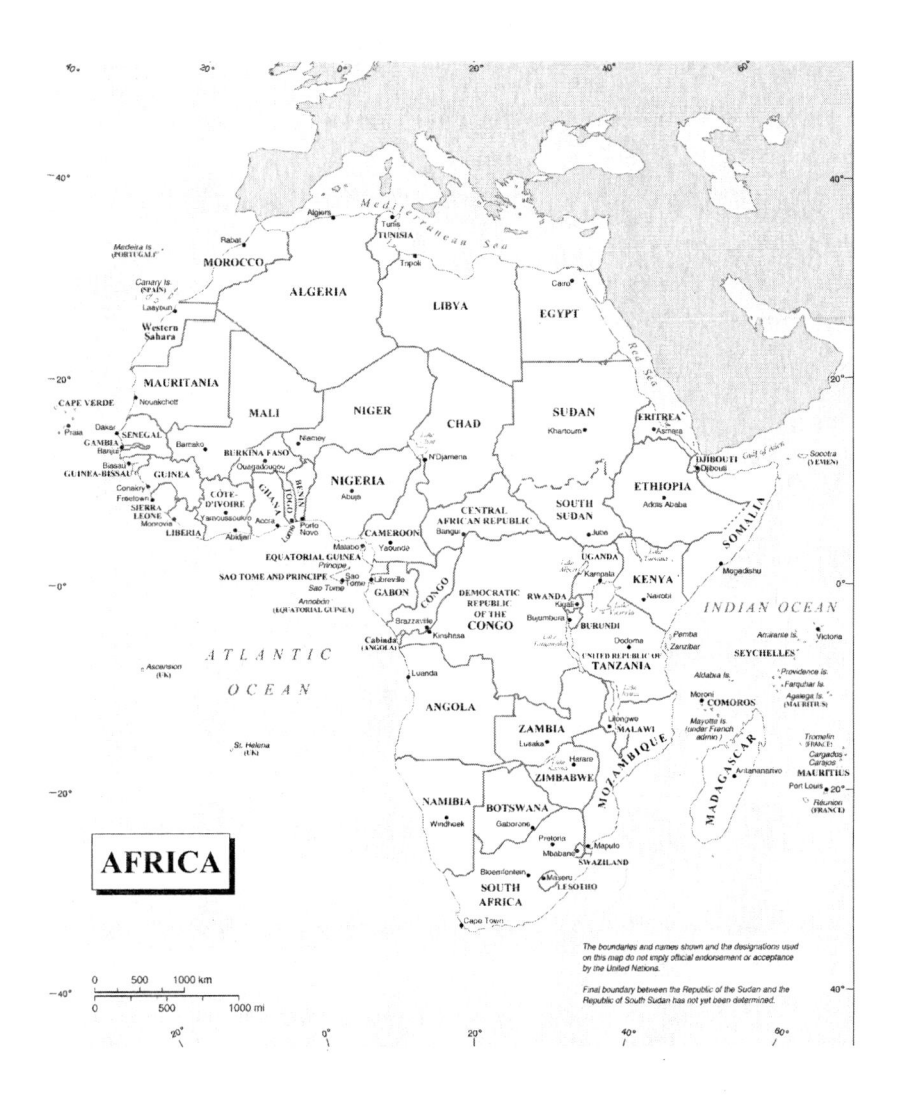

DEMOCRATIC
REPUBLIC OF THE
CONGO
National capital
District capital
City, town
Major airport
International boundary
District boundary
Main road
Secondary road
Railroad
0 100 200 300 km
0 100 200 mi
CENTRAL AFRICAN REPUBLIC
SUDAN
UGANDA
CONGO
RWANDA
BURUNDI
UNITED REPUBLIC OF TANZANIA
ZAMBIA
MALAWI
ANGOLA
Cabinda (ANGOLA)
ATLANTIC OCEAN
PROVINCE ORIENTALE
EQUATEUR
NORD KIVU
SUD KIVU
MANIEMA
KASAI ORIENTAL
KASAI OCCIDENTAL
BANDUNDU
BAS-CONGO
KATANGA
Katanga Plateau
Lake Victoria
Lake Albert
Lake Kyoga
Lake Edward
Lake Kivu
Lake Tanganyika
Lake Mweru
Lake Bangweulu
Lake Malawi
Lac Mai-Ndombe
Rukwa
Bangui
Zongo
Bangassou
Gbadolite
Bondo
Libenge
Businga
Gemena
Aketi
Buta
Isiro
Watsa
Faradje
Mungbere
Juba
Gulu
Impfondo
Imese
Lisala
Bumba
Ituri
Bunia
Ouesso
Basoko
Banalia
Bafwasende
Basankusu
Beni
Kampala
Jinja
Bolomba
Yangambi
Kisangani
Butembo
Kasese
Ekoli
Mbandaka
Liranga
Boende
Ubundu
Peneluta
Lubutu
Goma
Kigali
Ikela
Punia
Inongo
Bolobo
Kutu
Bukavu
Butare
Bandundu
Kole
Lodja
Kindu
Kilembwe
Uvira
Bujumbura
Kibombo
Makobola
Brazzaville
Kinshasa
Ilebo
Bena
Mwekа
Lusambo
Mamba
Kasongo
Kigoma
Pointe-Noire
Kenge
Bulungu
Kikwit
Tabora
Boma
Matadi
Mbanza-Ngungu
Lubao
Kongolo
Kananga
Mbuji-Mayi
Kabalo
Kalemie
Tshikapa
Kabinda
Mpala
N'zeto
Mwene-Ditu
Manono
Moba
Kahemba
Kabamba
Sumbawanga
Kapanga
Pweto
Moliro
Kamina
Luanda
Mbeya
Saurimo
Dilolo
Kolwezi
Kasenga
Likasi
Lubumbashi
Luena
Solwezi
Kipushi
Lobito
Sakania
Ndola
Ubangi
Uele
Kibali
Mongala
Congo
Lopori
Lulonga
Oubangui
Aruwimi
Tshuapa
Lomela
Lomami
Lualaba
Luilaka
Ulindi
Lukenie
Kasai
Kwilu
Sankuru
Kwango
Lukuga
Luvua
Lulua
Zambeze
10°
15°
20°
25°
30°
5°
0°
The boundaries and names shown and the designations used on this map do not imply official endorsement or acceptance by the United Nations.

Introduction

In early December 2010, as we were researching the final sections of this book, our local newspaper, *The Windsor Star*, ran a long editorial on the Congo entitled "The Congo's Plight: A Tragedy without End." In that editorial a Congolese clergyman was quoted as saying that "populations in the east of the country remain subject to a regime of growing terror and insecurity—violence, massacres, sexual violence and murder are recorded every day." It was further reported that 15,000 women had been raped in eastern Congo over the previous year, that 36,000 people died every month (roughly the population of a medium-sized Ontario town), and that the total death toll over the past decade approached 5.5 million, with another 2 million displaced from their homes. All this tragedy had been coupled with an ineffectual international response: in the words of *New York Times* columnist Nicholas Kristof, "The barbaric civil war being waged there is the most lethal conflict since the Second World War ... Yet no humanitarian crisis generates so little attention per million corpses, or such a pathetic international response" (both as quoted in *Windsor Star*, 2010, Dec. 6: A6). The editorial ended with a question: "Where are the world leaders acknowledging that this horrific crisis needs to be addressed?" Our interest in undertaking this project could not have been stated more clearly.

First published as an essay, "The Coming Anarchy" in 1994, Robert Kaplan's description of the disintegration of Sierra Leone in the early 1990s presages developments that were to ravage the Congo beginning two years later: "Sierra Leone is a microcosm of what is occurring, albeit in a more tempered and gradual manner, throughout West Africa and much of the underdeveloped world: the withering away of central governments, the rise of tribal and regional domains, the unchecked spread of disease, and the growing pervasiveness of war" (2000: 9). It is now clear that the Congo's near decade-and-a-half-long humanitarian disaster, like the atrocities in Darfur that took place during some of

Introduction

the same time period, presented a newly "Responsibility to Protect" (R2P)-equipped United Nations with challenges that it failed to address with anything approaching adequate responses. The question as to why this was the case remains. Was the concept of R2P fundamentally flawed or, as Kaplan's analysis would suggest, were the first two crises that occurred after it had gained acceptance by the international community simply too complex for any international involvement to bring under control?

The answer is a combination of the two explanations, and in the following chapters we hope to traverse in brief the troubled history of the Congo, examine the record of three UN attempts to deal with the fallout of that troubled history, as well as investigate the role of mass media in generating public support in developed nations either to support a UN-led intervention or to lead one authorized by the UN Security Council. Admittedly this is an ambitious a task to undertake within the covers of one volume. Nevertheless, in the following chapters we have attempted to weave together these disparate threads. To neglect any one of them would leave readers with an incomplete appreciation of the magnitude of the task entailed in controlling both inter- and intra-state violence in a country that, if it had ever gained control over all its territory, had clearly lost that control by 1997. In short, the story of why the Congo is mired in a never-ending humanitarian disaster and why the international community has been unable to mitigate that disaster to any meaningful extent does not provide easy answers. Readers should not expect to find in these pages a set of simplistically packaged solutions.

To understand how major US mass media, both television and print, treated the seemingly endless conflict in the Democratic Republic of the Congo (DRC) and what role they played in the international response, readers need to have background information relating to three major areas.

First, it is important to understand that the Congo is both blessed and cursed. It is blessed with size (the third-largest country in Africa), combined with an abundant range of valuable mineral resources and "more than one-quarter of the continent's total" supply of water (Williams, 2007: 1033). In turn, since the 1880s it has been cursed by a history of colonial subjugation as brutal as experienced anywhere (Hochschild, 1998); a tribally diverse population that complicates "nation-building" efforts; a chaotic independence process (including a near-fatal involvement in the Cold War), followed by three decades of rule by a corrupt, self-serving dictatorship; not to mention ambitions on the part of various neighbours, if not to poach territory, at least to enrich themselves at the Congo's expense (see Prunier, 2009).

Introduction

Jason Stearns tells us in his work on the Congo that "the historical legacy weighs heavily on the present" (2011: 330). Thus, chapter 1 is intended first to serve as a primer in Congolese history up to and including the Third Congo War, which started in 2003, drawing connections between the past and present. Second, the chapter gives readers two frameworks—regional analysis and "protracted social conflict" (Azar, 1990)—by which to understand the extremely difficult set of circumstances that coalesced in the Congo in the mid-1990s to create and sustain a horrific set of conflicts.

A second background component, reviewed in chapter 2, is the record of United Nations involvement in the Congo. This involvement began in 1960 at the time of Congolese independence, and it is arguable that had the UN peacekeeping force, Opération des Nations Unies au Congo (ONUC), not been dispatched at that time, the Congo would not have survived the initial tumultuous post-colonial period, or at least not survived with its present borders. For example, Ali Mazrui argues that anarchy nearly destroyed the nascent state and that "it was saved by the United Nations" (1998: 236). Chapter 2 also reviews the aborted UN mission Operation Assurance in 1996, which had been authorized to deal with the Rwandan Hutu refugee crisis in eastern Congo but was never dispatched (see Soderlund et al., 2008: chap. 8). Assessed as well in this chapter are the contributions of the Mission des Nations Unies en République démocratique du Congo (MONUC). The mission was authorized for deployment in 2000 but did not make a real contribution to peacekeeping until 2003, following a serious outbreak of violence in the Ituri region which necessitated the temporary deployment of a French-led European "stabilization force."

The third necessary background component is reviewed in the first section of chapter 3 and deals with the role of mass media in crisis intervention decision making—the mobilization of public opinion in favour of international intervention, generally thought of in terms of the "CNN effect." In understanding the role of mass media in this particular conflict, it is important to note that, as was the case with the involvement of the United Nations, US media were interested in the Congo long before the events of 1990s. In 1960, for example, the Congo accounted for over twelve pages of entries in *The New York Times Index*, second only to the United States itself (Berkeley, 2001, Aug. 2: A20). The longevity of the conflict indicates its "intractable" nature and thus brings into play Susan Moeller's concept of "compassion fatigue" (1999).

The crucial task performed by mass media in engaging public awareness and influencing interpretations of far-off crises is examined through the concepts of *agenda setting* and *framing*, vital components in the

Introduction

shaping of public opinion related to international actions, including the possibility of a military intervention. Also reviewed in this chapter are contemporary evaluations of media coverage of the current conflict in the Congo, which may be said to have been set in motion in 1994 by the large-scale movement of Rwandan Hutu refugees (some of whom were armed and had participated in that country's deadly genocide) into the border region of eastern Congo. The conflict was intensified in 1996 by the continuing cross-border efforts on the part of this group to destabilize the new government of its former homeland. This in turn led to what can best be described as a Rwandan military invasion of the Congo that began in late 1996 and resulted in the overthrow of long-serving dictator Mobutu Sese Seko in early 1997.

Chapter 3 continues with an explanation of the methods used to study and evaluate media coverage. In terms of research questions, we were primarily interested in assessing the cumulative effects of media coverage: (1) was coverage of the Congo sufficient to place the conflict on the policy agenda of foreign policy decision makers? (2) was it sufficient to keep it on that agenda over the long duration of the conflict? and (3) in terms of framing, did it tend to promote or discourage international involvement to bring the violence under control? In addition, we wanted to explore differences in Congo coverage on the part of television and print media as well as to compare Congo coverage with that generated by the crisis in Darfur, which competed for media attention at the same time as the Third Congo War began to take shape in the spring of 2003.

The final section of chapter 3 details US broadcast television news coverage of the conflict on prime-time newscasts on the ABC, CBS, and NBC networks during both the Second and Third Congo Wars. Quantitative data are presented on the performance of the "alerting function" (the number of stories aired) as well as on the nature of how the conflict was framed (the "evaluative function"), the latter based on in-depth examinations of visuals and descriptive language found in stories. Actual descriptive language used in stories with respect to major actors in the conflict, as coded by a panel of professors, is found in the appendix to the book.

Chapters 4 and 5, in turn, examine in detail *New York Times* coverage of the conflict: chapter 4 focuses on the Second Congo War, while chapter 5 deals with the Third. In these chapters conflict framing is analyzed through year-by-year narrative accounts of issues covered, as well as advice given to international decision makers based on important items of news content such as front-page stories, editorials, op-ed articles and letters to the editor, as well as selected news items dealing with ongoing international peacekeeping efforts.

Introduction

Chapter 6 first compares the performance of television and print journalism in covering the two Congo wars, and in so doing adds quantitative data relative to *New York Times* coverage on dimensions such as overall number of stories, type of content, support for international intervention, as well as where and by whom content originated. This quantitative data is combined with the qualitative material from the previous two chapters to give readers an overall evaluation of how adequately the *New York Times* covered the Congo. Congo coverage is then compared with the newspaper's treatment of the Darfur crisis that erupted in 2003 and began to attract significant media attention in 2004 (see Sidahmed, Soderlund, and Briggs, 2010). A range of factors leading to what is clearly lesser media interest in the Congo are reviewed and evaluated.

Chapter 7 offers our insights regarding how the problem-filled Congo peacekeeping experience may have affected the application of developing norms that relate to the international community's response to humanitarian disasters, subsumed under the concept of "Responsibility to Protect" (R2P). Under R2P the international community was tasked with three responsibilities: the *Responsibility to Prevent* massive abuses of human rights, the *Responsibility to React* in instances where a state either cannot or will not protect its population from mass killing, and the *Responsibility to Rebuild* war-torn societies following international intervention, all as brought forward in the 2001 report of the International Commission on Intervention and State Sovereignty (ICISS, 2001). We will comment on key aspects of each of these responsibilities, both generally and specifically as to how they applied to the Congo.

As the title of the book indicates, since the waning years of the last century the Congo has been the scene of "Africa's deadliest conflict," a conflict that has caused the greatest loss of life anywhere on earth since the end of the Second World War; unfortunately the deadly violence has not ended (Willis, 2011, Sept. 19). The final chapter provides an overall assessment of how media coverage may have affected the less-than-effective international response to the crisis. Central to this discussion is the idea of the lack of a "will to intervene" and the role of mass media in prodding hesitant governments into meaningful action (see Chalk et al., 2010). The book concludes with a postscript intended to update readers to ongoing developments in the Congo.

The Congo: Understanding the Conflict

PART ONE: HISTORICAL CONTEXT

Background

The Democratic Republic of the Congo (DRC) borders Tanzania, Burundi, Rwanda, Uganda, and the newly minted Republic of South Sudan to the east, Zambia and Angola to the south, the Central African Republic to the north, and the Republic of the Congo to the west; it is currently the third-largest country on the continent. In that it shares borders with nine countries, many of which have serious security issues of their own, it serves as a critical link between eastern and western components of what a decade ago Filip Reyntjens referred to as Africa's "war zone" (2000: 6). In addition to being a huge country (about the size of Western Europe), it is extraordinarily well endowed with natural resources, especially in its eastern provinces. Its tragedy, apart from the violence that has plagued its entire history as an independent state, is that these resources have never been harnessed in a way to provide much benefit to the majority of its population, estimated in 2010 to be around 71 million. Ironically, it may be argued that had the Congo possessed fewer resources, it might well have enjoyed greater security, stability, and perhaps even prosperity over the years. The fact that it enjoyed none of these, and has suffered in particular from a series of extremely bad political leaderships, presents a puzzle on which the following pages seek to cast some light.

Jason Stearns makes the point that "the lack of responsible politics, is not due to some genetic defect in Congolese DNA, a missing 'virtue gene,' or even something about Congolese culture. Instead, it is deeply rooted in the country's political history" (2011: 215). Robert Edgerton, on the other hand, notes that while no other country in the world can probably match the Congo in terms of the unremitting horrors which have occurred there, it "is hardly the only country in the world to have become known for its troubled history and uncertain future" (2002, XII). There is ample evidence, in any case, that on a world scale the Congo's deficiencies are almost unsurpassed. On the UN Human Development Index for 2010, for example, the DRC ranked 168th, next to last, only Zimbabwe finishing lower (*Human Development Indicators*, 2010). The historic continuities of exploitation and misrule in the Congo are consequently worth recalling in brief form as a background to, if not necessarily the sole cause of, the continued violence which has beset the country over the last decade and a half.

The details of the Congo's pre-colonial history are beyond the scope of this study, but for those who might be under the impression that the area was a kind of political and cultural vacuum prior to the appearance of Europeans, it is worth noting that it contained a number of well-developed and extensive political and commercial entities which did not in fact differ all that much from contemporary European states. When the Portuguese discovered the mouth of the Congo River in 1482, they came into contact with the Kingdom of the Kongo. The Kingdom governed extensive territories divided into provinces through a well-established hierarchical political system (see Leslie, 1993: passim). It was not a system which was entirely peaceful or stable, given the frequent rivalries for power and interregional conflicts, but in that respect it did not differ greatly from its European counterparts either.

A second extensive empire was that of the Lunda people. Their territory stretched from the Atlantic to the Great Lakes, including what is today the province of Katanga. They were primarily people of trade, whose commercial reach extended from the cities of Luanda and Benguela on the Atlantic to Dar es Salaam on the Indian Ocean (Bustin, 1975: see map, 19).

Europeans were, if nothing else, more technologically advanced than the inhabitants of such African states and thus were able to impose their will on the latter for their own purposes when that was thought necessary. Trade relations established between the Portuguese and the Kingdom of the Kongo in the late fifteenth century, for example, quickly became a matter of purchasing slaves to provide "cheap labor for plantations on nearby Portuguese islands and, subsequently, the Americas"

(Leslie, 1993: 6). This was a potent source of conflict, as were Portuguese efforts to Christianize the Kongolese as well as land issues such as those that developed between Kongo and the neighbouring Portuguese colony of Angola in the sixteenth century. It was, Winsome Leslie maintains, "friction [over land that] culminated in open conflict that effectively destroyed Kongo military and economic power and, indeed, the kingdom itself" (1993: 6).

The situation for local inhabitants and political authorities became even less comfortable when the territory of the Congo was seized as a personal possession by King Leopold II of Belgium in 1885 (see Nzongola-Ntalaja, 2002a: 1). Roger Anstey notes that African political thought, and political and social institutions were seriously undermined "at the commencement of Belgian rule" (1966: 25), and Bustin adds that with respect to the Lunda empire, for instance, "from the very first day it passed under Leopold's control [it drifted] into a state of marginality from which it never really re-emerged" (1975: 41). Edgerton summarizes the situation: "The impact of the European presence—slavers, traders, and missionaries—on most Congolese societies was profound" (2002: 23). But he also points out that the exploration and exploitation of the Congo was not restricted to Europeans. While the Portuguese were trading for slaves in the western Congo and sometimes

> a bit further into the interior, the eastern Congo had fallen prey to white-robed Arab slavers, who not only traded for slaves and ivory, but also stole them at the point of a gun ... The result was misery and death for millions of Congolese and a life of slavery for hundreds of thousands more. A few years later, a savage war would be fought to determine whether Arabs or King Leopold's forces would control the Congo's riches. (Edgerton, 2002: 79)

After King Leopold emerged victorious in that contest in 1893, the real exploitation of "the Congo's riches" began.[1]

The Congo under Leopold's Rule

The European seizure of the African continent, like the centuries-old pattern of conquest and reconquest in other parts of the world (as well as within Africa itself), resulted in the disruption, if not the destruction, of indigenous customs and systems and the virtual enslavement of peoples considered inferior and uncivilized. There were, of course, significant variations in the methods of subjugation and overlordship employed by the various European powers, but there can be little question that the devastation visited upon the Congo was among the worst experienced anywhere on the continent, especially during Leopold's terrorist rule (see Hochschild, 1998: passim; Young, 1965: 6).

Leopold had been able to persuade other European leaders at the 1884–85 Berlin Conference which divided Africa among them that "his ambitions for the nation were purely philanthropic." He wanted, he maintained, to wipe out the slave trade, spread civilization, encourage missionaries, and establish a free-trade zone open to all merchants (hence the name "Congo Free State" under which the territory was to be known). These ambitions "triggered unanimous applause" at the Berlin Conference (Wrong, 2000: 42–43). The reality was to be considerably different:

> Far from being a free traded zone, the colony's very *raison d'etre* was to make money for the king. Anxious to attract the foreign capital needed to build railways and bridges, Leopold divided part of the country into concessions held by companies in which he held a 50 per cent stake, with exclusive rights over tracts of forest, ivory, palm oil and mineral wealth. The rest of the country was defined as Crown property, where state agents enjoyed a business monopoly. Independent merchants who ventured into the area in search of ivory found their way physically blocked by Leopold's officials. (Wrong, 2000: 44)

It may be presumed that other European governments were less than enchanted with Leopold's broken promises, but it was the methods allowed and encouraged by him which eventually disgusted even colonialists, not themselves noted for their humanitarianism. Leopold himself stated his philosophy in the matter quite openly: "In dealing with a race composed of cannibals for thousands of years, it is necessary to use methods which will shake their idleness and make them realize the sanctity of work" (as quoted in Hochschild, 1998: 118). Consequently, the collection of ivory and natural rubber was pursued by Leopold's functionaries with the active assistance of the (by 1900) 19,000-strong Force publique.[2] Their methods included the use of chains, whips (the *chicotte*, made of dried hippopotamus hide), the practice of holding workers' families hostage against the fulfillment of production quotas, amputation of hands,[3] and sometimes executions (see Hochschild, 1998: chaps 8–10). Hochschild notes that "the death toll was particularly high among porters forced to carry heavy loads long distances. Of three hundred porters conscripted in 1891 ... for a forced march of more than six hundred miles to set up a new post, not one returned" (120). Following Leopold's reluctant transfer of control over the Congo to the Belgian government in 1908 (which yielded at last to continued pressures from other European colonizers), officials estimated that "*the country's population had been halved since the beginning of the Congo Free State,* implying that 10 million people either died or fled the Congo ... What had been laughingly dubbed the Congo Free State was an exploitative system premised on forced labour, terror, and repression" (Wrong, 2000: 45-46; italics added).[4]

Wrong echoes the earlier assessment of Roger Anstey, but the latter's account was somewhat more nuanced in that he found there had been several positive achievements during Leopold's reign of terror:

> The Congo Independent State lasted for twenty-four years. They were years of epic achievement. The period saw the exploration of the Upper Congo, the campaign against the Arabs and the Arab slave trade, the attempt to establish the Congo State on the Upper Nile, the occupation of Katanga, the establishment of some sort of European administration in many areas, the opening up of lines of communication, the extension of Christian missionary operations: the period also witnessed in the rubber-bearing regions of the forest, the subordination of sound administration to the obtaining of the maximum possible quantity of wild rubber. This came to involve atrocities on a large scale, atrocities which led to the inception of the Congo Reform campaign, and this was the principal immediate reason why Belgium took over the Congo in 1908. (1966: 2)

Ironically, the majority of these *achievements* betray attitudes prevalent in the early 1960s when Anstey wrote: they were achievements from a European rather than Congolese perspective and provided small compensation to the indigenous peoples for the atrocities committed.

The Congo under Belgian Rule

The official transfer of control over the Congo from the king to the elected government of Belgium resulted in little immediate change in the conditions there, despite high expectations to the contrary (see Anstey, 1966: 21). In the first place, Belgium's principal objective, like that of most colonial governors, was that "the Congo budget should be balanced," and that it should provide "economic opportunities for her children" (41-42). The extraction of wealth from the territory thus continued to be a priority. Second, unlike Portugal, Britain, and France, Belgium had no experience in administering a colonial empire. There were no archives of reports or developed legal and operational guidelines on which to rely (see Wrong, 2000: 51). Third, and perhaps most important, there was no easy or quick way to replace Leopold's Congo personnel (49); the same people tended to remain in the same positions and operate in the same long-established manner. The Congo thus continued for some time to be "strongly marked by the Leopoldian legacy as a system of economic exploitation, political repression and cultural oppression" (Nzongola-Ntalaja, 2002a: 26).

Progress *was* made, however, if slowly and erratically. The 1911 report of a commission appointed to study the impact of the new regime acknowledged that there were still instances of abuse of power "for personal gain," but, according to Anstey, there was also success in suppressing intertribal warfare and fewer instances of "naked oppression of Africans," even if the "really important aims of what was understandably a pedestrian-enough native policy were far from being generally attained" (1966: 48, 55). Infrastructural improvements were undertaken after the First World War—roads, ports, and the extension of electricity. Edgerton also acknowledges that "many Congolese greatly improved their standard of living, and much improved health care led to far greater chances of survival for their children and longer, happier lives for adults" (2002: 169).

On the negative side of the ledger, Belgian officials could still (until 1955) order the flogging of Congolese more or less at will (Wrong, 2000: 164); education beyond some agricultural and vocational training was deliberately avoided lest a Congolese elite emerge that might demand independence (Edgerton, 2002: 166); and, despite denials, racial segregation continued to be maintained "both by law and social practice" (Edgerton, 2002: 178-79). It was not, Wrong maintains, until "*after the Second World War that the Belgian Congo became 'a colony like the others'*" (2000: 49; italics added).

Probably the single greatest failure of the Belgian administration, however, was the lack of any significant preparation for independence, even after 1945. The French in Africa were by that time working assiduously to incorporate their African possessions into a "Greater France," including granting them limited representation in the French Chamber of Deputies, and the British were, however reluctantly, allowing themselves to be hauled in the direction of independence by a gradually expanding process of "Home Rule." However, the Belgians apparently considered until at least the late 1950s that such moves would not be necessary in the Congo for many years to come, if ever. In the words of Crawford Young, "The [Belgian] colonial behemoth, fixed on a given course by a ponderous set of procedures, was incapable of altering direction, even when it perceived that it was lumbering toward the precipice" (1965: 32).

The instances in which colonies have been said to be adequately prepared for independence are few and far between, but there is little doubt that the Congo was one of the least prepared of all. Wrong notes that "the Belgians did virtually nothing to pave the way for independence, expected in 1955 to be decades off" (2000: 50). Young maintains that it was not until 1957 that "there was a gradual realization that the sands were running out," and even then it was assumed that "decolonization would remain under full Belgian control" (1965: 36–37). But, he adds, "in eighteen months the Congo surged to independence on a tide over which neither colonizer nor colonized had much control" (1965: 4). At the time of the official hand-over (July 1, 1960), Congolese political parties had been in existence for only two years (Weiss, 1967: 3); there was a total of seventeen university graduates in the country (Wrong, 2000: 50); and few if any Congolese had served in any administrative capacity above the level of clerk. The result, as Jean-Claude Willame explained, was that "within a month after independence, the ... administration had collapsed with the departure of 10,000 Belgian civil servants, the major political parties were disintegrating, and the Force Publique, the military arm of the colonial administration, was in full rebellion" (1972: 1–2).[5]

In the chaos and violence that followed, abuses were inflicted on Belgian army officers who remained in nominal control of the Force publique and on those European civilians who remained in the country (only about 3,000 out of 29,000 by July 10, according to Edgerton). Priests and nuns, in particular, were subjected to humiliation and worse. Under the leadership of Moise Tshombe, Katanga, the richest of the Congo's provinces, also declared its succession. This added significantly to the overall turmoil and prompted the Belgians to dispatch paratroopers "to secure Leopoldville's airport and to protect the Congo's Europeans by whatever means they found necessary" (Edgerton, 2002: 185–86). This in turn was the cause of the UN's first intervention in Congolese affairs, a matter which will be explored in greater detail in the following chapter.

By way of summation one might say that Belgian rule in the Congo covered no one with glory. While conditions under the Belgian administration were less harsh than those imposed by Leopold, the net result of fifty years of Belgian rule was that by the time of independence the colonial power left a mass public totally uninitiated in the basic principles of self-government and an indigenous political elite that was largely uneducated, angry, and resentful. Such qualities were clearly manifested in the country's first prime minister, Patrice Lumumba, and contributed to problems in working with Belgian officials. Thus, in spite of numerous improvements in the country's infrastructure, the realities of neglect to the human side of development frustrated hopes for an orderly transition of power. It is difficult to quarrel with Michela Wrong's conclusion:

"For seventy-five years, from 1885 to 1960, Congo's population ... marinated in humiliation. No malevolent witch-doctor could have devised a better preparation of the coming of a second Great Dictator" (2000: 57).

The Congo under Mobutu's Rule

That "Great Dictator" was, of course, Joseph-Désiré Mobutu, who renamed himself Mobutu Sese Seko. Mobutu, described by Georges Nzongola-Ntalaja as "the *big man*, a new king for the Congo, and the true successor to King Leopold as the owner of the country and its resources" (2002a: 141; italics in original), ruled the country from 1965 until months prior to his death in 1997. He reached that position after serving as an army colonel and an aide to incoming Prime Minister Patrice Lumumba at the time of independence. He was appointed army chief of staff by Lumumba and then seized power for himself in the ensuing struggles for control of the country (see Young, 1965: 447-52; Wrong, 2000: 63-68; Edgerton, 2002: 198-201; Nzongola-Ntalaja, 2002a: 141-43).

Michela Wrong describes Mobutu as a shrewd and brave politician who favoured the financial carrot over the stick of repression to cement his rule. By institutionalizing corruption, he created a new elite (termed the "Big Vegetables") who were beholden to him personally for their positions, incomes, houses, automobiles, essentially everything. He viewed the national treasury, as well as international companies and financial institutions operating in the Congo, as personal resources to be exploited to finance spending excesses like constructing an elaborate new palace in the jungle, purchasing extensive real estate in Europe, and paying off supporters and adversaries alike. Edgerton estimates that during his thirty-two years in power he diverted between $4 and $15 billion of state funds into his own bank accounts (2002: 211). Such practices are of course by no means unique among autocrats, perhaps African autocrats in particular, but in Wrong's view, as expressed in her excellent study of Mobuto, *In the Footsteps of Mr. Kurtz*, "no other African autocrat had proved such a wily survivor. No other president had been presented with a country of such potential, yet achieved so little. No other leader had plundered his economy so effectively or lived the high life to such excess" (2000: 4).

Part of the explanation for his long survival was the fact that he was regarded in Washington, and the West generally, as an essential bulwark in central Africa against the menace of communism. If the price were right—and it usually was—he was prepared to allow Congolese territory to be used for whatever purpose his backers thought appropriate. It was, for instance, a very useful base from which to supply another anti-communist Cold War client of the United States, Jonas Savimbi, in his guerrilla war against the Soviet/Cuban-supported government in neighbouring Angola (Wrong, 2000: 196).

Unpalatable allies are tolerated, of course, as long as they are thought to be necessary. But as the Cold War began to thaw in the late 1980s Mobutu's usefulness faded with it, and Western patience with him (except that of France) began to ebb. Factors other than global political concerns played a part in his eventual downfall, however. First, Mobutu's prolonged financial excesses led to internal economic chaos bordering on collapse—for example, a national debt of over $14 billion and an inflation rate that reached 9,800 percent in 1994. Second, toward the end of his rule he was weakened by prostate cancer and unable to control the army as effectively as had been the case earlier: his generals became increasingly independent, and, as the troops often went unpaid, they became more and more undisciplined and exploitive of the population.[6] Third, as will be reviewed in greater detail in the following chapter, the aftermath of the 1994 Rwandan genocide had a significant, and decisive, impact on Mobutu's survival. The presence in the eastern Congo of thousands of Hutu refugees hostile to the new Tutsi-dominated regime in Rwanda prompted Rwandan President Paul Kagame in 1996 to organize and lend military support to the ongoing efforts of long-time opponent Laurent-Désiré Kabila to overthrow Mobutu. It is significant that the United States refused to come to Mobutu's assistance in the vicious war that ensued, as it would probably have done twenty years earlier.[7] The Rwandan/Kabila campaign brought about Mobutu's fall in the spring of 1997 (see Wrong, 2000: esp. chaps 4-10; Reyntjens, 2009: chap. 4).[8]

Wrong's succinct summary of Mobutu's rule is worth noting: "In Mobutu's hands, the country had become a paradigm of all that was wrong with post-colonial Africa. *A vacuum at the heart of the continent delineated by the national frontiers of nine neighbouring countries, it was a parody of a functioning state.* Here the anarchy and absurdity that simmered in so many sub-Saharan nations were taken to their logical extremes" (2000: 10; italics added).

PART TWO: THE CONGO CONFLICT, 1996 AND BEYOND

Framing the Conflict

The year 1996 is often cited as marking the beginning of the series of conflicts in the Congo, which at the time of writing still show no sign of coming to a conclusion, though this is more a matter of choosing a convenient place to begin analysis than a clear and indisputable fact. But in any case, since 1996 there have been three more or less distinct periods to the conflict, each with its own dynamic and complexity (see Weiss and Carayannis, 2005): (1) the First Congo War (1996–97), which saw the overthrow of President Mobutu and the coming to power of Laurent-Désiré Kabila; (2) the Second Congo War (1998–2002), also known as Africa's World War (see Prunier, 2009), in which armies from at least six African countries participated; and (3) the Third Congo War (2003 and onwards), which, despite a peace agreement in 2002 that in theory ended formal regional participation, saw the continuation of violence in many regions of the country, especially in the eastern region, where there is still little evidence of change for the better. As we noted in the Introduction, it is estimated that an astounding 5.5 million people have perished in the Congo, making it the most deadly conflict the world has known since the Second World War. The conflict in the Congo cannot be described as wholly domestic or interstate. Stearns has likened it to "layers of an onion [in that it] contains wars within wars. There is not one Congo war, or even two, but at least forty of fifty different interlocking wars. Local conflicts fed into regional and international conflicts and vice versa" (2011: 69; see also Turner, 2007; Lemarchand, 2009a; Prunier, 2009; Reyntjens, 2009; and Autesserre, 2010).

The Congo conflict is not, however, unlike a number of others which have plagued the developing world toward the end of the twentieth century and the first decade of the twenty-first. Writing in 1990, international relations and conflict-resolution theorist Edward Azar explained: "Many conflicts currently active in the underdeveloped parts of the world are characterized by a blurred demarcation between internal and external sources and actors. Moreover, there are multiple causal factors and dynamics, reflected in changing goals, actors and targets. Finally, these conflicts do not show clear starting and termination points" (1990: 6).

Azar also noted that these conflicts differed from our traditional understanding of the roots of conflict as arising out of material interests, big-power politics, and territorial rivalry. Instead, he argued, most contemporary conflicts are about "developmental needs expressed in terms of cultural values, human rights, and security." While the majority of these conflicts "may remain dormant for a period of time and then suddenly break into open warfare" (2), they invariably revolve around questions of *communal identity*, which he identified as "political groups whose members share ethnic, religious, linguistic or other cultural identity characteristics" (7).

Azar's important contribution to the understanding of contemporary conflict was contained in *The Management of Protracted Social*

Conflict, published in 1990. It focused heavily on the internal dynamics of societies, especially the relationship between *communal* or *identity groups* and the state, which he believed drive conflict (14). He specifically identified the deprivation of human needs as the underlying source of protracted social conflict, and the state's failure to address those needs as leading to outbreaks of violence. As he explained, protracted social conflict is most likely to occur in those parts of the world characterized by multi-communal compositions and by "incompetent, parochial, fragile and authoritarian governments that fail to satisfy basic human needs" (10).

There is certainly much merit in viewing the enduring Congo morass (as well as other conflicts in the region such as those in Rwanda and Burundi) from the perspective of the protracted social conflict model. Indeed, much of the violence that continues to wreak havoc there can be understood within this context. This is especially true with respect to the eastern Congo (including North Kivu, South Kivu, North Katanga, and Ituri), where underlying communal problems, which grew in intensity in the years leading up to 1996, spun out of control from that point onward and took on a life of their own.[9] The shorthand explanation for this sort of occurrence has frequently been *ethnicity*, or even *tribal rivalries*. William Zartman, for instance, observes that "it is the collapse of old orders, notably the state that brings about the retreat to ethnic nationalisms as the residual, viable identity" (1995: 1). Similarly, Ali Mazrui points out that even in cases where the state has not collapsed, "in post-colonial Africa, ethnicity continues to be a major factor influencing the success or failure of the state" (1998: 237).

Many scholars, however, are uncomfortable with the "e" word, because it is thought to smack of racism reminiscent of colonial times and/or because it is regarded as a simplification that obscures complex social factors.[10] Consciously used as shorthand for the latter, ethnicity is a useful and not inaccurate term, since ethnic identity is a natural pole around which members of society may coalesce or which may be used by ambitious leaders to build group cohesion in support of their particular cause. In cases like the eastern Congo, though, it must be recognized that many of the difficulties are local/community ones—what Séverine Autesserre refers to as "bottom-up tensions" (2010: esp. chap. 4). These revolve around issues of land, citizenship, resources, access to status and power, and indigenousness, though they may often assume an "ethnic" colouring. It was issues of this kind that were ignited by the breakdown of state power during the latter years of Mobutu's rule and with which no subsequent government has been able to deal successfully.

While Azar's protracted social conflict theory assigns a somewhat secondary role to the external dimensions of intrastate conflict, it is essential to our understanding of the regional influences at work in the Congo as well as elsewhere. Oliver Ramsbotham and colleagues suggest that, in general, the end of the Cold War has made possible a *regionalization* of world politics, raising in importance that "level of explanation" (2009: 98). Probably nowhere does this hold more true than in the Great Lakes region of Africa. Though Mobutu was already under considerable pressure from a variety of sources, it is arguable that he would not have fallen had it not been for Rwandan, and subsequently other states', military intervention. In fact, from 1996 through 2002 the fate of the Congo was largely in the hands of its various neighbours, and even when their armed forces retired from the fray at the end of 2002, their influence in the form of proxy militia sponsorship continued. Thus, further examination of the interplay of regional forces is important to our comprehension of the Congo wars.

The First Congo War (1996-1997)

The consensus among scholars is that the immediate origin of the First Congo War was the Rwandan civil war of 1990-94 between the Hutu-dominated government of the time and Ugandan-based, Tutsi-dominated rebel group, the Rwandan Patriotic Front (RPF), led by Paul Kagame. The conflict climaxed in the 1994 genocide in which approximately 800,000 mostly Tutsi Rwandans were butchered.[11] When the RPF took control of Kigali and subsequently the government of Rwanda in July 1994, approximately 1.5 million Hutus fled across the border into the eastern Congo and settled in refugee camps stretching along the Congo-Rwandan/Burundi border from north of Goma to south of Bukavu. Among the refugees were members of the notorious Interahamwe militia that had carried out the genocide, as well as members of the former Rwandan government thought to have orchestrated the massacres, and members of the former Rwandan armed forces. Although Reyntjens maintains that no more than 15 percent of the refugees were involved in the genocide (2009: 20-21), the Interahamwe and their allies were able to gain control of the refugee camps and use them as bases from which to attack Kagame's new government in the hope of overthrowing it and recapturing power in Kigali (Stearns, 2011: 34-44).

The Rwandan government saw the Interahamwe and the Hutu refugees as a significant threat and accordingly increased its involvement in the Congo (see Jones, 2001: 150-51). This included, ultimately, an armed invasion aimed at deposing Mobutu, who had had close ties with the former Rwandan regime and who was considered sympathetic to the ambitions of the refugees. In cooperation with Laurent-Désiré Kabila, a long-time Congolese Marxist rebel leader (Stearns, 2011: 69, 86-88), the Rwandan military created the Alliance des forces démocratiques pour la libération du Congo-Zaïre (AFDL). The AFDL included a number of small (and even obscure) opposition movements, which on their own would probably not have been able to do more than harass Mobutu's regime, but became a potent force when joined together and, particularly, when bolstered by significant military support from Rwanda and its allies, Uganda and Angola. In 1995 *The Economist* described the Congolese state as "just a Zaire-shaped hole in the middle of Africa" (quoted in Stearns, 2011: 113). A year later, its army, weakened by long neglect and without a leader (Mobutu had left the country to seek medical treatment), was thoroughly demoralized and no match for the Rwandan-spearheaded forces. As previously noted, the United States refused to come to the aid of its erstwhile ally. The AFDL and its allies were consequently able to march across the country to seize Kinshasa and the reins of power. Laurent-Désiré Kabila named himself president of the Congo in May 1997, thus bringing the First Congo War to an end. Stearns observes that "Kabila came to power on the wings of a rebellion sponsored and, to a large degree, fought by other armies" (2011: 171), and few appear to contest that conclusion.

In its march across the Congo, the Rwandan military, one of the best armed in the region, conducted a bloody campaign against the fleeing Hutu refugees; Stearns offers a compelling account of their pursuit and killing across the interior of the country (2011: 133-44).[12] Rwanda also provided support to ethnic Congolese Tutsi (referred to as Banyamulenge) who were in conflict with indigenous Congolese groups in the eastern provinces. The reality was that Rwandan and Congolese Tutsi forces took control of most of the eastern area. This exacerbated existing bottom-up tensions caused in part by the arrival of the large refugee contingent and further displacements caused by marauding bands of thugs of various kinds.

The Second Congo War: "Africa's World War" (1998-2002)

Within a year of assuming power, Kabila fell out with his Rwandan sponsors. They had propelled him into the presidency but had also continued to occupy dominant positions in the Congolese army and to provide many civilian "advisers," in effect controlling the government in all meaningful respects. This was not a situation that any independent-minded leader could tolerate, nor was it likely to enhance

Kabila's popular support. The unravelling of the relationship, however, led Rwanda, together with Uganda and Burundi, to shift their backing to groups who were opposed to Kabila's rule. A new rebel compilation, the Rassemblement congolais pour la démocratie (RCD), was created.[13] It was dominated by Congolese Tutsis and initially led by a US-educated university professor, Ernest Wamba dia Wamba. Its sole aim was to overthrow Kabila. The emergence of this movement in turn alarmed others of the Congo's neighbours for a variety of reasons—geo-strategic and otherwise. Angola and Zimbabwe accordingly intervened on the side of Kabila, and Namibia, Sudan, and Chad did likewise, though they played a less significant role in the hostilities which followed.[14] At least six armies, however, were involved to varying degrees in Africa's World War, which needless to say meant that the Great Lakes region was submerged in even greater turmoil than it had previously experienced.

The external support for Kabila meant that only a perpetual stalemate could be achieved. Kabila held on to nominal power but had no control over large parts of his country, the eastern region in particular. In effect, the country was divided between the Kinshasa government and its allies on the one hand, and the rebels with their external backers on the other. This did not mean, however, that there were only two jurisdictions. The RCD, for example, promptly split into two groups, and Uganda helped to create the Mouvement de libération du Congo (MLC), led by businessman Jean-Pierre Bemba, which, with the strong backing of the Ugandan army, took control of large tracts of the northern Congo, while the residue of the RCD continued to control other areas.

Stability and order, not to mention personal safety, were now scarce commodities in most parts of the Congo, but the situation in the eastern provinces could only be described as one of complete disintegration. As Crawford Young explains:

> A pattern of permanent disorder in the eastern border regions took hold. Insurgent groups proliferated; some began as community self-defense militias (Mai Mai), while others formed as armed groups reflecting ethnic rivalries. Former Rwandan Hutu soldiers or youth militia, stained by their involvement in the genocide, operated from the sanctuary of the Congo, as did Ugandan rebel fragments. (2006: 307)

To this it should be added that none of these groups, government supporters, or rebel supporters was stable from one day to the next. Rather, they were like a cauldron of shifting and complicated alliances in which it was often impossible to know who was siding with whom and for what community, regional, national, or extra-Congo purpose.

The Congo: Understanding the Conflict

As far as the principal players' motives for their intervention in the conflict are concerned, Rwanda had the greatest and most direct interest, as has already been indicated. Kigali made it plain that it would not withdraw from the Congo until its government was willing, and able, to reign in the Interahamwe and render the border between the two countries secure. It is possible that this was not the full story, but for public consumption it was a credible one. There was some similarity, too, between Rwandan and other countries' interests. Many of these struggled with one or more insurgencies of their own, and prior to the First Congo War at least ten rebel groups from neighbouring states were using the Congo as a base from which to pursue their objectives at home (Stearns, 2011: 51). Mobutu, in fact, had knowingly harboured some of these groups when it served his political interests. But given the size and ruggedness of the territory in question, the porousness of the Congo's borders, and the weakness of both its administrative and military capabilities, it is likely that he could not have done much about these incursions in any case. Uganda, Burundi, and Angola, for instance, were all being challenged by rebel groups operating from the Congo, and the outbreak of the Second Congo War provided new or enhanced opportunities to seek their eradication.

But there were other motivations as well. Domestic considerations that had little to do with conditions in the Congo itself may also have played a part. In the case of Rwanda, for example, critics of Kagame's Tutsi minority-dominated regime charged that, to at least some extent, he used the border/Interahamwe issue as an excuse for maintaining near dictatorial rule in Kigali.[15] In addition, the eastern Congo's mineral resources—gold, diamonds, and coltan, not to mention valuable timber—were a perpetual temptation. In the absence of any significant control by Kabila, it was wealth for the taking, or wealth to be denied to those working to unseat governments in Luanda or Kampala or Harare. According to Ian Fisher and Norimitsu Onishi, at least Rwanda, Uganda, and Zimbabwe were guilty of appropriating Congolese resources for their own use and reluctant to surrender the privilege (2000, Feb. 6).

A final motivating factor relates to regional balances of power and traditional rivalries among the involved states. No country was anxious to see others benefit disproportionately from meddling in the Congo, and the only way to ensure this did not happen was to dive into the melee themselves and grab what they could before someone else got it. In other words, almost all of the Congo's neighbours had concerns that failure to join the game might mean the loss of important immediate or future opportunities, especially if the conflict should ultimately result in the country's dismemberment—an outcome that was widely predicted (see chapter 4 in this volume).

As we will note throughout this book, the wider international community watched developments in the Congo with a combination of alarm and misgiving. There was scarce sympathy for Kabila himself, and certainly no inclination to fly to his rescue. Key Western players like the United States, France, and Belgium were unhappy with the manner of his rule, which appeared to differ little from that of Mobutu (see Young, 2006: 306), and, in particular, with his intransigence concerning international investigations into the fate of tens of thousands of the Hutu refugees. On the other hand, there were clear humanitarian and well as strategic concerns. The UN, for its part, could scarcely ignore a conflict which was already widespread and deadly for millions of people and had every prospect of becoming more so. There appears, however, to have been little or no consideration of any form of international intervention, save on the diplomatic front.

Diplomatic efforts, however, met with a degree of success when the main protagonists fought to a stalemate by the summer of 1999 and agreed, under urging from members of the Southern African Development Community (SADC) and with the support of the international community in general, to sign the Lusaka Accords, calling for a ceasefire to be monitored by the United Nations (see chapter 2 for details of UN operations). At least partly because of Kabila's continuing lack of cooperation, however, little changed. Between 1999 and 2002 thousands of additional people lost their lives in continued fighting.

In January 2001, a disgruntled bodyguard assassinated Laurent Kabila. His son Joseph succeeded him and proved to be a more adept political leader than his father, even though he had not yet turned thirty years of age. By 2002 the warring parties were back at the negotiating table. Under the strong leadership of South Africa (the most powerful state in the region) peace talks held in that country between April and December 2002 led to the signing of a "comprehensive peace agreement." Its main provisions were for a power-sharing government in Kinshasa, elections to be held within two years, and the withdrawal of foreign forces from the country. This marked the official end of the Second Congo War.

The Third Congo War: Continuation of Violence in Eastern Congo (2003–2011)

The peace agreement brought relative calm to Kinshasa and other parts of the Congo, and the foreign armies did for the most part withdraw. But in the eastern provinces, what Prunier describes as "confused post-conflict violence" (2009: 353) continued without apparent interruption. It is here that Azar's theory of protracted social conflict is most applicable.

Many, if not most, of the problems in the eastern region stem from local causes, as was suggested earlier and emphasized by Séverine Autesserre's *The Trouble with the Congo* (2010). Involving issues such as land tenure and citizenship, these problems have deep historical roots; hence the protracted nature of the conflicts. These issues were exacerbated in the present conflict by the existence of predatory militias and outsiders like the Rwandan refugees. It should also be recognized that neighbouring states continued to interfere, sometimes militarily—Rwanda, for example, supported the insurrection led by Congolese Tutsi General Laurent Nkunda from 2004 until early 2009.

The more prolonged the conflict becomes, the more difficult it is to resolve. As Azar explains:

> Societies undergoing protracted social conflict find it difficult to initiate the search for answers to their problems and grievances. As the protracted social conflict becomes part of the culture of the ravaged nation, it builds a sense of paralysis which afflicts the collective consciousness of the population. An environment of hopelessness permeates all strata of society, and a siege mentality develops which inhibits constructive negotiation for any resolution of the conflict. (1990: 16)

A complicating factor is that once violence begins, a conflict becomes even harder to resolve. This is the case in eastern Congo, where rebel groups live off villages to survive, brutalizing their inhabitants and leaving them little option but to respond in kind or to flee elsewhere. The latter course of action creates additional problems as the newcomers impinge on territory and resources belonging to others and fall prey to malnutrition and diseases like malaria, measles, dysentery, and typhoid. Based on 2008 statistics (five years after the Congo war officially ended), 45,000 people were dying every month in the Congo, and the mortality rate, at 57 percent, was the highest in sub-Saharan Africa (Polgreen, 2008, Jan. 23). In addition, the level of sexual violence appears unparalleled.[16] Jason Stearns offered a sobering assessment of the situation:

> The story of the Congo wars is one of state weakness and failure, which has made possible the ceaseless proliferation of insurgent groups, still numbering twenty-nine ... These armed groups fight brutal insurgencies and counterinsurgencies that, as the United States discovered in Viet Nam and Iraq, are not so much about controlling territory as about controlling

civilians, who are brutalized in order to obtain resources and as retaliation for attacks by their rivals. (2011: 329)

It is difficult to describe these conditions in terms other than *a continuing humanitarian disaster*.

It is a situation, moreover, with which neither the Congolese army nor United Nations peacekeepers have so far been able to deal successfully. In theory it is the army which is supposed to extend state control and stability to the eastern region. However, it has not been up to the task, in part because, as a force made up of units from former rebel groups, it has lacked professionalism, discipline, and loyalty. In 2010 the UN reported that:

> the army is accused of having criminal networks that are pillaging resources and jeopardizing security in the mineral-rich east of the country. Some army officers, including the head of Congo's ground forces (General Gabriel Amisi), are allegedly using operations against rebels as a pretext to smuggle gold, tin ore and timber. Prioritization of personal economic interests by these officers has undermined the capacity of the armed force to execute its mandate. The officers are running criminal networks that have disrupted the chain of command, hindered the fight against illegal armed groups and put civilian lives at risk. (Kavanagh, 2010, Nov. 29)

UN peacekeeping, too, has been severely criticized. As one seasoned reporter put it, "despite more than 10 years of experience and billions of dollars, the peacekeeping force still seems to be failing at its most elemental task: protecting civilians" (Gettleman, 2010, Oct. 3). This will be discussed in greater detail in the next chapter.

We have pointed out that two different theoretical frameworks are needed to fully understand the Congo conflict: a regional level of analysis framework combined with the theory of protracted social conflict. The first emphasizes regional dynamics, having their roots in the Rwandan genocide; the second focuses on internal state dynamics, including the breakdown of governance under Mobutu and the impact of this, as well as continuous low-intensity warfare, on long-standing tribal/ethnic rivalries. While the regional level of analysis framework is primarily useful in understanding the First and Second Congo Wars, and the protracted social conflict theory for understanding the Third, as Stearns has pointed out, it is the interaction of the two (especially in eastern Congo) that captures the unique nature of the conflict.

The UN Response: From ONUC to MONUSCO

The UN has been deeply involved in Congolese affairs for most of that country's fifty years of independence. In truth, it has been one of the many parties involved in the shifting kaleidoscope of internal, regional, and international conflicts that has been the defining characteristic of Congolese life. Conversely, the Congo has provided, and is continuing to provide, what is arguably the severest test of the UN mandate to maintain a semblance of order in this fractious world. At this writing, it is by no means clear whether, in another fifty years, it will be possible to say that the UN has defined the Congo or that the Congo has defined the UN. Certainly their interaction has had profound implications for both. The UN's first venture into the Congo in 1960, while generally considered more successful than not, in fact presaged a great many of the problems later missions of the same type were to experience, and more than a few for which solutions are still wanting. For that reason, this seminal experience is worth reviewing in some detail.

ONUC: 1960–1964

Opération des Nations Unies au Congo (ONUC) was launched by Security Council (SC) Resolution S/4387 on July 14, 1960, precisely fifteen days after Belgium's formal transfer of power to Leopoldville's hastily assembled government. The resolution was a response to the urgent requests of President Joseph Kasavubu and Prime Minister Patrice Lumumba to Secretary-General Dag Hammarskjöld for assistance against alleged aggression by the former colonial power. The resolution studiously avoided using the word "aggression" and, further, refrained from any determination of threat to international peace and security. Thus, it is clear that from the outset the international consensus with respect to the situation differed sharply from that of the Congo's leaders. That this would continue to be a significant, if not central, problem in the UN's efforts quickly became apparent.

Unlike many peacekeeping operations undertaken by the UN in later years, ONUC was launched quickly: an advance party of Tunisian troops was in the Congo within twenty-four hours of the passage of Security Council Resolution 4387. It was quickly followed by contingents from Ethiopia, Ghana, and Morocco, and, because Hammarskjöld insisted that the force be representative of the UN membership as a whole, ultimately by units from Brazil, Canada, Ceylon (Sri Lanka), Denmark, India, Ireland, Liberia, Mali, Norway, Sweden, and Yugoslavia. A total of thirty countries participated directly in the mission in one way or another over the four-year lifespan of the mission. The force reached its maximum troop strength of just under 20,000 in July, 1961 (see Boulden, 1999: 44, note 9).

UN peacekeeping experience prior to 1960 was limited. Apart from three small observer missions in the Balkans and on the Indian-Pakistani border established during the early years of its existence, and two similar operations in Lebanon and Jordan in 1958—none of which constituted peacekeeping in any real sense—the only model for ONUC was the emergency force (UNEF) occasioned by the 1956 Suez Crisis. The latter had been a clearly defined, limited, and highly successful matter of sitting astride a border and ensuring a degree of honesty between parties who were antagonistic but who had already agreed to cease hostilities, thus allowing the diplomats time to work out more permanent solutions (Burns and Heathcote, 1963: chap. II).

The Congo operation obviously differed in a number of ways from UNEF, but in justice it could still reasonably be seen in July 1960 as a relatively simple matter of creating conditions which would allow the overt Belgian presence to be removed, and the fledgling regime in Leopoldville to begin establishing effective control over the vast country. Moise Tshombe's declaration of Katangan independence on July 11 complicated the picture, but that too might be attributed to the Belgian military presence and thus could be expected to dissolve with the latter's departure. In any case, internal political disputes, it was assumed, were not matters ONUC needed to address, except by providing the security necessary for the Congolese to deal with these issues themselves. The task thus appeared manageable enough.

The UN Response: From ONUC to MONUSCO

The differing perspectives of Prime Minister Lumumba and Secretary-General Hammarskjöld, however, resulted in unanticipated complications. From Lumumba's point of view, the UN's mission was simple and straightforward: expel the Belgians and put down Katanga's drive for independence. Hammarskjöld insisted, however, that while the UN was in the Congo to cooperate with Congolese authorities in the restoration of order, it must not become an instrument of the central government for the achievement of particular objectives (see Spooner, 2009: passim; Lefever, 1965: passim).

Katanga was the principal problem. The majority of independent Afro-Asian states, not to mention both Hammarskjöld and after him U Thant, were adamantly opposed to Katangese secession. Some took that position because they considered Tshombe a Belgian puppet created to ensure continued European control of the province's rich mineral resources. Belgium itself gave credence to this belief by announcing, after some vacillation, that "the Katanga position has Belgium's complete sympathy" (quoted in Gordon, 1967: 36). According to Lefever's very precise figures, it also proceeded to supply 114 army officers, and 117 other ranks, to command the Katangan military, plus another 58 officers in the service of the police (1965: 51-52). Others opposed the secession because they quaked at the thought of any precedent for challenging the integrity of inherited borders. Given the number of states in Africa for whom the latter issue was important at the dawn of independence, it was also a matter of concern for international peace and security in general.

Several weeks of negotiation with the Katangese leaders were required before UN forces were able to deploy in the province. And, having reluctantly allowed this, Tshombe "ceased all further cooperation with the UN" (Boulden, 1999: 30). Lumumba also was unhappy with the manner of the deployment—it had not been forceful or decisive enough—and accordingly announced that "the government and people of the Congo" had lost all confidence in the Secretary-General (Burns and Heathcote, 1963: 41).

The complexities of the overall Congo situation multiplied when the central government disintegrated and a number of pretenders to the throne emerged. It became, in fact, *the* classic case of "dammed if you do and damned if you don't," because any action, including none at all, was inevitably favourable to someone and unfavourable to someone else. When reasonable precautions were taken to prevent serious violence in Leopoldville after the Kasavubu-Lumumba split, they clearly favoured (though not necessarily intentionally) the former over the latter. When Leopoldville was restrained from mounting civil war against Katanga, the latter was favoured over the former. And when ONUC forced the expulsion of the Belgian mercenaries from Katanga, it favoured the centre over the province. There was no such thing as neutrality, as Major General Lewis MacKenzie was to bluntly point out many years later with respect to UN peacekeeping in Bosnia. He recounted how even transporting the dead and wounded of one faction to hospital was considered a hostile act to be resisted by force by other factions (MacKenzie, 1993: 157).

The neutrality/impartiality flag under which all UN peacekeeping operations fly is, however, a necessary political fiction. That, along with stated mandates which are sufficiently imprecise to allow radically different interpretations by political opponents, is what permits such operations to be undertaken in the first place. But it should not be supposed that proclaimed neutrality will endear those wearing blue helmets to the parties among whom they are attempting to mediate, or that their assignments can ever be as precise and straightforward as military minds would like.

In the case of the 1960s Congo, criticism of the UN force on the neutrality issue was based on a number of alleged sins of both commission and omission, but the principal bones of contention were the death of Lumumba and the military operations that eventually ended Katanga's attempted secession. The USSR in particular considered that Lumumba's escape from his UN-guarded home, as well as his capture and later execution by ANC forces, was a deliberate Western-generated ploy to remove a socialist-minded stalwart from the Congo picture and led to the protracted Soviet campaign to force the removal of Hammarskjöld.[1] It appears, in fact, that Soviet suspicions were not entirely unfounded. As early as 1965 Royal Institute of International Affairs researcher Catherine Hoskyns maintained that once Lumumba had left his protected premises, ONUC peacekeepers "all over the Congo were given orders 'to refrain from any interference in regard to Mr. Lumumba's movements or those of his official pursuers'" (quoted in Spooner, 2009: 115). Moreover, by his own admission, Lieutenant Colonel J.A. Berthiaume, the Canadian aide to UN force commander General Carl von Horne, advised the ANC on how and where to capture Lumumba (115–16).

In Katanga UN forces eventually undertook a series of military operations in response to continual harassment by Katangan personnel, including the construction of roadblocks from which UN forces were fired upon, and obstructionism as far as the expulsion of foreign mercenaries was concerned (Boulden, 1999: 40). These actions culminated on January 28, 1962, with Operation Grandslam, when U Thant had become convinced that Tshombe could not be satisfied through negotiations.

This was a full offensive against Katangan troops, carried out throughout the province and resulted in "Tshombe's surrender of Elizabethville in January, 1993, [and] signalled the end of the Katangan secession" (Dobbins et al., 2005: 15-17).

In the opinion of James Dobbins and colleagues, this "conquest of Katanga" (2005: 17) amounted to the abandonment "of all pretence of political neutrality" (15). At the time perhaps not many would have been prepared to openly accept that judgment, taking refuge instead in U Thant's explanation that ONUC was merely seeking "to regain and assure our freedom of movement, [and] to restore law and order," and that military means could be utilized if necessary to accomplish those ends (Boulden, 1999: 39). Fewer would probably quarrel with it today but at the same time would defend the necessity of ONUC's action, thus underlining the inherent truth in General MacKenzie's opinion about the paradox faced by UN peacekeepers each time they intervene in complex conflict situations.

ONUC pioneered a variety of other problems which would also become standard features of peacekeeping operations. For example, contingents arrived in the Congo with little of the equipment they were supposed to have, or with equipment quite unsuitable for the circumstances they faced. The Irish, for example, arrived wearing heavy winter uniforms, despite the fact that they would not have been wearing such clothing in midsummer even in Ireland (Spooner, 2009: 63). There were, inevitably, communications problems within a force consisting of speakers of at least a dozen different languages, and difficulties communicating with the Congolese because of the shortage of English-French bilinguals. More serious in terms of operational integrity was the problem of contingent commanders communicating directly with, and taking direction from, their home governments rather than the force commander or UN personnel. Kevin Spooner has detailed this phenomenon extensively with respect to Canadian contributions to ONUC (Spooner, 2009: 101-2, 156-57; see also Lefever, 1965: 183-88). In May 1961, for example, a planned use of Canadian personnel was aborted because protests to Ottawa that it was too risky resulted in the Canadian ambassador to the UN telling the Secretariat that Canadians would not participate in the mission (Spooner, 2009: 156). Later, following the settlement of the Katanga issue in early 1963, the Canadian government wished to withdraw or at least reduce the bilingual Signals Squadron which had been the "backbone of ONUC" operations, according to Brigadier Indar Rikhye (Spooner, 2009: 207). UN headquarters considered this alarmingly premature. Ottawa nonetheless dispatched its armed forces' director of signals to the Congo to make an independent determination of the need there (207).

There is no reason to think that Canada's behaviour in these respects was unique. Nor should any participant in peacekeeping operations be expected to behave differently. Governments, even those not noted for their adherence to democratic principles, are ultimately answerable for the safety and "good conduct" of their nationals, and that fact is not altered by their being seconded for international service. Indeed, the circumstances in which states would find it possible to surrender complete control of a portion of their armed forces to foreign, and largely unknown, control are difficult to imagine. Another abiding characteristic of humanitarian peacekeeping is therefore that it will always lack the unity of command that is both militarily and politically desirable. It must instead muddle through with perpetual uncertainty and continuous multi-dimensional negotiations with numerous centres of control concerning almost every facet of its operations. Too often, it seems, this is forgotten in discussions of UN peacekeeping efforts.

ONUC came to an end in June 1964. The question is, had it been a success? For most, the answer was uncertain. The geographical integrity of the country had been preserved, and what might have been a very bloody civil war had been prevented, but the reformulation of the ANC into a capable security force had scarcely begun. In Spooner's words, "ONUC's failure to use its presence to reform the Congolese military was lamentable" (2009: 212) and paved the way for the Mobutu dictatorship which began a scant two years later.

Operation Assurance

Mobutu's rule over the Congo was reviewed in the previous chapter. It has been suggested that had it not been for events external to the country, his dictatorship of thirty-plus years might have passed into the hands of equally corrupt successors, and the country continued a fractious but marginally stable existence for considerably longer (see Weiss, 1995: 159). As has already been indicated, it was the arrival of large numbers of Hutu refugees from Rwanda in 1994 that changed that assessment. The refugees promptly became an international *cause célèbre* in and of themselves, quite apart from the political and security ramifications of their presence in the Congo. Alarmed by the number of refugees, the deplorable conditions in which they were forced to live, and the escalating cross-border conflict, human rights activists began calling for an international observer force to be sent to the region.

A number of countries, notably France and Germany, also campaigned for a more robust military intervention (Hennessy, 2001: 12). France, indeed, "became increasingly shrill and insistent" on the matter, while maintaining stoutly that it did so only from the highest of humanitarian motives (Massey, 1998: 5). Most observers found it difficult to believe in French protestations of personal disinterest. France had, after all, been close to the former Hutu government of Rwanda, had trained and armed its forces, and contributed legionnaires to repulse RPF incursions in 1990 and 1993. Most offensive of all, it had launched Operation Turquoise during the heat of the genocide, an operation which many believed had aided the escape of large numbers of the guilty to the Congo (see Soderlund et al., 2008: chap. 5). Those of a suspicious turn of mind saw the French plan to use helicopters to lay down a trail of food, water, and medicine along corridors that would allow refugees to escape westward, deeper into the Congo (when all others were looking to arrange their return to Rwanda) as a self-interested scheme to ensure the fortunes of the Hutu extremists and to rescue Mobutu from serious difficulties at the same time (see Massey, 1998: 5). Needless to say, the possibility of Rwandan or AFDL acceptance of any such intervention was minimal—so obviously so that one cannot help wondering how France could have thought its proposition worth the predictable derision it generated. It could only have done so, one might surmise, from a deep desperation to regain some of its rapidly disappearing influence in central Africa.

France was not alone, however, in advocating some sort of mission to deal with the situation. Regional African leaders convened a summit in Nairobi on November 5, 1996, to consider the matter. Mobutu, however, refused to attend. The summit expressed "grave concern" about what it described as the "threat posed to peace and stability of the entire Great Lakes region," called for the "intensification of efforts towards voluntary repatriation of refugees to Rwanda," the separation of "the intimidators from bona fide refugees," and accepted a need for a "neutral force to secure safe corridors and temporary sanctuaries for the provision of supplies" (as quoted in Massey, 2000: 3; see also Hennessy, 2001: 13).

These calls were greeted with a distinct lack of enthusiasm by the world at large, and perhaps most of all by those most immediately concerned. For one thing, the wounds inflicted by the 1992–93 Somali debacle were still fresh, especially in the United States (see Soderlund et al., 2008: chap. 3). Involvement in yet another complex, quasi-understood morass of a situation in terrain even less hospitable than that of Somalia was not something to which anyone was likely to look forward. Apart from that general consideration, there were several specific difficulties, both practical and political:

1. It was unclear what could be done. The mainly humanitarian-based calls for the repatriation of the refugees, for instance, were more emotional than rational. Insofar as they were perpetrators of

genocide, Rwanda did not want them back, except perhaps to be able to deal with them with greater impunity on home ground. In turn, the refugees could not have been anxious to return to the inhospitable jurisdiction from which they had fled.
2. Calls for the separation of criminals from innocent refugees were equally impractical, especially when undertaken by outsiders. On what basis, and according to what process, could a just distinction be made? And was such a delicate matter appropriate for a multilateral military force?
3. A sufficiently large military force could perhaps have formed a kind of cordon around each of the refugee camps and shielded them from external predation while facilitating the provision of humanitarian aid to relieve their suffering. But that solution would have given extremists even greater freedom of operation within the camps while doing nothing to bring about a permanent solution to the basic problem.
4. An international force would, by its very presence, have constituted interference in the ongoing political and military process in the country and beyond it. It would have hindered Rwandan/AFDL efforts to deal with the remains of FAR and inhibited the drive to dispose of the Mobutu regime. As has been mentioned, few apart from France had any sympathy for Mobutu (see Massey, 2000: 5). On the other hand, there *was* sympathy for Kagame's new regime in Rwanda and a willingness to allow him considerable latitude. This stemmed partly from genuine feelings of guilt about the inadequacy of the international response to the genocide, and partly from concern to avoid further criticism by appearing to come to the aid of his enemies a scant two years later.

However, the international community could scarcely afford to appear indifferent to a situation that was not only desperate in human terms, but also capable of engendering still larger conflict in central Africa. That may have prompted Canada to offer to lead a multinational mercy mission to the Congo. To some this was a case of Canada rendering noble, self-sacrificing service to the world: "In the absence of the Canadian proposal for a multinational force (MNF) under Canadian command, it is unlikely that the international community would have organized a force to intervene" (Appathurai and Lysyshyn, 1998: 93). Other commentators have hinted that it was at least partly a matter of Prime Minister Jean Chrétien grandstanding on the eve of his retirement (see Massey, 2000: 8). Retired colonel and military analyst Sean Henry observed that "this was a political exercise aimed at raising Canada's and the prime minister's profile." The *Globe and Mail* editorially agreed: "Mr. Chretien was 'grabbing the lead in a global morality play' ... which should prove 'a political home run with the bases loaded'" (both quoted in Koch, 1996).

It appears, however, that the initiative was less Chrétien's than US President Clinton's. According to James Bartleman, who had been Chrétien's diplomatic adviser between 1994 and 1998,

> in surprising back-channel calls to me from the president's national security advisor, Tony Lake ... the Americans offered to place their military forces under Canadian command if we would lead the international mission ... perhaps the [US] turned to us, because lacking a colonial past, we would be more credible ... than France, or for that matter [the US]. Perhaps the Pentagon was comfortable working with the Canadian Armed Forces ... Perhaps the [US] expected that Canada would allow it to lead the operations behind the scenes. (as quoted in Cooper, 2005: 7)

In any case, on November 12, 1996, Canada formally offered to lead a UN force to central Africa (Hennessy, 2001: 13). Four days later the Security Council unanimously approved Resolution 1080, which authorized a multinational force under Chapter VII of the Charter, "to use commensurate force to secure specific humanitarian objectives—the 'effective provision' of aid to refugees and the local population, and the 'voluntary and orderly repatriation' of the refugees" (Massey, 2000: 7). The mission was to be commanded by Lieutenant General Maurice Baril, a veteran of the legendary Canadian Vandoos battalion, and who had headed the military component of the UN Department of Peace-keeping Operations (DPKO) during the Rwandan crisis of 1994 (Dallaire, 2003: 33, 44, 48). He was to have an American deputy. Several European countries, including Britain and France, and several developing countries, including Senegal and Ethiopia, also offered troops.

Preparations for launching the operation began immediately, including the establishment of a rear headquarters in Stuttgart and an operational headquarters in Kampala, but in fact no troops other than a few hundred Canadians ever joined the enterprise. Michael Hennessy somewhat curiously remarks in this context that "despite taking the lead, Canada could not convince others to follow, and could do little itself to fill the void" (Hennessy, 2001: 15; see also Appathurai and Lysyshyn, 1998: 95). As Hennessy goes on to admit, however, "events unfolded faster than mandates or the MNF could develop" (16). On the same day the SC authorized the mission, Rwandan-backed AFDL forces of Laurent Kabila began a major offensive against the refugee camps (Soderlund et al., 2008: 189). Hennessy argues, probably correctly, that this was a deliberate attempt to forestall international intervention: "Allowing international intervention to stabilize the region—and halt the fighting—ran contrary to [the local wielders-of-power] designs for toppling the government of Zaire" (Hennessy, 2001: 16). The offensive had the effect of causing several hundred thousand refugees (exactly how many is a matter of much dispute) to recross the border into Rwanda, where, as might have been expected, they were not gently treated by the Tutsi-dominated Rwandan army.[2]

With evident relief, reassessment of the need for a rescue mission began in various capitals, not least in Washington. Since the rationale for the international force had always been the "voluntary repatriation" of the refugees, the fact that this had, apparently, now occurred allowed other issues to be put on the back shelf. The safety of the returnees within Rwanda, the fate of those who remained in the Congo, and the well-being of the inhabitants of Kivu and the region were matters for another day. The US announced as early as November 20, 1996, that American forces would not be participating in Operation Assurance (Soderlund et al., 2008: 189). Canadian Minister of Foreign Affairs Lloyd Axworthy persisted in believing that there was still a role for an intervention, and the UNHCR warned, as did French officials, that as many as 700,000 people were still "missing" in the eastern Congo. But the Rwandan response was direct and clear: "We don't need ... [peacekeepers]. Unless they are edible, they won't be much good," said Claude Dusaidi, an aide to Paul Kagame (as quoted in Massey, 1998: 8). However, by December 8 even France had bowed to the inevitable, and on December 14 the UN abandoned the planned deployment.[3]

From MONUC to MONUSCO: 1999–2011

Until now, the two most glaring failures of UN peacekeeping have been Somalia and Rwanda, the first largely by commission, the second almost entirely by omission. After eleven plus years in the field, the current international operation in the Congo, the largest and most expensive UN endeavour in history, may well outdo both. If such were the case it would deliver a stunning setback not only to the doctrine of the Responsibility to Protect, but to the concept of peacekeeping in general, and perhaps to the overall credibility of the United Nations.

Judging the success or failure of international interventions in situations which are complex and difficult depends on the criteria used for measurement, and particularly on the time frame employed. But certainly the current Congo operation has suffered from perceptions of failure for most of its existence. *The Economist,* for instance, could ask in

December 2005, "Is this the world's least effective peacekeeping force?" Internal reports at the UN itself admitted that the mission laboured under perceptions of "impotence and cowardice" (both cited in Tull, 2009: 215; see also Grignon and Kroslak, 2008). An important new academic study of the UN efforts has accordingly been titled *The Trouble with the Congo: Local Violence and the Failure of International Peacebuilding* (Autesserre, 2010).

The multi-sided turmoil in the Congo's eastern provinces continued and intensified through 1997 and 1998, to the alarm of many outside the region itself. As Roessler and Prendergast observe, there were "almost two dozen peace initiatives ... in the first nine months of the conflict" (2006: 243). These included a meeting in Onagodougou, Burkino Faso, of the Organization of African Unity's (OAU) Central Organ Mechanism for Conflict Prevention, Management and Resolution in December 1998. The OAU played only a marginal role in the peacemaking attempts, however, because it "was not disposed to undertake robust peacekeeping (303) and did not in any case have the capacity to do so. It had, in fact, "many handicaps," including the lack of "relevant tradition, financial resources, political prestige, and operational capacity," not to mention the fact that the organization was "managed and controlled by state elites, many of whom were ... responsible for the conflicts their 'club' [was] supposed to address" (van Nieuwkerk, 2001: 83; see also Diehl, 2008: 71-72; Keller, 2002).[4]

It was the Southern African Development Community (SADC),[5] under the leadership of Fredrick Chiluba of Zambia, which spearheaded the process that led to the Lusaka Conference of July 1999. Despite the fact that several of SADC's members were parties to the Congo morass, the gathering was able to hammer out an agreement, which called for the disarmament of all foreign-armed rebel forces (referred to as "negative forces"), the withdrawal of foreign armies, and the reform of the Congolese government through an Inter-Congolese dialogue (Roessler and Prendergast, 2006: 246-47). In what was to be the beginning of a slippery slope for the United Nations, that body was charged with the responsibility for deploying a peacekeeping force "to ensure implementation of this Agreement; and taking into consideration the peculiar situation in the DRC, mandate the peacekeeping force to track down all armed groups in the DRC" (Paragraph 11 of the Lusaka Agreement, as quoted in Roessler and Prendergast, 2006: 248-49).

Once more, this was not an assignment that the world's capitals welcomed. Apart from many other considerations, if "African solutions to African problems" consisted only of writing ambitious documents and then passing the responsibility for their implementation to the UN, little progress or change had been made in the peacekeeping realm. Both US and EU observers at Lusaka had warned that extensive UN intervention was not to be expected, but, as before, it was not an assignment that could be turned down, given the UN's overall mandate and the seriousness of the Congolese conundrum. Indeed, UN spokesmen had underlined the gravity of the situation in a number of statements and resolutions beginning as early as August 1998, and had also strongly encouraged the regional peace efforts that were taking place (see UN, S/PRST/1998/26). These sentiments were reiterated in the statement of the President of the Security Council on December 11, 1998, with the addition that:

> the Security Council is prepared to consider, in the light of the efforts toward peaceful resolution of the conflict, *the active involvement of the United Nations* in coordination with the OAU, including through concrete, sustainable and effective measures, to assist in the implementation of an effective cease-fire agreement and in an agreed process for a political settlement of the conflict. (UN, S/PRST/1998/36; italics added)

Security Council Resolution 1234 of April 9, 1999, repeated and reaffirmed the above. Therefore, contrary to what appears to be implied by Roessler and Prendergast (2006: 249), the participants in the Lusaka Conference were not entirely unjustified in assuming that the UN was ready to offer substantial and concrete assistance in resolving the Congo problem.

The form and extent of that assistance, however, were another matter. US Ambassador to the UN Richard Holbrooke took the lead in persuading the Security Council to authorize a peacekeeping force for the Congo, but on condition that the parties to the Lusaka Agreement first showed full respect for its provisions (Roessler and Prendergast, 2006: 250). In his view, and in that of his government, the force should literally be *peacekeeping*, not *peacemaking*, and it should be both modest in size (a maximum of 5,000 troops) and of short duration. African leaders, in contrast, called for "robust peacekeeping" and "a force between 15,000 and 20,000 UN troops" (250).

In his report to the Security Council of July 15, 1999, the Secretary-General had announced the appointment of a Special Representative to lead an observer mission to the troubled country, to be called the United Nations Mission to the Democratic Republic of the Congo (MONUC), and suggested that on the basis of its reports a further deployment of up to 500 military observers might be authorized (UN, S/1999/790). Security Council Resolution 1291, sponsored by the United States and passed on February 24, 2000, authorized the expansion of MONUC to 5,537 military personnel, with a mandate to, among other things: (1) monitor the implementation of the ceasefire; (2) establish liaison with all the parties' military forces; (3) supervise and verify the disengagement and redeployment of forces; and (4) develop an action plan for carrying out the provisions of the Agreement. It also, referencing Chapter VII of the Charter, authorized the mission to "take the necessary action" to protect UN personnel and installations and "civilians under imminent threat of physical violence" (UN, S/Res/1291, Paragraphs 4, 7, and 8). Interestingly, the latter went beyond, indeed was contrary to, what the Secretary-General had recommended in January 2000 (UN, S/2000/30, Paragraph 67; see also Mansson, 2005: 4). It should also be noted that the resolution requested the Secretary-General "to continue to plan for any additional United Nations deployments" (UN, S/Res/1291, paragraph 11).

The immediate reaction to Resolution 1291, not only by African spokespersons, but also by media commentators and even UN officials (Roessler and Prendergast, 2006: 252-53), "concerned primarily the mismatch between its mandate and the resources allocated for its implementation: 5,537 troops ... authorized to carry out complex tasks throughout a territory the size of Western Europe" (Mansson, 2005: 4). However, the caution that the resolution reflected was not inappropriate for the situation at hand. It proved, in the first place, not easy to recruit even the modest force envisioned. Two years after the passage of Resolution 1291, there were still only 200 UN military personnel in the Congo, a fact that may have prompted the Secretary-General to actually reduce the requirement for troops to only 3,000 (Mansson, 2005: 5). Another factor was the difficulty encountered in deploying the force, something which probably did not come as a surprise given the complexities on the ground. In the opinion of Roessler and Prendergast, "the greatest obstacle to the success of MONUC in its first three years ... [was] the warring parties' own violations of the Lusaka Agreement and their obstruction of the UN peacekeeping mission" (2006: 254). Kabila himself was among the worst offenders. For instance, he took the position that UN peacekeepers could be deployed on territory held by rebel groups, but not on that under the control of Kinshasa, and insisted that MONUC could operate aircraft only with case-by-case approval from his government (Prunier, 2009: 247, 265). But Rwanda, Uganda, and Zimbabwe also continued to meddle in Congolese affairs, helping to further undermine the processes outlined by the Lusaka Agreement (Roessler and Prendergast, 2006: 255).

If anything, during 2000 the conflict escalated, with serious fighting between supposed allies, Rwanda and Uganda, at Kisangani among other incidents. In his report to the Security Council in September of that year

Kofi Annan threatened to terminate MONUC altogether (Roessler and Prendergast, 2006: 266). However, when Laurent Kabila was succeeded by his son Joseph in January 2001, confidence was restored to the point that the Secretary-General recommended "the gradual build-up of capability that encourages the parties to cease hostilities" (as quoted in Roesssler and Prendergast, 2006: 268). By May 2001 nearly 2,000 mostly African troops had been deployed to various centres around the country. For the most part, both the foreign forces within the Congo (Rwandan, Ugandan, Angolan, Namibian, and Zimbabwean) and the major local factions (Rassemblement congolais pour la démocratie and Forces armées congolaises) took up defensive positions, and by October the Secretary-General could declare that the disengagement phase of the operation had been largely completed (Roessler and Prendergast, 2006: 269). Further progress was made in July 2002, when agreements between Kinshasa and both Kigali and Kampala (the Pretoria Peace Agreement) brought about the withdrawal of the latter states' military forces, in exchange for Kabila's promise to dismantle the remaining Interahamwe groups within his borders. This set the scene for the further expansion of MONUC's personnel (to 8,700, though only about half that number had been deployed by April 2003) and an expanded focus on bringing about the disarmament of contending groups in the principal conflict area of the eastern Congo. The Secretary-General made clear, however, that the *"tracking down of armed groups and their disarmament by force are not peacekeeping functions"* (UN, S/2001/373, Paragraph 103; italics added). In effect, MONUC's role in this respect would be one of persuasion and diplomatic pressure and the facilitation of whatever arrangements could be arrived at among the volatile kaleidoscope of armed groups.

During his lifetime, Laurent Kabila had stonewalled the initiation of the Inter-Congolese Dialogue which had been called for in the Lusaka Agreement and which aimed at the overall rehabilitation of Congolese political life. Under Joseph Kabila the process was revived, and although it by no means proceeded smoothly, a supposedly all-inclusive peace agreement was reached in December 2002. It provided for the sharing of power among the main internal Congolese factions (Kabila was to remain president, and there were to be four vice-presidents representing the other groups) and nationwide elections following a two-year interim period (Roessler and Prendergast, 2006: 278). Officially, the agreement marked the end of the conflict phase in the Congo; henceforth, references were made to a "post-conflict" situation, and attention was turned primarily to advancing national political processes, especially the achievement of the elections which it was assumed would bring "democracy" (and therefore peace), to the country (Autesserre, 2010: 100). Between 2002 and 2006 (when the elections were actually held), "foreign embassies, many UN agencies and, most important, MONUC devoted the largest part of their human, logistical, military, and financial resources to the organization of the elections" (111).

Logistical and security costs of the election alone totalled around $670 million, not to mention indirect costs such as those associated with trying to prepare the population for this strange and little understood new event (Autesserre, 2010: 111-12). In effect, everything that occurred during this period, including often serious outbreaks of violence, was interpreted in terms of their effect on the electoral process. For instance, when large-scale fighting broke out between government troops and Mai-Mai militias in Katanga in mid-2005, the Secretary-General requested additional troops for the area, but these were "to ensure the security of the elections" rather than to deal with the violence itself, and when the Security Council authorized the increased deployment, it did so only for the duration of the electoral period (113). According to Séverine Autesserre, what explains this singular preoccupation is the simple fact that organizing elections, even in as difficult a place as the Congo, was something UN officials knew how to do—because they had previously done so with apparent success in Cambodia and Namibia:

> International actors could rely on a body of knowledge, standard operating procedures, preexisting bureaucracies, and predefined indicators; these tools enabled peacebuilders to consider the existing constraints on organizing elections as difficulties they could overcome. By contrast, no such intellectual and material toolkits were available for local conflict resolution. (221)[6]

The elections, though hailed as a great success, solved little other than to confirm Joseph Kabila in office and confer on him a legitimacy he previously lacked. A number of serious crises had occurred during the period leading up to the elections. One, in May 2003 in Bunia (Ituri district), saw local militias fight for control of the city, witnessed the massacre of 400 civilians, and needed the intercession of a 1,400-strong Interim Emergency Multinational Force (Operation Artemis) by the European Union to re-establish order. Another erupted in 2004 when forces led by Laurent Nkunda created havoc in Bukavu. In both of these cases MONUC troops had been bystanders to the events. After each, the Security Council authorized increases in MONUC's force level, but without noticeable impact on the incidence or the outcome of either violent outbreaks or the serious human rights abuses which constantly occurred

(Tull, 2009: 217-18). Repeated fighting in various parts of the eastern Congo—involving a variety of local and foreign groups, and causing significant numbers of deaths, atrocious human rights violations, and massive displacements of people—was more or less constant even after the 2006 election. There was little indication, when these pages were written, that a democratically elected government in Kinshasa or UN-sponsored intervention in the country had achieved much (see, for example, York, 2010, Dec. 3; Marlow and El Akkad, 2010, Dec. 7 and 8).

Media, humanitarian, and to some extent academic observers have been critical of MONUC's performance on a number of grounds. First and foremost, they see the Congolese situation as at best only marginally less chaotic today than it was in 1998. It is true that on any given day there are probably fewer neighbouring states' armies on Congolese territory, but they do periodically return for several reasons. For instance, despite the commitment of the Kabila government to contain the ex-Rwandan Hutu armed forces (FAR), it has been unable to do so, and this provides Kigali with a temptation, and an excuse, to continue to meddle in the Congo for both security and economic reasons. Second, Uganda arguably has justification for military involvement in the Congo as well. The Lord's Resistance Army (LRA), a bizarre and savage quasi-religious cult which had been conducting hostilities against the Ugandan government for decades, now operates from bases in the Congo as well as South Sudan and other neighbouring countries. The eastern Congo is particularly attractive to the LRA (as well as many others) because of the mineral wealth there that provides the means of financing its operations and enriching its cohorts.[7]

Internally, too, there is apparently no end to the number and variety of would-be military strongmen, perhaps consciously or unconsciously emulating the pattern established by Laurent Kabila, who emerge to seize control of lucrative territory and brutalize people indiscriminately. These warlords may or may not be proxies for external powers. Power vacuums caused by the withdrawal of previously occupying forces also tempt others to try to take their place, especially local, often ethnically based, militia (Mai-Mai) groups. They also allow "spoiler organizations" (those for whom a decrease in disorder is not seen as advantageous), like Laurent Nkunda's National Congress for the Defense of the People, greater incentive for wildcat operations which have little regard for human life, let alone human rights. Nkunda himself has been under detention in Kigali since January 2009, awaiting legal disposition of his fate (which has been repeatedly postponed), but there is certainly no guarantee that similar figures will not emerge tomorrow or the next day.

The UN Response: From ONUC to MONUSCO

The UN-led strategy for dealing with hydra-like monsters of this kind has been to avoid confronting them directly, but to try to induce the individuals making up their multiple heads to voluntarily lay down their arms and either be reintegrated into civil society or become part of the Congolese National Army (FAC), a process called DDR, for Disarmament, Demobilization, and Reintegration. DDR was mandated by the Lusaka Agreement and placed in the hands of the (Congolese) National Commission for Demobilization and Reinsertion (CONADER) for implementation. This process has suffered from several problems. In the first place, it would appear not to be a mechanism which is of high priority to Kinshasa: "It has been marred by delays, limited funding, and the fact that ... some of [those] who have integrated remain loyal to their former rebel commanders" (Mobekk, 2009: 276). In addition, those who choose demobilization (the majority according to Eirin Mobekk) wait so long for assistance in civil reintegration that they give up on the exercise and re-resort to violence and pillage in order to support themselves and their families (276-77).

In the view of many critics, the greatest failure of MONUC has been its inability to protect ordinary people from unimaginable violations of their lives and persons. Despite one of the most aggressive mandates in UN history, which allows the use of "all means deemed necessary to protect civilians and improve security" (Perry, 2009, Feb. 9; see also Roessler and Prendergast, 2006: 294-95), observers nearly universally agree that MONUC not only has provided little protection, but has not tried very hard to do so. The Congo today remains the rape capital of the world, with thousands of women and girls (and, somewhat surprisingly, some men) being violated each year, and even more gruesome atrocities a common occurrence. Séverine Autesserre, for instance, recounts the story told to her by a humanitarian worker of the case in which rampaging soldiers "took a family, they killed the father, they took the mother, they told the children to support the mama while they were raping her. They took out the heart and liver of the father, and they told the children to eat them" (2010: 77).

Autesserre thinks she knows why MONUC personnel have rarely intervened in such rampages—essentially because they consider that such events are more or less the norm for Congolese society:

In the words of a UN official, violence was the "usual mode of relations between the Congolese state and its population." The Congo was "a country with a history of abuses" and "a constant pattern of violence against the population by people in power." Therefore, the violence and the "armed men ... preying on the population"... were present "in the same way" as they had "always" been before ... An experienced aid worker explained to me that a high level of rape had always existed in Congolese society: "For generations, eight women out of ten have been raped by their father, their uncle, or a neighbor." A French diplomat further claimed that rape perpetrators considered sexual violence as natural because the Congolese population's approach to violence was essentially identical to that of European citizens in the Middle Ages. (2010: 75-76)[8]

The implication of such statements is clear: these are ingrained practices which outsiders cannot, and perhaps should not, try to change. Apart from anything else, the fact that the Congo's undisciplined and often unpaid army is responsible for many of the atrocities is a complicating factor (Mobekk, 2009: 277; York, 2010, Dec. 3; see also UN, S/2010/512, paras. 7 and 8). It should also not be forgotten that MONUC's own personnel were involved in "a major sexual exploitation scandal in 2005" (Autesserre, 2010: 90).

More generally, Autesserre criticizes the international community (not only MONUC, but Western and African diplomats and the staffs of other international organizations as well) for concentrating almost exclusively on what she calls a "top-down" strategy for dealing with the Congolese situation.

> Because of earlier socialization processes, UN officials, diplomats, and the staff of most nongovernmental organizations interpreted continued fighting and massacres as the consequence of national and regional tensions. They viewed local conflicts as the result of insufficient state authority and of the Congolese people's inherent propensity to violence. The dominant peacebuilding culture also shaped the international actors' understanding of their role and of the paths toward peace. It constructed intervention at the national and regional levels as the only "natural" and "legitimate" task for UN staffers and diplomats. (2010: 11)

She does not argue that national and regional problems did not need addressing, but rather than in addition to these, much more attention should have been given to "conflicts at the grassroots level," because "appeasing micro-level tensions was essential to ending collective violence on the ground and to ensuring the stability of the national and regional settlements" (2010: 178; see also Lemarchand, 2009). Autesserre makes several specific suggestions about what could (admittedly with difficulty) have been done:

1. International actors should have devoted greater resources to supporting, training, advising, and financing local actors, if necessary

by "shifting their priorities away from elections" and devoting some or all of the $670 million to local peacebuilding. She believes that little harm would have been done by postponing the election for several years (181-83).
2. "The very first priority should have been to resolve land disputes in the eastern Congo" because these were plentiful due in part to the coming and going of thousands of displaced persons, and thus fuelled conflict both in and of themselves and because they created situations which could be exploited by outside parties (183).
3. Assistance should also have been available to help restore social links and mechanisms for conflict resolution at the community level, which could have provided local populations, for instance, with "ways of deciding how to deal with war criminals" (185). Such mechanisms, Autesserre asserts, "could have helped stem violence, address many of the grievances that give rise to local militias, shrink the pool of local recruits for regional and national warlords, reintegrate refugees and displaced persons, and start rebuilding state institutions" (186).

During Autesserre's exhaustive interviewing of officials of every kind in the Congo over several years, her suggestions were greeted with incredulity or it was explained that it was impossible to devise any comprehensive strategy to deal with such complex problems, and, even if it could be done, the financial, logistical, and political obstacles were such that it was out of the question (181).

Autesserre's argument is persuasive, and her work is perhaps the most original contribution to the peacekeeping literature in some time. Yet the objections that may be raised to her formula are by no means trivial. There is no doubt, for instance, that implementing her suggestions would require massive personnel resources, and that these would have to possess a cultural sensitivity and a flexibility not likely to be found in soldiers from Asia, Latin America, other African states, or in fact anywhere else. One wonders, therefore, how any comprehensive operation of the sort Autesserre envisions could possibly be manned. In addition, most authorities would probably still maintain that the essential job of peacebuilding is to assist in the emergence of central institutions capable of carrying out such tasks themselves, and that it would be counterproductive to divert any significant resources from that effort to the local level (see, for instance, Durch and Berkman, 2006: 19 passim).

Yet the problem of violence in the Congo, and the failure to deal with it in any satisfactory way, remains. Commentators, however, generally stop short of suggesting that the international effort in the Congo has been a complete failure. Though also critical of the record with regard to the protection of civilians, Eirin Mobekk observes that "MONUC has played a crucial role in providing security in the DRC and it must be acknowledged that without MONUC's presence the situation would probably be significantly worse" (2009: 274). In similar fashion, Denis Tull suggests that MONUC's "steadily growing presence in the DRC's war-torn eastern parts may have enabled the peace process to move forward and may have resulted, despite pervasive insecurity, in less fighting overall and hence less human suffering" (2009: 222). Autesserre also refers, without apparent disagreement, to interviewee arguments that UN troops acted as a deterrent to violence on the local level because potential warring parties could not afford to break a ceasefire under the eyes of UN staff (2010: 201). She credits MONUC with two accomplishments: the organization of the 2006 elections and the "easing of macro-level tensions" (233).

In the final analysis, however, such "accomplishments" are very much a matter of "damning with faint praise." It can hardly be claimed that UN efforts in the Congo have been an outstanding success, though, as mentioned earlier, a good deal depends on the expectations with which one begins. Too often, perhaps, our expectations of peace operations undertaken in extremely difficult situations like the Congo are not entirely realistic. It may be the case that improving things somewhat and creating some base upon which further progress might be built is all that can be hoped for.

In June 2010 the operation in the Congo was rechristened the United Nations' Organization Stabilization Mission in the Congo (MONUSCO), reflecting a "new phase reached in the country" (MONUC, 2010, July 1). Moreover, the Secretary-General's report of October 8, 2010, claimed that "the country has made significant progress ... Most of the country remains free of armed conflict, and the Democratic Republic of the Congo is at peace with its neighbors ... In this context, I welcome the decision of the Security Council to rename MONUC as MONUSCO, reflecting a new partnership between the Democratic Republic of the Congo and the United Nations" (UN, S/2010/512, paras. 77 and 78). The report also announced the withdrawal of 1,494 troops and the decrease of Indian logistical support for MONUSCO (para. 67), without any indication that efforts would be made to replace these resources. Given that there still appears to be substantial violence, lawlessness, and human rights violations in the eastern provinces of the country, for civilians in the region the security situation is far from adequate. In short, what most people would consider a stable future seems problematic at best. In the summer of 2011 the Security Council extended MONUSCO's mandate until June 30, 2012, and in so doing made "it clear they would stay put until Kinshasa shows it can govern its turbulent east" (Charbonneau, 2011, June 28). Specifically, the UN demanded "that all armed groups ... immediately cease all forms of violence and human rights violations, including rape and other forms of sexual abuse against civilians, in particular women and children" (reliefweb, 2011, June 28).

In the Postscript to this book we review recent events in the Congo, focusing on the 2011 election and its aftermath. While predicted large-scale violence was avoided, the outcome of the election was contested by Joseph Kabila's chief opponent, and the resulting situation can probably best described as uncertain. History's final judgment on the UN's latest Congo mission will not be quickly reached. "Africa's most under achieving country" (*Globe and Mail*, 2011, Nov. 11: A18) is yet a long way from achieving either peace or security, and we suspect that MONUSCO may well not be the UN's last venture in the Congo.

Mass Media, Public Awareness, and Television News Coverage of the Congo

Theories of Media Influence

Over the past half-century, the role of the mass media in political processes, both domestic and international, has been the focus of increasing academic attention. Theories regarding media influence have ranged from the robust "hypodermic needle" analogy (Lasswell, 1938), to the more conservative concept of "limited effects" (Klapper, 1960; Chaffee and Hochheimer, 1985), to a position somewhere in between (Katz and Lazarsfeld, 1955). However, in the early 1970s Maxwell McCombs and Donald Shaw (1972) added the theory of "agenda setting" to the theoretical tool bag of media analysts, setting in motion a productive series of studies documenting media influence on public opinion and public policy that has continued to this day (see Rogers and Dearing, 1988; McCombs and Shaw, 1993; Kosicki, 1993; McCombs, Shaw, and Weaver, 1997; Weaver, 2007).

Agenda Setting: The "Alerting" Function of Mass Media

Agenda setting relates to the role of mass media in the formation of *public opinion*, a crucial component in democratic governance. For our study of mass media coverage of the Congo, agenda setting is important specifically in terms of its ability to "alert" the American mass public to a crisis situation in a far-off land that otherwise would likely escape their attention—a function of the press that Harold Lasswell identified as "surveillance of the environment" (1948: 38). Further, as pointed out by

Elizabeth Perse, unlike the case for political elites for whom mass media is but one source of information, "for nonelites, media coverage is not only a source of new data, but their only source of information. For nonelites, media content is both foreground and background" (2001: 94).

This observation is critical for understanding how crises occurring in the post-colonial world gain popular attention, especially those in Africa, which appears to occupy a particularly low position in the hierarchy of Western media interest (Livingston and Eachus, 1999; Hachten, 2004). In cases of conflict leading to humanitarian disaster such as the Congo, it is important to understand that in the absence of pressing security or economic interests, an energized mass public is essential to the process of getting an issue on the policy agenda of governments—the so-called "CNN effect."[1] In this regard, the International Commission on Intervention and State Sovereignty makes the point that following 9/11,

> killing and conflict occurring not only in major capitals but in distant places around the world has been brought right into the homes and living rooms of people all over the world. In a number of cases, *popular concern over what has been seen has put political pressure on governments to respond. For many of these governments, it has created a domestic political cost for inaction and indifference.* (ICISS, 2001: 7; italics added)

The idea underlying agenda setting was first broached by Walter Lippmann in the early 1920s, when the phrase "Pictures in Our Heads" appeared in the title of the first chapter of his book *Public Opinion*. In explaining the deadly gap between the signing of the armistice and the actual ending of the First World War some five hours later, Lippmann reminded us "that looking back, we can see how indirectly we know the environment in which nevertheless we live. We can see that the news of it comes to us now fast, now slowly; but whatever we believe to be a true picture, we treat it as if it were the environment itself" (1922: 4). While Lippmann emphasized the importance of media in creating people's impression of reality (whether true or false), in the 1960s it was Bernard Cohen who introduced the idea that media could influence mass publics through what has become known as the *transfer of issue salience*. However, by focusing on issue salience he also set for a time the limits of media effects with respect to what was to become agenda-setting theory with his often-quoted assessment that while the press "may not be successful much of the time in telling people what to think ... it is stunningly successful in telling its readers what to think *about*" (1963: 14; italics in original). It was this notion that the salience of an issue could be transferred from the agenda of mass media to the agenda of the mass public that McCombs and Shaw first detected empirically in their study of Chapel Hill, North Carolina voters in the 1968 election. They termed this phenomenon *agenda setting*. It is important, because as Maxwell McCombs and Amy Reynolds have argued, establishing the "salience among the public so that an issue becomes the focus of public attention, thought, and perhaps even action *is the initial stage in the formation of public opinion*" (2002: 1; italics added).

Framing: The "Evaluation" Function of Mass Media

Over the years agenda-setting theory has been expanded in scope to encompass more than the mere transfer of issue salience. It suggests in fact, that media not only tell us *what* to think about, but *how* we should think about events and leaders. This dimension is referred to in the literature as "second-level" or "attribute agenda-setting" (Ghanem, 1997). As explained by McCombs and Reynolds, "an important part of the news agenda and its set of objects are the attributes that journalists and, subsequently, members of the public have in mind when they think about and talk about each object. How these news agendas of attributes influence the public agenda is the second level of agenda-setting" (2002: 10).

This enhancement of agenda-setting theory comes very close to what had been studied previously under the rubric of *framing*, defined by Robert Entman as "selecting and highlighting some facets of events or issues, and making connections among them so as to promote a particular interpretation, evaluation, and/or solution" (2004: 5). Kathleen Hall Jamieson and Peter Waldman contend that "by choosing a common frame to describe an event, condition, or political personage, journalists shape public opinion" (2003: xiii). So as not to confuse the issue unnecessarily, in our research on media coverage of the wars in the Congo we will continue to deal with the "what to think about" role of the press under the concept of *agenda setting*, while its "how to think about" role is considered under the more established concept of *framing* (see Goffman, 1974; Entman, 1993, Scheufele, 1999; Entman, 2004).

Todd Gitlin explains that "media frames are persistent patterns of cognition, interpretation, and presentation, of selection, emphasis and exclusion, by which symbol-handlers routinely organize discourse" (1980: 7). The purpose of a frame, according to William Gamson and Andre Modigliani, is to serve as "a central organizing idea ... for making sense of relevant events, suggesting what is at issue" (1989: 3),[2] and Robert Entman tells us that beyond selection, emphasis, problem definition and interpretation, framing can involve moral evaluation and policy recommendation (1993: 52).

The importance of media framing lies in its ability to influence the way in which various audiences come to gain their understanding of what developing events actually mean—the "pictures in their heads." Pertinent to the present study, Shanto Iyengar has identified two types of framing—*episodic* and *thematic*. In the former an event is portrayed as idiosyncratic (a one-time occurrence), while in the latter it is explained in the context of a larger set of ongoing events (1991). Further, Piers Robinson has introduced the terms *empathy* (supporting) and *distance* framing (discouraging) with respect to support for possible international intervention in situations of humanitarian disaster (2000: 614–16; see also Robinson, 2002).

For this book, the "alerting function" of mass media was initially documented through a *story count* of broadcast television news coverage as well as of material appearing in the *New York Times*. Over a nearly twelve-year period, we addressed the question of whether media coverage was sufficient, first to impact public opinion so as to "push" the humanitarian disaster in the Congo on to the national policy agenda, and second, whether it was adequate to keep it on that agenda over the long duration of the conflict.

The "evaluative function" of television news was assessed through an in-depth analysis of the content appearing in selected broadcast stories, the details of which will be explained later in this chapter. In this examination of framing we determined what issues were highlighted, which sources appeared in stories, and the extent to which visuals promoted empathy towards the victims of the conflict; we then identified and evaluated the positive or negative valence of the language used to describe key participants in the conflict, a key component of "attribute agenda setting." In addition, we coded descriptions of the Congo itself. *New York Times* coverage was assessed through both qualitative narrative analyses of content and quantitative indicators of news importance.

Media Coverage of the Congo: The Literature

Assessments of mass media coverage of the continuing violence that consumed the Congo from the mid-1990s onward are not extensive and focus overwhelmingly on two features: (1) the Congo's lack of salience to US media, and (2) a framing of the conflict that reinforced "the common western assumption that little can be done" (Fair and Parks, 2001: 37; see discussion in chapter 6 of this volume).

In their study of the refugee crisis in the Congo's eastern border region with Rwanda and Burundi in the latter months of 1996, Jo Ellen Fair and Lisa Parks studied both the extent of coverage and its framing by leading US television news organizations. While ABC, CBS, NBC, and CNN news featured forty-six stories on the crisis from late October to the end of 1996, the authors focused their attention on framing of the crisis that they characterized as distancing "American television viewers from conditions in the region" (2001: 38). They concluded that the use of satellite images to track the movement of huge numbers of refugees led to an unintended consequence:

> While these images might reveal the scale of the crisis, they also reinforce and further elaborate Western distance from the political and social turmoil and trauma in Africa. The aerial image visually constructs refugees as an enigmatic nationless body, a moving target, a wandering collective rather than as a group of socially situated individuals with distinct histories and interests. (Fair and Parks, 2001: 46)

Examining the same 1996 post-Rwanda genocide refugee crisis, Soderlund and colleagues examined forty-four stories aired on ABC, CBS, and NBC prime-time news programs over the final six months of that year. The vast majority of these stories appeared between late October and the end of that year; the first story that featured a reporter on the ground in the region of conflict aired on November 1. In total, twenty-five stories contained reports from reporters in the field. Two issues dominated the coverage: the plight of the refugees and the need for some sort of international intervention to deal with their distress. Contrary to the conclusion of Fair and Parks, these issues in combination were judged to have constituted *empathy* framing that pushed the international community to respond. Among the ten humanitarian crises included in *Humanitarian Crises and Intervention* (2008), combined television and *New York Times* coverage of the Congo ranked sixth in volume, and, in the opinion of the authors, was sufficient (although barely so) to create a "CNN effect" which helped lead to the decision to create a UN intervention mission, Operation Assurance.[3] In the wake of perceived positive developments on the ground (the so-called voluntary repatriation of refugees back to Rwanda), this peacekeeping force was never deployed (see chapter 2 in this volume).

Johan Pottier's work on framing focuses on the merger of "information and misinformation" and traces journalistic failures to adequately frame the refugee crisis in the Congo to earlier failures to understand what had happened in Rwanda (2001: 1):

> Journalists fudged the issue of ADFL/RPA [Rwandan Patriotic Army] aggression, war crimes and crimes against humanity and realized only too late that they had fallen victim to Kagame's powerful doctrine of

> information control. The price paid—the "fixation" that all Hutu were "genocidal maniacs"—originated in the guilt-ridden failure to cover, and thus help prevent the 1994 Rwandan genocide. (2002: 81)

Further, once the Rwandan and Congolese Tutsi forces had established control in eastern Congo, "if journalists wanted to avoid eviction from eastern Zaire, a real threat, they did well not to upset the powers in the land" (90).

With respect to the Second Congo War that began in the summer of 1998, a *lack of media coverage* was added to the concerns over crisis framing, a theme that continued to dominate critical commentary in the years that followed.

In attempting to explain the media's lack of interest, Michela Wrong claims that changes in the international system worked to reduce the Congo's newsworthiness in the eyes of Western media. In 1960, at a high point in Cold War tensions, she argues that

> the UN responded to the crisis [in the Congo] with extraordinary speed. Its reaction time, like the hordes of journalists who flooded into the Congo to cover those years, was a measure of the enormous hope the West was pinning on Africa during those years. Impossible as it is to imagine in the year 2000, when the renewed threat of national fragmentation raises barely a flicker of national interest, the Congo of the 1960s was one of the world's biggest news stories. (2000: 65)[4]

In a paper presented to the International Studies Association in 2004, John F. Clark agreed that the Congo crisis, which he described as "one of the most deadly, but also most interesting, conflicts of the post-Cold War world," was largely ignored, not only by mass media, but by academics as well:

> In general, the Congo war has been grossly under-covered in the Western media and grossly under-analyzed by Western academics. In the media, when the Congo war has been covered, it is typically presented as a mysterious conflict taking place in an impenetrable and alien country that cannot be understood by the Western audiences ... Western academia, meanwhile, has had virtually nothing to say about the Congo at all. (2004)

However, Clark attributed "the relatively complete inattention to the Congo war on the part of the world community [to a] pernicious form of the global hegemony of the empowered." Specifically, he argued that "the dominant forces of the world community, most obviously represented by the diplomats on the UN Security Council, have simply tried to keep Congo off the agenda of world politics ... The Western media and academic communities have been willing collaborators, for the most part, in caching the Congo's misery before any sympathetic audience" (2004).

By 2005, the situation had not improved, according to Andrew Stroehlein, who complained that "with so many dying and so much at stake, it is simply astounding that Congo isn't in the newspapers and on nightly news regularly." In response to queries from his puzzled colleagues, he addressed the question of "why aren't the media covering the Congo?" His answer was that "field-hardened correspondents often tell me they'd like to go but can't convince their editors. News editors have long assumed [incorrectly in Stroehlein's view] 'no one is interested in Africa,' supposing their audience sees only hopeless African problems eternally defying solution and thus not worth attention" (2005, June 14).

A year later Keith Harmon Snow and David Barouski again decried the paucity of media coverage dealing with the horrific conditions in the Congo:

> The British medical journal Lancet recently took greater notice of the Democratic Republic of the Congo (DRC) than all western media outlets combined. A group of physicians reported that about 4 million people have died since the "official" outbreak of the Congolese war in 1998. The BBC reported that the war in Congo has claimed more lives than any armed conflict since World War II. However, experts working in the Congo, and Congolese survivors, count over 10 million dead since the war began in 1996—not 1998—with the U.S.-backed invasion to overthrow Zaire's President [Mobutu Sese Seko] ... While the western press quantifies African deaths all the time, no statistic can quantify the suffering of the Congolese. (2006, Mar. 1)[5]

Moreover, according to the authors, the lack of media coverage should not be attributed to simple inattention. A virtual "A-list" of US publications was cited for a conspiracy of misinformation designed to "blackout the truth" behind the war, which they described as "organized crime perpetrated through multi-national businesses."[6]

> The international media is completely silent on virtually every major issue of significance with respect to war in DRC—and the international and criminal networks behind it. Misinformation about Africa prevails due to *a concerted effort by the mainstream media to blackout the truth*. A boycott of key publications is imperative, and must include the most offensive: Boston Globe, Washington Post, Newsweek, Time, US News & World Report, USA Today, New York Times, the New Yorker (Conde Nast

Publications), Harper's, Atlantic Monthly (highly subsidized by Lockheed Martin and Northrup Grumman), and, especially, National Geographic. (Snow and Barouski, 2006, Mar. 1: footnote 8; italics added)

In 2006 Ken Reich claimed that "even The New York Times, it seems, seldom ventures into this country of 63 million" (2006, June 2), and, in a news analysis article comparing the Congo and Darfur crises, *New York Times* correspondent Lydia Polgreen noted that while Darfur had "finally burst into the world's consciousness" by 2006, the Congo, with four million dead since 1998, "remains largely forgotten." She reported that "though the war officially ended in 2002, its deadly legacy of violence and decay will kill twice as many people this year as have died in the entire Darfur conflict which began in 2003" (2006, July 23: IV3).[7]

In 2007 Bob Harris claimed that it should come as no surprise that Americans were unaware of the grave situation in the Congo: "According to its online archive, the Washington Post, whose coverage seems to have been much better than most, has noted the entire war and its horrifying aftermath an average of about once every two months since 1998" (2007, Nov. 26). Glen Ford's 2007 comparison of the Congo and Darfur crises cited figures of 5 million dead in the former, as opposed to a quarter million dead in the latter and asked why is the "exponentially more massive carnage in Congo unworthy of mention?" His answer was that "in Congo, it is U.S. allies [Uganda and Rwanda] and European and American corporate interests that benefit from the slaughter" (2007, July 18).

David Kampf acknowledged that elections in 2006 did bring the international media back to the Congo, but pointed out that this attention "was fleeting." His overall assessment can be added to the consensus of other critics:

> Despite the severity, the war received limited international attention. There was a widespread perception that the DRC possessed little geopolitical significance. For instance, notwithstanding its inclusion in Médecins Sans Frontières' (MSF) annual list of *Ten most underreported humanitarian stories* for the past eight years, the country has gone "virtually unnoticed to the rest of the world" despite the "extreme deprivation and violence endured by millions of Congolese" (*Médecins Sans Frontières, 2006*). World powers and international media simply ignored the tragedy. (Kampf, 2007, Mar. 1; italics in original)

Intensification of violence in eastern Congo in the fall of 2008, related to the insurgency mounted by General Laurent Nkunda, and which opened the possibility of yet another region-wide conflict, likewise resulted in a spike in media attention. But Rachel Levitt asked, "how long will that coverage last?" Her answer was "probably not long considering that foreign affairs, especially those not directly related to the United States, make up *only a fraction* of what Americans read, see, and hear: 9 percent of network news, 13 percent of newspaper coverage, 4 percent of cable news" (2008, Nov. 11; italics in original).[8]

Gérard Prunier has also cited the "poverty of media coverage" of the Congo, adding that in what meagre coverage there was, the Rwandan genocide occupied a "hegemonic position ... as a global frame of explanation."[9] As evidence for the lack of coverage, a Nexis-based figure of 1,600 articles was cited as having been published on Darfur in 2005, compared with only 300 on the Congo, "which means that media coverage of the Darfur crisis was over five times that of the Congo, though the Congo situation killed over three time as many people as Darfur" (2009: 353).[10]

Jason Stearns acknowledges as well that the Congo conflict, described as one of the "great cataclysms of our times ... has received little sustained attention from the rest of the world." His explanation is that "from the outside, *the war seems to possess no overarching narrative or ideology to explain it, no easy tribal conflict or socialist revolution to use as a peg in a news frame.*" He asks, "How do you cover a war that involves at least twenty different rebel groups and the armies of nine countries, yet does not seem to have a clear cause or objective?" (2011: 5; italics added).

Research Methods

The goal of this research is to document the amount of media coverage of the Congo (the "alerting" function), as well as the framing of the conflict (the "evaluative" function), that was presented to the American public and its political leaders by key US television and print media. The study covers the period that begins in mid-May 1997 with the fall of Mobutu Sese Seko and the coming to power of Laurent-Désiré Kabila and continues through to the end of 2008. Because our study period covers the run-ups to and active phases of both the Second and Third Congo Wars, where appropriate we did separate analyses for the periods prior to and after the initial withdrawal of the major international combatants at the end of 2002. This provided us with two roughly equal time periods during which the nature of the war changed from primarily regional/civil to primarily tribal/regional proxy, with changes in at least some issues and participants involved in the conflict, along with the need for greater international peace enforcement activity. Both quantitative and qualitative methods were used in the research; quantitative methods to document media's "alerting function" and qualitative methods to address their "evaluative function," carried out largely through framing devices. Both television and print news coverage was studied.[11]

To document the "alerting function" as carried out by television news analyzed in the pages that follow immediately, stories on the Congo aired on prime-time evening news programs of the ABC, CBS, and NBC broadcast networks were first identified from the Vanderbilt Television News Archive. All stories broadcast between May 17, 1997, and December 31, 2008 (N=89), were categorized by date, network, and running time. Second, those stories with running times of at least one minute in length were selected, and at this point videotapes of 47 stories were ordered, accounting for just over half of all those aired during the study period. It is these stories that make up the database for the assessment of broadcast TV news coverage. The date the story aired, major issues covered, interpretations offered, and sources used were coded. As well, the impact of visuals and descriptive language contained in the stories were accorded a critical in-depth examination to establish the nature of media framing employed. As a part of this analysis the language used to describe various participants, as well as the Congo itself ("attribute framing"), was submitted to an academic panel for their judgments as to whether specific words and phrases appearing in stories would likely to be seen by audiences as reflecting *positively* or *negatively* on the subjects being described.

The *New York Times*, the newspaper of record in the United States and in 2011 ranked first among world newspapers (4International Media & Newspapers, 2011), served as our source of print media coverage reported in chapters 4, 5, and 6. Initially, we checked *The New York Times Index* for all items dealing with the Congo that appeared during our study period—in total 515 items in coverage of the Second Congo War and 304 items in coverage of the Third Congo War. These 819 stories were subsequently retrieved, read, and coded for date of publication, dateline, source, and type of material. The totals for these variables are reported in tables in chapter 6 which show relevant data by year for both the Second and Third Congo Wars, and provide material for the further evaluation of the adequacy of the media alert that was presented earlier with respect to television news as well as for a comparison of Congo-Darfur coverage.

Primarily, however, for the *New York Times* all major "opinion-leading/opinion-reflecting" articles (front-page stories, editorials, op-ed articles, "news analysis" pieces, and letters to the editor), plus stories dealing specifically with UN (MONUC) and French-led European peacekeeping efforts, were identified and read for issues covered, interpretations offered, and evaluations of the parties to the conflict, including international peacekeeping forces. As well, any prescriptions that were offered with respect to how the international community, especially the United Nations and the United States, should deal with the conflict were noted. Based on this material, *narrative analyses* of conflict framing were constructed for each year of the study. These appear in chapter 4 for the Second Congo War (primarily regional) and chapter 5 for the Third Congo War, which was characterized by tribal and proxy militia insurgencies that actively engaged international peacekeeping forces.

We believe that the combination of quantitative and qualitative research approaches has yielded a relatively complete picture of the extent of media coverage of the long-running and complex humanitarian disaster in the Congo, as well as the interpretations and preferred options for dealing with it that over time were offered to television audiences and newspaper readers. Specifically, we want to assess whether the level of media coverage was adequate to alert the American public to the catastrophic situation on the ground in the Congo, and whether the level of attention and the issues given media prominence changed as the conflict progressed through its different phases. Further, in terms of framing, we want to know what explanations were offered regarding the meaning and implications of the violence that was occurring in the Congo, and whether these changed significantly over the nearly twelve years covered in the study. Also, how were the major participants (both domestic and international) and the Congo itself presented? Had identifiable "good guys" and "bad guys" emerged in the coverage, or were all parties to the conflict painted with more or less the same brush? Finally, with respect to the role of the international community in the conflict, how were the French-led European and later MONUC peacekeeping operations evaluated in terms of their effectiveness once they took an active role in the field in 2003?

Broadcast Television News Coverage of the Congo

Of the total of 89 stories dealing with the Congo broadcast on ABC, CBS, and NBC prime-time newscasts between May 17, 1997, and December 31, 2008, two-thirds (N=59) aired from 1997 through 2002, while one-third (N=30) aired from 2003 through 2008. Of the total stories, ABC accounted for just about half (N=44), posting almost equal numbers in the two periods, while CBS ran 26 stories and NBC ran 19, with coverage falling off substantially for both the latter networks following the end of the

Second Congo War in 2002. From this story list, video recordings of the 47 stories that ran at least one minute in length were ordered from the Vanderbilt Television News Archive for in-depth analysis.

Findings

Our findings confirm the "worst-case scenario" regarding media attention to the war in the Congo reviewed in the previous pages; thus, with respect to mass media's "alerting function," broadcast television news clearly has to be given a failing grade. Over nearly twelve years of a complex regional/civil/proxy/tribal war, an average of less than eight stories per year appeared on the three major US networks, with somewhat fewer than half (N=42) appearing in the 10- to 20- to 30-second anchor-read summary format. Moreover, of the 47 stories that ran at least a minute in length, 13 focused primarily on the Mt. Nyiragongo volcano eruption in 2002, and most of these mentioned the war tangentially, if at all.[12]

It is likely that viewers of network television news in the United States would have had at least some awareness of 1997 events that resulted in the transition from Mobutu Sese Seko to Laurent-Désiré Kabila, along with perhaps a perception that Mr. Kabila was not the man to lead the Congo out of its difficulties. Beyond this, however, audiences would have had little consciousness of the catastrophic conflict that followed, or information on strategy and key battles, much less any clear understanding of its link to the 1994 Rwandan genocide. With the exception of the assassination of President Kabila in January 2001 (covered in four 20- to 30-second accounts) and the volcanic eruption in early 2002 (which attracted a relatively large amount of media attention), the years following 1997 were characterized by a significant lack of interest—one in-depth story in 1998, none in 1999, and two in 2000. Not only were the implications of the apparent "end" of Africa's first world war in December 2002 never addressed, the event was not even reported in short anchor-read accounts. (See table 3.1a.)

Numbers, however, do not tell the full story of media indifference. Only three stories dealt in any detail with the war itself. These reviewed the major regional participants in the war, but only one (reported by Jim Wooten) featured a visual of what was actually happening on the ground—a person shown being thrown off a bridge into a river and subsequently shot (ABC, 2001, May 7). The first indication of the number of people killed in the Congo (at that point, almost three years into the war, estimated at 2.5 million) appeared at the end of April 2001 in a story prompted by a report commissioned by the International Rescue Committee (ABC, 2001, Apr. 30). As well, another four stories aired at various

Public Awareness and News Coverage of the Congo

TABLE 3.1a
Network TV Coverage of the Second Congo War, by Year

	1997	1998	1999	2000	2001	2002	Total
All stories	15	9	0	4	14	17	59
Stories 1 minute and over	8	1	0	2	5	13	29

points during the Second Congo War explained the economic reasons why the broader international community had little interest in bringing the war to an end—profits to be gained from diamonds and coltan.[13]

While four stories focused on the killing of Rwandan refugees during Laurent Kabila's Rwandan-backed successful march across the country to Kinshasa in 1997, none adequately explained the origins and continuing role of the Hutu Interahamwe in the conflict. A particularly glaring omission was the failure to mention that beginning in 1998, President Kabila had recruited the former *génocidaires* to support his government against Rwandan and Ugandan forces aiming to overthrow him. The volcanic eruption near the eastern Congo city of Goma in January 2002 prompted some comparisons to the 1994 refugee crisis in the same area triggered by the Rwandan genocide, and provided what little contextual material there was in coverage linking 1994 events in Rwanda to the subsequent outbreak and persistence of warfare in eastern Congo (NBC, 2002, Jan. 25). As mentioned, there was little coverage and no analysis of two conferences convened to bring about peace in the Congo, the second of which, with South African encouragement, resulted in the end of formal regional participation in the war at the end of 2002.

Although there was substantially less television coverage during the Third Congo War, the war itself (especially the role of the international community in attempting to quell the violence), figured far more prominently, as half of the 18 in-depth stories focused on various aspects of the war. In addition to peacekeeping (including one about the sex scandal involving UN peacekeepers), these stories dealt with the war's impact on refugees and its extensive use of child soldiers. As shown in table 3.1b, coverage peaked at the beginning and end of the study period, with comparatively little interest demonstrated in between. Somewhat ironically, it was not until February 2005 that a story by Brian Ross presented a comprehensive account of the role of Rwandan Hutu refugees both as a trigger to the conflict and as a factor contributing to its persistence in eastern Congo (ABC, 2005, Feb. 10). Also, in 2008 NBC's Ann Curry reported two stories in the human interest frame characteristic of her

TABLE 3.1b
Network TV Coverage of the Third Congo War, by Year

	2003	2004	2005	2006	2007	2008	Total
All stories	11	1	4	4	1	9	30
Stories 1 minute and over	8	1	2	1	0	6	18

reporting on Darfur: an empathic personal account of the aftermath of a vicious rape (NBC, 2008, Feb. 13), and another of two ex-child soldiers who had fought against each other earlier in the war (NBC, 2008, Feb. 14). Next to stories focused on the impact of the war, the plight of Congo's gorillas received the greatest amount of attention by television news, featured in a total of four stories between 2003 and 2008.

At first glance, the data in table 3.2 might lead one to believe that there was a significant "evaluative component" in visuals accompanying stories. However, especially with respect to the Second Congo War, this would be a mistake.

Between 1997 and the end of 2002, 15 stories (52 percent) were judged to contain visuals promoting "empathy" for victims/refugees. However, perhaps due to the difficulty and danger of getting adequate video from remote areas of conflict, in only three cases was this empathy focused on the hardships suffered by refugees. These refugees were Rwandan Hutus (only once identified as such) who had been targeted in the Rwandan Tutsi-led operation to oust Mobutu in 1996–97. The remaining 12 focused on the plight of refugees fleeing the 2002 eruption of the Nyiragongo volcano. In one story dealing with US Ambassador to the UN Richard Holbrooke's visit to Africa in May 2000, the graphics painted an unusually bleak picture of the progress made against violence on the continent as a whole and were coded as promoting international "distance" from Congo's problems (ABC, 2000, May 12). During the Third Congo War, the prevalence of empathic visuals continued, but this time their focus was on suffering experienced by refugees displaced by the continuing chaotic war in eastern Congo (6 stories), plus the war's impact on child soldiers (3 stories) and victims of systematic rape (1 story).

Unlike crises in Somalia, East Timor, and Darfur (see Soderlund et al., 2008; Sidahmed, Soderlund, and Briggs, 2010), only after the Second Congo War had "ended" in 2002 did US television news advocate, even in a limited way, an international intervention to help deal with the humanitarian suffering in Congo. At this juncture, the conflict had morphed into "tribal warfare" that was seen as perhaps serious enough

Public Awareness and News Coverage of the Congo

TABLE 3.2
Number of Stories Containing Empathy- or Distance-Producing Visuals, 1997–2008

	1997–2002		2003–2008	
	Empathy	Distance	Empathy	Distance
	N=15	N=1	N=10	N=0

to escalate into another Rwanda-type genocide. As reviewed in chapter 2, the resulting dispatch of a French-led, UN-sanctioned European "stabilization force" (Operation Artemis) to the Ituri region in the spring of 2003 for a three-month period to control tribal violence triggered the first discussion of what would constitute an appropriate international response to the Congo's enduring distress.

In light of the severity of the Congo conflict, it is somewhat surprising that the possibility of the international community's mounting some sort of effective peacekeeping response did not receive more serious and compassionate media attention. Be this as it may, what is clear from the data in table 3.3 is that when international peacekeeping did finally find its way onto the agenda of television news beginning in 2003, it came in for severe criticism. The major issue brought to the attention of viewers was that insufficient numbers of troops and mandates that were inadequate for the task at hand had led to past failures on the part of UN peacekeeping missions, and that this was very likely to be the case in the Congo (CBS, 2003, June 7; ABC, 2003, June 13; ABC, 2005, Feb. 10). As well, one story dealt with the scandal involving peacekeepers under UN command bartering various items for sex with Congolese women and the UN's inadequate response (ABC, 2005, Feb. 11). In terms of evaluation, the French-led stabilization force fared slightly better, but reporters tended to be unimpressed that the force had no authority to disarm tribal militias or to act outside the city of Bunia, and that in any event it would be gone in three months.

Table 3.4a shows both the major sources used in coverage of the Second Congo War and the number of times these sources appeared in stories. Not surprisingly, ordinary Congolese, mainly as refugees, headed

TABLE 3.3
Evaluation of European and UN Peacekeeping Operations in the Third Congo War, by Year

2003	2004	2005	2006	2007	2008
POS NEG	POS NEG	POS NEG	POS NEG	POS NEG	POS NEG
1 3	/ /	/ 2	/ /	/ /	/ /

TABLE 3.4a
Major Sources and Number of Times Used during the Second Congo War, by Year

	1997	1998	1999	2000	2001	2002	Total
Congolese citizens	5	/	/	/	2	14	21
Non-governmental organizations	3	1	/	1	7	8	20
US government	7	/	/	1	/	/	8
Experts	1	1	/	/	/	6	8
President Laurent Kabila	7	/	/	/	/	/	7
Congolese politicians	2	/	/	/	/	/	2
Rebel leaders	/	/	/	/	1	/	1
United Nations	/	/	/	/	1	/	1
British politicians	/	/	/	1	/	/	1

up the source list, followed by spokespersons for a variety of non-governmental humanitarian aid groups active in the Congo.[14] However, it must be stressed that the spike in the appearance of the latter sources seen in 2002 was related to the eruption of Mt. Nyiragongo, the refugees caused by it and the humanitarian aid agencies responding to it, not due to the war itself.

Besides Congolese citizens and NGO spokespersons, the only other significant sources appearing were US government spokespersons Bill Richardson and Richard Holbrooke (on trips of Africa), President Kabila (all in 1997 and associated with the transition in power from Mobutu Sese Seko), and various "experts" (mostly associated with the volcanic eruption in 2002). Significant by his total absence as a source is President Joseph Kabila, who took over the presidency from his assassinated father in January 2001 and emerged as a surprisingly adept leader. As well, no spokespersons for the major regional combatants (Rwanda, Uganda, Angola, and Zimbabwe) appeared as sources. There was only one appearance of a spokesperson representing any of the domestic rebel groups (Rassemblement congolais pour la démocratie) and this was in the context of an economic story dealing with the role of coltan in funding the war (CBS, 2001, June 13).

Television news coverage of the Third Congo War evidenced the same basic pattern of source use seen earlier, with NGO spokespersons, Congolese citizens, and various experts appearing most frequently. Beyond these sources was the limited appearance of child soldiers, UN spokespersons (mainly William Swing, chief of the UN mission in the Congo, who attempted to control the damage in the wake of the 2005 sex scandal), and French peacekeepers in the field.

Public Awareness and News Coverage of the Congo

TABLE 3.4b
Major Sources and Number of Times Used during the Third Congo War, by Year

	2003	2004	2005	2006	2007	2008	Total
Non-governmental organizations	3	/	1	1	/	6	11
Congolese citizens	4	/	1	/	/	2	7
Experts	3	/	1	/	/	2	5
Child soldiers	2	/	/	/	/	2	4
United Nations	1	/	2	/	/	/	3
French peacekeepers	2	/	/	/	/	/	2
Congolese politicians	/	/	1	/	/	/	1
Rebel leaders	1	/	/	/	/	/	1

During the Third Congo War there was no use of US government spokespersons as sources. Of course, US presidents have the power to be consistent newsmakers and news shapers should they choose to use it, and it must be noted from their absence in both Tables 3.4a and 3.4b, that neither Presidents Clinton nor Bush, nor their various secretaries of state, ever appeared as sources in news stories dealing with the Congo (see Bennett, Lawrence, and Livingston, 2007). Nor, we might add, had any celebrities embraced the Congo to the extent that they were able to attract network attention to the crisis. This is in sharp contrast to Darfur, which we will discuss further in chapter 6.

Along with visuals, language (especially evaluative descriptors) is a key component in media framing.[15] As shown in table 3.5, with the exception of Mobutu Sese Seko, Laurent-Désiré Kabila, the United States, and UN- and French-led peacekeeping forces, none of the participants involved in the Congo's wars appeared to catch the attention of television news to the extent that any firm evaluation could be made regarding how they were presented to American audiences. Among the above, while Kabila fared somewhat better than Mobutu in press evaluation, only the United States emerged with a favourable image. However, in reviewing the use of descriptive language (see Appendix, this volume), it is important to note that all the language used with respect to Mobutu and Kabila appeared in the context of the 1997 power transition; this means that none of the descriptive language related to Laurent Kabila related in any way to his role in the Second Congo War, which erupted just over a year after he came to power. For the United States, in addition to its role in the transition from Mobutu to Kabila, descriptive language appeared in coverage of the foreign aid response to the 2002 volcanic eruption and in both instances was largely positive. During the Third Congo War

TABLE 3.5
Use of Positive and Negative Descriptors, 1997–2008

	1997–2002	
Mobutu Sese Seko	Positive (N=2) 13%	Negative (N=13) 87%
Laurent-Désiré Kabila	Positive (N=8) 22%	Negative (N=28) 78%
	1997–2008	
United States policy	Positive (N=8) 62%	Negative (N=5) 38%
The Congo	Positive (N=9) 25%	Negative (N=27) 75%
	2003–2008	
UN peacekeeping force (MONUC)	Positive (N=2) 12.5%	Negative (N=14) 87.5%
French-led European stabilization force	Positive (N=8) 57%	Negative (N=6) 43%

descriptive language focused on lack of contributions to international peacekeeping efforts on the part of the United States, and in this case our panel coded all such references as negative.

As noted previously, UN peacekeeping efforts in the Congo received pervasively negative evaluations, chiefly for reasons related to past peacekeeping failures (insufficient force levels and inadequate mandates for proposed missions), plus involvement in sex scandals. As a point of interest, following the initial arrival of the European stabilization force in June 2003, especially in view of the speculation that it couldn't get the job done, there was no appraisal of the results of the three-month-long mission, which did in fact restore some degree of law and order to the conflict-beset city of Bunia.

Not surprisingly, language used to describe the Congo tended to focus on the negative outcomes of the long-running conflict—loss of life, plus economic and societal collapse—along with some limited references to both the beauty and economic wealth of the country. On balance, this language tended to confirm the "intractable conflict" frame and thus would discourage attempts by the international community to find solutions to the Congo's problems.[16]

Conclusion

It is difficult to imagine a more inadequate treatment of a major international story than was seen in US television news coverage of the conflict that wreaked havoc on the Congo for a dozen years. While ABC turned in by far the best performance, the overall lack of television coverage is especially troubling, since during this nearly twelve-year period the war had resulted in the deaths of an estimated 5.4 million Congolese (Polgreen, 2008, Jan. 23: A8) and had engaged the armed forces of much of Central Africa, not to mention drawing in United Nations and European peacekeeping forces. What accounts for this performance on the part of television news, which can only be described as extremely disappointing?

While various "conspiracies of silence" theories noted in the literature have been reviewed above, to our minds none of these appears compelling. In fact, among relatively few stories aired, four focused specifically on international complicity in prolonging the conflict due to trade in diamonds and coltan (NBC, 2000, June 11; CBS, 2001, June 13; CBS, 2001, Aug. 1; ABC, 2002, Jan. 21). There are, however, a number of more plausible explanations (though certainly no excuses) for lack of television interest in the Congo.

Gadi Wolfsfeld has explained the connection between news events (those that drive media coverage) and "framing" (the interpretations that journalists place on those happenings). For Wolfsfeld, "news" is presented as a combination of information and framing (1997: 31-36). He contends that in the process of story construction information collected about an event from various sources has to be placed into some existing, well-known interpretive frame in order for audiences to gain some understanding of what they are seeing or reading about. For example, during the Cold War years the spectre of the *communist menace* was one such key frame applied by US media to situations such as Guyana, Guatemala, Grenada, and Nicaragua (see Soderlund, 2001). During the post-Cold War period, Wolfsfeld identifies *aggressor-victim*, *brutal repression*, and *ethnic cleansing* and *genocide* as examples of frames that have been widely used to make sense of far-off conflicts for Western audiences.

In the case of the Congo, as a number of reporters have pointed out, television news coverage was confounded by the difficulty of finding any suitable frame (other than *intractable conflict*) to explain the exceedingly complex, multi-actor, multi-dimensional nature of the violence they were attempting to report. For example, Jason Stearns pointed out that the unique nature of the violence in the Congo, "a war of the ordinary person, with many combatants unknown and unnamed, who fight for complex reasons that are difficult to distill in a few sentences," led to frustration on the part of international journalists (2011: 5). As well, ABC *Nightline*'s Ted Koppel confirmed that "Africa, particularly Congo, was difficult to pin down" (as cited in Salamon, 2001, Sept. 6: E8).

In a book that focuses on the role of media in processes of peace negotiations, Wolfsfeld offers further insights that help us understand the lack of television coverage of the Congo conflict. He explains that "journalists tell stories [and that] all other things being equal, journalists prefer to tell stories about conflict. News is first and foremost about conflict and disorder. Protests, violence, crime, wars, and disasters provide the most natural material for news reports" (2004: 15). Against that backdrop, which suggests that media should be interested in the Congo, he goes on to identify four "professional norms and routines" that influence the production of news: *immediacy, drama, simplicity,* and *ethnocentrism*. Let us examine these points to understand why the conflict failed to generate media interest.

Immediacy relates to the reality that "the press covers events, not processes" (2004: 17). The "protracted social conflict" nature of conflict in the Congo (see chapter 1 of this volume) could clearly lead to what Susan Moeller has described as *compassion fatigue* (1999). For example, Bill Berkeley reports that in 1960 in the midst of the Cuban revolution, the Congo had more pages of entries in *The New York Times Index* than "Fidel Castro's Cuba" (2001, Aug. 2: A20). That some forty years later the Congo was still embroiled in conflict has to place it in the top echelon of the world's "intractable conflicts."

In his comprehensive book on Congo's problems, Gérard Prunier has divided African humanitarian emergencies into two categories based on what he terms their "media-sexiness." Among those crises embraced by the media were Ethiopia (1985-86), described as "the mother of all emergencies," Somalia (1992), Rwanda (1994), Zaire-Congo (1994-95), and Darfur (beginning in 2004). In addition to the Congo, Prunier's "unsexy" conflicts included the Ugandan civil war (1981-86), Southern Sudan (1983-2005), and Somalia (after 1995). He argues that the long duration of the latter group of conflicts was a major factor leading to reduced media attention (2009: 352-53).

A sense of *drama* refers to the fact that "every act of violence, every crisis, and every sign of conflict is considered news" (Wolfsfeld, 2004: 18). In this context, the problem with the Congo was that, with the exception of the initial Rwandan-led attempt in 1998 to unseat the newly installed President Laurent-Désiré Kabila, by and large the war was not carried out in a series of dramatic "big battles," nor did it feature conventional military campaigns.[17] In fact, as was the case with most of the African wars, the majority of casualties were seen to be the very young and the very old, who succumbed to either disease or starvation. As confirmed by Jason Stearns, "the dying was not spectacular. Violence only directly caused 2 percent of the reported deaths" (2011: 249-50).

Third, as Wolfsfeld points out, "simple story lines, especially when they are accompanied by good visuals, are the key to reaching a mass audience" (2004: 20). It was this need for *simplicity* that was perhaps the most important factor discouraging television news coverage of the Congo conflict, which was anything but simple and lacked a coherent story line (see Prunier, 2009; Reyntjens, 2009; Stearns, 2011).

The conflicts in Rwanda (Hutu vs. Tutsi), East Timor (East Timorese vs. Indonesian-sponsored militias), and Darfur (Arab Janjaweed militias vs. African farmers) fit nicely into the "two camp-good vs. bad" method of presentation much favoured by the media. The Congo, with its multiple regional and internal combatants, who tended to be driven by different motives and goals, was quite complex and hard to deal with in simplistic terms. For example, Julie Salamon, reporting in the *New York Times*, noted that "Congo is a slippery subject for television, which likes its stories, even real ones, to follow a dramatic structure ... with the forces of evil clearly delineated." Such was not the case in Congo, where "seven or eight governments and factions are involved, and righteousness is elusive" (2001, Sept. 6: E8).

Along similar lines, Lydia Polgreen's explanation of the lack of attention to the Congo centres on the degree of "moral clarity" involved in the conflict. Such moral clarity was seen to be present in Darfur (where Sudanese aircraft and Janjaweed militias attacked and burned African villages, with survivors raped or killed), but was absent in the Congo, which she described as a many-sided "free-for-all [characterized by] a mind-numbing collection of combatants known by a jumble of acronyms" (2006, July 23: IV3).

The final factor that characterizes media coverage is *ethnocentrism*. It is well recognized that, even at the best of times in its presentations of Africa, Western media coverage is loaded with Eurocentric stereotypes (Hawk, 1992; Keim, 1999; Quist-Adade, 2001; Grzyb, 2009b). Wolfsfeld argues further that "every news medium operates from a certain political and cultural base that defines its language, beliefs, values, attitudes, and prejudices." This leads to a situation where "news stories are almost always about 'us': about what is happening or could happen to us. When there is news about 'others,' it centers on how they affect us" (2004: 22). As has been noted, the wars in the Congo did not attract the attention of any recognizable celebrities who might have brought greater visibility to the conflict. Thus, in terms of attracting media attention, the Congo wars were not easily translated into domestic consequences that were likely to raise concerns among US viewers (for an extended discussion of these points, see chapter 6 in this volume).

Two other factors must be considered as well: the danger to reporters and the impact of competing crises, not only in Africa, but elsewhere in the world as well. In a review of the ABC network's September 2001 *Nightline* series on the Congo, "Heart of Darkness," Julie Salamon reports that Ted Koppel admitted that the program had "come late to the Congo story, in part because 'the place is distant and dangerous and not easily accessible'" (as quoted in Salamon, 2001, Sept. 6: E8). It is perhaps no coincidence that a spike in reporting on the Congo occurred in 2003, precisely at the time of the arrival of the French-led force in June of that year, which afforded reporters some measure of safety in the zone of conflict.

Jennifer Parmlee has commented that "the world seems to have an appetite for only one crisis at a time" (as quoted in Livingston, 1996: 83), and during our study period the Congo had no shortage of competition. The 9/11 attacks and the US-led invasions of Afghanistan and Iraq that followed, plus an armed intervention in Haiti in 2004, not to mention the 2004 Asian tsunami, and electoral violence in Kenya in 2008, entailed huge commitments of media resources.[18] With respect to competition from Africa, Gérard Prunier notes in particular the "disastrous effect" of the Darfur crisis on media coverage of the Congo—a conflict garnering "over five times" the amount of coverage given the Congo (2009: 353). Added to the problem is that Africa in general (and the Congo in particular) appears not to occupy a high position in the interests of the American public, or indeed the American government (see our discussion in chapter 6). According to Prunier, the nearly 4 million victims of the Congolese conflict were not really news because "they belonged (together with Angola, Ethiopia, Somalia, Burundi, Liberia, and Sierra Leone) to the abominable and hardly comprehensive world of African civil wars. That particular war was simply a bit bigger than the others, but it did not mean anything more" (2009: 352).

Unfortunately, the combined impact of these factors provided little incentive for television networks to commit costly resources to cover what, as Ian Stewart lamented with respect to the fighting in Sierra Leone in the late 1990s, was seen by his editors in the United States as "just another story about a little war in Africa" (2002: 185). Indeed, at least two television news stories openly acknowledged that TV news had done a less than credible job in covering the conflict (ABC, 2001, May 7;

CBS, 2001, Aug. 1). The former story outlined reasons not unlike the ones we have presented, but emphasized the danger inherent in reporting on the Congo. Our own conclusion is that the "alerting" function of television news was virtually non-existent and that its "framing" of the crisis in the relatively few stories that did appear was at best (and perhaps understandably so) confused. Whatever the explanation (and we suggest that a combination of factors all pushed in the same direction), the US mass public was poorly served with respect to coverage of the Congo by their major television networks. The medium that was most capable of generating an emotional response to the horrors of the Congo failed in the basic task of covering the conflict.

New York Times Framing of the Second Congo War

4

1997: Initial Framing of the Congo under Laurent Kabila

According to Todd Gitlin, a critical function of mass media is "to certify reality as reality" (1980: 2). In its role as a domestic and international agenda setter, it is arguable that no newspaper is better positioned to carry out this role than the *New York Times*. In the process of media construction of reality, the initial "pictures in our heads" that we acquire about a situation are especially important. As Karl Deutsch and Richard Merritt (1965) have argued, once these images are in place, they act as screens or filters through which new information on a subject must inevitably pass.

Immediately following the fall of Mobutu Sese Seko in the Congo in 1997, the *New York Times* offered its readers a significant volume of reporting, with thirty-three items of content appearing between May 18 and the end of the month. Major contributors to this coverage included such established correspondents as Howard W. French, James McKinley Jr., Raymond Bonner, Nicholas D. Kristof, Donald McNeil Jr., and Barbara Crossette. This initial content included eight front-page news stories, fifteen inside-page news stories, four op-ed or news analysis pieces, one stand-alone photo, four letters to the editor, and one correction item. From this assortment of material emerged a reasonably full discussion of the problems facing the newly liberated Congo, not the least of which was its new leader, Laurent-Désiré Kabila. There were, however, no editorials during this period and little clear direction about what the end of the Mobutu dictatorship meant for the people of the Congo, the region, or the United States. Nor was there much discussion of what policy the West should adopt with respect to the new ruler of the Congo, other than the fact that much patience would be required in dealing with him.

There was certainly no lament expressed for the long-time US-supported dictator, the departed Mobutu Sese Seko; nor, significantly, was there any enthusiasm expressed for his self-declared successor. In a front-page story on May 18, Howard French described Kabila's accession to power as "the improbable victory of a lifelong rebel whose past is marked more by obscurity and failure than inspiration" (1997, May 18: A1). On the same day, in a second Congo story appearing on the front page, James McKinley pointed to Kabila's Marxist past, in 1997 still a potent indicator of anti-Americanism in Third World politics. Kabila was described as "an obscure rebel leader with a history of Quixotic Marxist revolts that fell apart," while his most notable administrative experience was said to involve running "a small socialist commune in the mountains of eastern Zaire in the 1970s." Kabila's history of Marxism, however, was seen to have been tempered by his apparent recent embrace of a "free market philosophy."[1] The fragmentation of the Congo was also mentioned as a possible outcome of an uncertain situation (McKinley, 1997, May 18: A1).

On the following day, in another front-page story, Raymond Bonner and Howard French introduced regional politics into the mix of issues facing the Congo, citing the key role played by the Rwandan army in Kabila's military victory, although the problems inherent in what was truly a marriage of convenience were not discussed (1997, May 19: A1). These problems were raised a few days later, however, when McKinley pointed out that Rwandan support in the war against Mobutu was "almost certain to complicate Mr. Kabila's efforts to govern this fractious country of more than 200 tribes, since it essentially brought to power the Tutsi, who in the Congo are a minority group with strong ties to Rwanda" (1997, May 22: A1).

The first mention of international politics beyond Africa came in a "Reporter's Notebook" piece by Howard French in which he argued that the influence of France in the region was waning—this to the extent that even "the word France was almost a curse." It was argued that continued support for Mobutu on the part of Paris during the war, combined with a grudge against Kabila, left France in the rare position of not "calling the shots" in the region. In the opinion of one Congolese source, "The old days are over" (1997, May 20: A11).[2]

Another issue raised by Howard French in early Congo coverage was Kabila's seemingly weak commitment to democracy: "For many Zairians, after living lives stunted by a ruinous dictatorship [freedom combined with hard work] sounded almost like a complete deliverance. Often, however, even on the first day of the county's new leadership, there were questions about democracy" (1997, May 19: A10). A more optimistic assessment of the power transition was offered by Nicholas Kristof, who in a long background piece on the Congo introduced the first *thematic*, as opposed to *episodic*, frame. Here the Congo was portrayed as "emblematic of a group of countries in Africa that have been disasters for their inhabitants." Stressing the "rich country/poor people" reality of life in the Congo, Kristof maintained that with the fall of the Mobutu dictatorship, the Congo "has a chance to remake itself" (1997, May 20: A1). In an op-ed article a few days later, Kristof offered his formula for successful development in post-Cold War Africa—follow the example of Asia in pursuing "an outward-oriented, market-based economic policy coupled with an emphasis on education and health care" (1997, May 25: IV1).

It was the issue of how far the United States should press Kabila on holding early elections that give rise to the first set of letters to the editor, all three of which were critical of US concerns over Kabila's commitment to democratic practice. On May 23, University of Chicago Professor Andrew Apter cautioned the Clinton administration against pressuring Kabila into holding quick elections, arguing that "in its myopic rush to promote democracy ... the Administration is putting the development of a real democracy at risk." He argued that prior to holding any elections, the "patronage model of big-man politics" needed to be replaced, and a system of accountability "applying to all politicians," including the president, had to be put in place. Only when these were accomplished, he argued, could "viable elections" be held (1997, May 23: A30). Martin Mbuga claimed that Western criticism of Kabila was "hypocritical," arguing that the new ruler should not be held "to Western standards of government and bench-marks for human rights, which have proved disastrous in many African countries." He went on to point out that since "neither the United States nor the United Nations provided viable solutions for Zaire in the past, their new role as Monday morning quarterbacks is laughable" (1997, May 23: A30). A third letter claimed that rather than being interested in "political and economic democracy," the real interest of the United States lay in "the right of American-based corporations to exploit the resources of the indigenous population. In other words, democracy for transnational corporations and the American interests that profit from them" (Laderman, 1997, May 23: A30). On May 30, it was reported that Kabila had promised "a transition to democracy with elections in April 1999," to which John Dinger, commenting for the US State Department, indicated that "a two-year period does not seem unreasonable to us" (as quoted in McKinley, 1997, May 30: A1).

Another dimension stemming from Rwandan support for Kabila in the removal of Mobutu was added to the agenda of problems on May 27. In a front-page story, Donald McNeil reported "some form of systematic killing of [Hutu] refugees" in eastern Congo, coupled with a destruction of evidence. Moreover, the implications of this abuse of human rights extended beyond the Congo: "Assuming that Rwanda may be behind the killings ... diplomats and aid workers have begun to suggest that the United States, Britain and other donors should threaten to cut off the $600 million a year they give to Rwanda." As one source put it, "Pressure, massive pressure, is all these regimes understand" (1997, May 27: A1). In a letter responding to that story, Helen Fein, executive director of the Institute for the Study of Genocide, called for pressure on the Kabila government "to protect the right to life and to acknowledge its responsibility ... to prevent further mass killings of Rwandan refugees ... to allow international observers to investigate and to bring those responsible for such murder to justice" (1997, May 30: A28).

The first op-ed article offering specific direction for US foreign policy appeared on May 29. Harvard academics Jeffrey Sachs and Robert Rotberg argued that because the West was responsible for creating Mobutu, it now "has a moral duty to help rebuild Congo ... even if the new leader isn't making the task an easy one." Specifically, they told the US to "abandon its calls for early elections," and added: "There can be no illusions of quick progress in Congo. Its wealth has been pillaged for decades, and the Belgian colonizers did nothing to build the foundations for self-government before they left in 1960. Today, the western nations, once agents of despair in Zaire, can help start the rebuilding of one of the most troubled parts of the world" (1997, May 29: A21).

The first *New York Times* editorial dealing with the Congo following Kabila's accession to power appeared on June 12, and it recapped the problems facing the new government: its alleged involvement in mass killings of refugees, its reputed shallow commitment to democracy, its restrictions on human rights, its deferral of elections, and its failure to incorporate other anti-Mobutu groups into government. In view of past US failures to rein in the excesses of Mobutu, the Clinton administration was advised to preach "civic virtue to Mr. Kabila." In addition, a policy of "tough love" was advocated: "America should provide aid *only if he* [Kabila] *begins to move Congo away from the human rights abuses and dictatorship* it suffered for so long under Mr. Mobutu" (*NYT*, 1997, June 12: A28; italics added).

The issue that dominated June coverage was the question of what had happened to the Hutus who had fled Rwanda in 1994 and did not return in late 1996: "How could 220,000 people simply vanish?" The answer, Donald McNeil suggested, was that Rwandan troops took revenge against suspected Hutu *génocidaires*, "massacring refugees, including women and children, and burning the bodies" (1997, June 1: IV4). As well, Susan Moeller's idea of "compassion fatigue" on the part of the West was already evident as one unnamed UN official advised that "the international community is tired of the Tutsi-Hutu mess" (as quoted in Bonner, 1997, June 6: A1).

It was, however, specifically on the issue of refugee massacres that US envoy to the Congo, Bill Richardson, appeared to make some progress, securing President Kabila's commitment to a UN investigation of accusations of the "killing of thousands of refugees." Assistant Secretary of State for Human Rights John Shattuck placed the following spin on what was called "a major breakthrough": "I think [Kabila] realized that he could not get American support or assistance unless he took the right steps" (as quoted in Bonner, 1997, June 8: A1). A second *New York Times* editorial dealt specifically with the killing of refugees, elevating it to a defining issue for Kabila: "The coming days will show what kind of ruler Congo's new President ... is likely to be." Beyond facilitating the work of a UN team investigating alleged massacres, "Mr. Kabila must also see that United Nations refugee workers and the Red Cross are allowed access to all remaining refugees." The editorial ended by placing Kabila on a short leash: "He needs to start delivering on the humanitarian agenda raised by Mr. Richardson if he wants continued American support" (*NYT*, 1997, June 26: A26).

At the same time, the US strategy of linking aid to good behaviour on the part of Mr. Kabila was called into question. In an article dealing in general with the effectiveness of foreign aid, Bonner asked whether "financial aid from the West would save Congo from becoming another Rwanda?" *Not very likely* was the answer given by Douglas Bandow, Senior Fellow at the Cato Institute, who offered the thematic assessment that "foreign aid has not delivered self-sustaining economic growth or prevented collapse of numerous poor societies into chaos." Of significance as well, Bonner's article ended with a pessimistic appraisal of Mr. Kabila: "There is nothing in [Kabila's] background to suggest that he will be a democrat, though some men around him have democratic desires" (1997, June 22: IV5). Moreover, the new president was reported to have taken a "hard line against dissent" by arresting long-time opponent of Mobutu, Étienne Tshisekedi. According to Howard French, the arrest appeared "to confirm the fears of many that political intolerance and arbitrary use of power would be watchwords of the Kabila era" (1997, June 27: A1).

Kabila's continuous sparring with the UN in its attempts to investigate charges of the mass killing of Rwandan Hutu refugees and attempts to stifle political dissent were the focus of reportage over the summer and fall of 1997. On these issues evaluations of the new Congolese president were not favourable. In early September an editorial wove together two Rwanda-related problems facing Kabila, one domestic and one international. The domestic problem focused on the lack of legitimacy faced by his government: "Many Congolese now distrust the Kabila forces as an instrument of Rwandan foreign policy and inadequately representative of the country's ethnic diversity." The international problem centred on his need to protect his Rwandan allies from a UN investigation of alleged massacres of refugees, an issue on which "the Kabila Government seems to show that its real goal is endless delay." The editorial argued that while the United States had a responsibility to rebuild the Congo, there were limits to this enterprise: "Washington should not repeat its original mistake [of supporting Mobutu] by giving a blank check to a new strongman who refuses to be accountable to his own people and to the international community" (*NYT*, 1997, Sept. 2: A20). By mid-September Howard French reported that Kabila was "locked in a showdown with the United Nations [the outcome of which] could critically influence his government's prospects for survival and how it is seen by much of the world" (1997, Sept. 15: A1).

Key international financial donors served notice on Kabila that continued loans to his government would "be contingent on human rights improvements and a real commitment to democratic elections," but the Congolese government did not appear impressed. Biyoya Makutu Kahandja, a senior official in Congo's Foreign Ministry, voiced his government's dissatisfaction with the UN, commenting that "the history of our country and the United Nations is a history of failed romance." In turn, Bill Richardson reflected US displeasure with Kabila's actions: "We very much wanted to give him the benefit of the doubt and to help him ... But when it appears that his government turns its back on important commitments made to the international community, he leaves us with few options" (both as quoted in French, 1997, Sept. 15: A1). By the end of the month French concluded that the new government had "given its citizens little real sense of where it is leading the country"; as well, clashes were reported between Kabila's Rwandan and Angolan allies, signalling the beginning of future problems. A foreign businessman highlighted the president's dilemma: "The West is telling Kabila to allow the U.N. to start digging up mass graves or else ... and Rwanda is whispering back in Kabila's ear: Dig a hole and we'll put you in it." A Western diplomat offered what turned out to be a prophetic assessment of the situation: "What we have is a lot of instability in [eastern Congo] with no quick end in sight" (both as quoted in French, 1997, Sept. 28: A10).

A five-month assessment of Kabila's rule concluded that he had not been able "to gain control over the eastern provinces ... and his rise to power has not brought peace to Central Africa." The chief problem identified by James McKinley was "the age-old animosity between the Tutsi and Hutu ethnic groups" (1997, Oct. 13: A1). Specifically, "since Mr. Kabila's victory, Congolese Tutsi have become more and more dominant in local administration and in the army. Resentment has grown among other ethnic groups, many of whom regard the Tutsi as invaders from Rwanda." An unnamed local journalist claimed that "the longer the Tutsi soldiers stay here, the more insecurity there will be in this area" (as quoted in McKinley, 1997, Oct. 13: A6).

In a mid-October front page "news analysis" article, Howard French discussed a new model of regime change in Africa which he termed "change by the gun" (1997, Oct. 18: A1). At least in part due to a lack of response on the part of the West to Mobutu's neighbours' military intervention to oust him, French argued that African states had come to believe they had "a green light to violently replace unfriendly governments on their borders with regimes more to their liking." And, he claimed that in the case of the Congo, in the eyes of many Africans, the result has been a close identification of the United States with the Kabila government, leading them to interpret "Washington's relative quietness on issues of human rights and democracy as a sign that the United States is mostly preoccupied with securing a new ally in a country immensely rich in natural resources" (French, 1997, Oct. 18: A7).

The final issue to gain prominence in 1997 was the mid-December visit of US Secretary of State Madeleine Albright to the Congo as part of a seven-nation trip to Africa. This visit, seen as an attempt to bolster Kabila's presidency, was generally not viewed favourably by the *New York Times*. A mid-December editorial claimed that although "Ms. Albright broadly defended democratic principles, she too often glossed over the abusive practices she met, most notably Mr. Kabila." It argued that the Congolese president "has shoved aside opposition leaders, stymied United Nations human rights investigators and failed to deliver on his promises to end corruption" (*NYT*, 1997, Dec. 17, A30). Three letters to the editor related to the Albright visit appeared, two of which supported the critical position expressed in the editorial, along with one (from the Congo's UN representative) that supported Kabila's actions, which, it was pointed out, were taken in the face of most difficult circumstances.

It is safe to say that President Kabila's media "honeymoon period," to the degree that it can be said to have existed at all, was at best characterized by skepticism and at worst by hostility. By the end of 1997 it should have been clear to all who read the influential newspaper that the *New*

York Times was not pleased with a US policy that it saw as supporting a president who was not likely to provide solutions to the Congo's many problems.

1998: The Start of the Second Congo War

In early 1998 reporting on the Congo was sparse, with only seven inside-page and "World News Briefings" appearing from January through March. The most notable of these was a report of President Clinton's Africa visit in late March during which he met with President Kabila, among other leaders. The media issue agenda remained focused on human rights abuses, both past and present. In a letter to the editor, human rights advocate Lesley Carson linked the two, arguing that in addition to pushing the investigation of what had happened to the Rwandan Hutu refugees, "the United Nations and the United States should also condemn the increasing attacks by the Government on human rights groups in Congo" (1998, Apr. 18: A18). In mid-April the forced withdrawal of the UN team investigating atrocities was reported and UN Bureau Chief Barbara Crossette described the Congo as "steadily sliding back into repression since the overthrow of Mobutu Sese Seko last May" (1998, Apr. 16: A1). While State Department spokesperson James P. Rubin expressed "disappointment at the Congo's unwillingness to assist the U.N. in this mission," it was also reported that the administration had asked UN Secretary-General Kofi Annan to cut Kabila some slack as "Washington was interested in building good relations and influence with the new Congo Government." Reed Brody of Human Rights Watch was skeptical about the benefits of such an approach: "Kabila should not be rewarded for this stonewalling by stopping the investigation now, when we haven't got to the bottom of who was responsible" (both as quoted in Crossette, 1998, Apr. 16: A6).

A *New York Times* editorial in early May provided a one-year anniversary assessment of Kabila's rule, concluding that "far too much of the Mobutu style remains." The United States was credited with having done its share in reaching out to Kabila, but the Congolese leader was described as "a rigid and intolerant autocrat who scorns democracy, jails rivals and has stonewalled the United Nations." The editorial took the position that the $50 million aid package promised the Congo should be reviewed: "Those [parts] that can be administered independently of the Kabila Government and directed to humanitarian and development needs should continue. But programs likely to tighten Mr. Kabila's grip or signal Washington's support for his methods should not" (*NYT*, 1998, May 4: A18). A letter from Congolese native Sozi Sozinho agreed:

"If Laurent Kabila ... is going to move away from the demagogy of Mr. Mobutu, the United States will have to make it clear that it is not going to tolerate the brutality it once ignored" (1998, May 6: A22).

Howard French delivered his own one-year assessment on Kabila's rule, saying that much was expected, but "the last year has seen one of Africa's most dramatic unravelings of a political honeymoon" (1998, May 21: A1). An African diplomat commented as well that "when [the Kabila government] came to power, they had the world at their feet. But ever since it is almost as if they had deliberately gone out of their way to turn people off." A diplomat assessed the difficult situation facing the United States: "Our policy calls for supporting the Government, but at this point it is pretty much for lack of an alternative ... That means searching around for the few bright spots, because there is an awful lot of darkness out there" (both as quoted in French, 1998, May 21: A6).

The Second Congo War that followed the critical split between Kabila and his Rwandan and Ugandan backers in August 1998 began with the news that Tutsi troops had "seized control of several cities in Eastern Congo ... threatening [Kabila's] hold on power." A rebel leader claimed that he "had decided to remove [the president on grounds of] nepotism, corruption and bad governance" (as quoted in French, 1998, Aug. 4: A1). According to French, "Mr. Kabila now faces the problem that bedeviled his predecessor ... keeping the Congo whole. But he does so with far fewer friends within Africa and abroad than he had a year ago." It was also noted that Kabila had now identified Rwanda as "the enemy" and was leaning on Angola for support (1998, Aug. 4: A6). An editorial laid the blame for the new conflict squarely on Mr. Kabila: "Few African leaders have squandered political opportunities faster than Congo's President ... His authoritarianism and ineptitude have cost the Congolese people their best chance in a generation for democracy and economic renewal." It went on to point out that "the United States, which has given him crucial diplomatic support, has become disenchanted with his performance" and that "his record to date provided no basis for optimism" that he would be able to broaden and democratize his rule (*NYT*, 1998, Aug. 5: A22).

Belgian African expert Felip Reyntjens identified "two unresolved problems" as being at the root of the conflict, both thematic: "the legal status of eastern Congo's so-called Banyamulenge [Tutsi] population, and Rwanda's own festering conflict between its large and disenfranchised Hutu majority and the Tutsi regime that seized power in the midst of a campaign of genocide aimed against its people in 1994" (French, 1998, Aug. 9: IV3). According to a Central African diplomat quoted by French, "what we are all realizing is that over the long term there is going to be trouble in our region until the problem of Rwanda itself can be sorted out. And almost no one seems to focus on that."

Moreover, French made very explicit the subordinate role Kabila had played in the removal of Mobutu: "Suddenly, as the Rwandan-led 'rebellion' swept Zaire, Mr. Kabila, *the Rwandan-selected front man for the invasion*, went from being an obscure and inconsequential Mobutu opponent to President-in-waiting" (1998, Aug. 9: IV3; italics added). For his part, Kabila labelled "the uprising as a thinly veiled Rwandan invasion" and insisted that "Rwanda has territorial and economic designs on his country" (French, 1998, Aug. 14: A5).

While the United States had reconciled itself to the departure of Mobutu under the concept of "African solutions to African problems," it was now clear that the Congo's problems had not been solved by Mobutu's removal. According to a news analysis piece by French, the immediate effects of the new war were "still unpredictable. But what is feared ... is that the rivalries and instability the tensions create will eventually be played out on a far larger stage [and that] the outcome of this conflict ... is likely to be decided by more powerful neighbors" (1998, Aug. 19: A3).

The fate of the Congo as a unified state was the issue that dominated media coverage throughout the remainder of 1998. It was reported that South African President Nelson Mandela had attempted "to negotiate a peaceful resolution to the conflict" that was feared would lead to the break-up of the Congo: specifically that "the rebels would end up controlling the northeast region near Rwanda and Uganda, while the Government would dominate in the West and South" (Onishi, 1998, Aug. 24: A1). However, according the Suzanne Daley, "Mr. Mandela was basically told to go home" (1998, Aug. 24: A4).

Fearing both the regionalization of the conflict and the break-up of the country, the *New York Times* threw its weight behind a negotiated settlement in which the United States was urged to use its influence to get Rwanda, Uganda, and Angola to end their participation in the conflict. Specifically, "Washington must insist that [Rwanda and Uganda] halt their assistance to rebels and commit to keeping Congo unified" (*NYT*, 1998, Aug. 26: A20). In a letter to the editor, Angola's ambassador to the United States defended his country's intervention, pointing out that Angola had "very specific, short-term goals ... to contain the conflict and facilitate a negotiated solution to an unfortunate and dangerous rebellion" (Dos Santos Franca, 1998, Sept. 1: A24). Southern Illinois University history professor Anthony Cheeseboro disagreed with the editorial, arguing that a ceasefire might have unintended negative consequences: "If regional powers obtained their own zones of influence as a result ... Congo would become a de facto partitioned state. It would be better if one side or the other won rather than having a stalemate involving negotiations and peacekeepers" (1998, Aug. 30: IV4).

In early December Donald McNeil reviewed the status of the conflict in thematic fashion. He pointed out that contrary to past practice in Africa (whereby states generally respected the territorial integrity of their neighbours), the Congo was different, with "troops from as far south as Namibia and as far north as Chad ... fighting inside the vast equatorial basin of the Congo River." Nor was McNeil optimistic regarding the future for the Congo, pointing out that historically the east was tied economically to Uganda and Kenya, while the south traded with Zambia and South Africa, with "only the west and interior answering to the capital, Kinshasa." It was feared that prolonged fighting could lead to "a formal division" along these lines. Two factors were cited as driving the conflict: at the societal level, *tribalism*, and at the state level, *self-interest*. The result was a Congo that was described as "prone to fracture ... With Congo as weak as it is, it is simply too big, too central and too rich in resources for its neighbors not to encroach" (McNeil, 1998, Dec. 6: IV5). In a Christmas Day news analysis article, Ian Fisher wrapped up the 1998 framing of the crisis by exploring one of these problematic resources: diamonds. He emphasized the central role played by diamonds in sustaining the conflict: "Now that the foreigners have fled, industry analysts and dealers say, the rebels as well as Ugandans and Rwandans whose countries back the rebels, are buying up diamonds, presumably to finance the war" (1998, Dec. 25: A4).

1999: The Initial Search for Conflict Resolution

Reporting in January 1999 continued with a focus on the issue of the possible fragmentation of the Congo and ways to deal with it. Continuing in the thematic mode, Ian Fisher and Norimitsu Onishi pointed out that in fact the "Congo has rarely belonged to itself alone. Now, this vast unsteady state has become a battlefield for soldiers from no fewer than six foreign nations who are fighting a war that has as much to do with problems outside of Congo as inside it." The result was that the Congo had split into two parts, "perhaps for good" (1999, Jan. 12: A1). Moreover, it was feared that "the Congo war may become a point of departure from which African nations begin to re-imagine themselves in ways not possible under the old rules" and that "the national boundary lines that have defined African security for a century, and lent some stability, may slowly come apart." A senior European diplomat referred to the Congo War as "the first big test of national boundaries [in Africa, offering that] nobody is happy with the borders they have but nobody wants to open

Pardora's box" (as quoted in Fisher and Norimitsu, 1999, Jan. 12: A9). That story prompted a letter from Florida Atlantic University geography professor Martin Kenzen, who argued that in spite of obvious difficulties, the Congo conflict merited international intervention: "The West must try to prevent what could surpass the Rwandan genocide. Foreign intervention is seldom a sensible option, but foreign intervention created the situation, and, with ethnic factions possessing modern weaponry furnished by the West during the cold war, it is the most ethical thing to do" (1999, Jan. 15: A22).

In a June news analysis piece, Donald McNeil addressed the role of the international community in the ongoing ceasefire process and found little that was reassuring:

> Although the world has been willing to bomb Slobadan Milosevic into submission and to lean heavily on India and Pakistan to stop fighting, the pressure on the warring parties in Congo is fraternal, and relatively weak. The United Nations would like the fighting to end, and so would regional powers from Libya to South Africa. But nations that might contribute peacekeepers—including South Africa, Nigeria and Egypt—cannot offer the legions of trained forces needed to police a country 200 times the size of Kosovo, *and the rest of the world is not volunteering*. (1999, June 30: A3; italics added)

McNeil further noted that "the United States, the United Nations and the European Union are attending the [peace] talks, but seem content to sit and watch ... hoping for the best."

July 1999 saw the signing of a peace agreement, the Lusaka Accord. Norimitsu Onishi claimed that if it held, it would "bring closure to the single event that has destabilized all of Central Africa: the genocide in Rwanda." He acknowledged, however, that the task would not be easy. Among the key provisions of the agreement were the disarmament of the Hutu Interahamwe militia (which had taken refuge in eastern Congo following the Rwandan genocide), the withdrawal of all foreign troops within 180 days, and the granting of equal status to all ethnic groups in the Congo, a provision which was described as "clearly intended to protect the Tutsi minority" (1999, July 9: A8). McNeil, however, pointed to an immediate problem: neither of the two major rebel groups (the Movement for the Liberation of the Congo and the Congolese Rally for Democracy) had signed the agreement. He went on to probe the broader implications of the agreement: "In some ways the document reflects a triumphant trend for the continent: finding African solutions to African problems. In others, it betrays the continent's deadly weakness—because no great powers are guaranteeing the peace, the participants are forced to accept language that virtually begs for help" (1999, July 11: A9).

To find such help, "the United Nations so far has pledged only 500 peace observers. South Africa, Nigeria, Egypt and others might offer some troops—but these would number only in the low thousands." In a follow-up news analysis article, McNeil offered a pessimistic take on the outcome of the agreement, pointing to the anomaly "that everyone had endorsed it ... except the rebels who started this last round of the war." Especially troublesome in his view was that "even a fully subscribed cease-fire agreement would have proved difficult since crucial issues—particularly disarming Hutu militias in eastern Congo—were left vague." It was pointed out that "they were not represented at the talks, and they have everything to lose" (1999, July 12: A9).

It was at this point that a significant involvement in the conflict on the part of the UN was called for: "Kofi Annan [was] reported to favor sending up to 20,000 peacekeepers, drawn mostly from African countries, to Congo, feeling the organization must do at least as much as it did in the Balkans to keep peace." This position, however, appeared less than realistic as it was "not clear that the United Nations peacekeepers would be willing to take heavy casualties to disarm any of the factions" (McNeil, 1999, July 12: A9). An editorial in early August argued that for the Lusaka Agreement to have a chance for success, "Rwanda and Uganda must press their rebel clients to sign" the negotiated settlement (*NYT*, 1999, Aug. 3: A14).

Ian Fisher further examined the destabilizing role that the Hutu Interahamwe militia (estimated to number between 5,000 and 25,000) played in the conflict. Given their "status as international outlaws," Hannelie de Beer, a senior researcher with the South African Institute of Strategic Studies, claimed that "it will be very difficult to disarm them, if not impossible," especially since President Kabila had recruited them as allies in his struggle against the rebel forces that threatened his government (as quoted in Fisher, 1999, Aug. 4: A1). Fisher emphasized the regional connections of the conflict, indicating that "the war in Congo is in part the last chapter of the mass killings in Rwanda in 1994." Moreover, he claimed that at least part of the solution to the conflict was to be found in Rwanda: "Critics of Rwanda say that there can be no real solution to the interahamwe until the Rwandan government greatly expands power sharing with the Hutu majority. The United States also comes under heavy criticism in the region—and much suspicion in Congo itself—for its close relationship with the Rwandan Government" (1999, Aug. 4: A10).

In late September it was reported that a small number of UN military observers had been sent to major countries participating in the conflict. However, failure of these same parties to agree on a facilitator for the peace process led US Ambassador to the UN Richard Holbrooke to issue a warning that no "political or financial support" would be forthcoming from Washington for "the planned deployment of 500 United Nations peacekeepers." On a trip to Rwanda, Holbrooke advised: "We have made it clear that the United States will be unable to support a move to the next step of U.N. peacekeeping if the Lusaka parties do not themselves choose the facilitator called for under their own accord" (as quoted in AP, 1999, Dec. 10: A9). Two days later Holbrooke added: "The United States, this administration, is committed to help in the region ... But we are not going to go blindly with a United Nations peacekeeping operation just to make it look as if we are doing something" (as quoted in Crossette, 1999, Dec. 12: I13).

2000: "Africa's First World War"

Congo reporting in 2000 began with a historical review of the circumstances that had given rise to the seemingly endless bloodshed between Hutu and Tutsi, not only in Rwanda and Burundi, but in eastern Congo as well. Ian Fisher pointed out that "all this fighting makes the Great Lakes region one of the most grim and complicated places on earth." Moreover, the conflict was seen as "one where well-intentioned outsiders periodically wonder whether, and how, they might step in to halt the violence" The key thematic question addressed was whether the Congo's pervasive violence could be attributed to "old hatreds" or to "political manipulation." Fisher chose the latter, arguing that while "ancient divisions, even animosities, exist ... it takes a political elite to seize on them and transform them into something far more violent as politicians seek power for themselves." Human Rights Watch Congo consultant Alison Des Forges expressed some optimism, arguing that "trust-building" and "evenhandedness" in dealing with abuses perpetrated by both Hutu and Tutsi should be the focus of international attention, while Jan van Eck of the Center for Conflict Resolution in Cape Town pointed out the paradox that the "mutually awful pasts [of both Hutu and Tutsi] may offer an opportunity for starting anew" (as quoted in Fisher, 2000, Jan. 2: IV10).

The first *New York Times* editorial on the Congo in the new century also took a cautiously optimistic stance. Presenting the Congo as "a key link in the chain of interconnected conflicts that are ravaging a vast swath of Africa from the Horn of Africa to Namibia," the editorial highlighted the consequences of the conflict: "thousands of civilians" killed, "many more ... dying from disease and hunger [and] nearly a million Congolese" driven from their homes. However, referring to an "American-led focus on the conflict in the United Nations Security Council" which resulted in US support for a peacekeeping force of about

5,000 troops to support 500 ceasefire monitors, the editorial saw "a small glimmer of hope." The proposed force would have no American troops involved, nor would it, or should it, "interpose itself between active combatants. Rather it would provide security in relatively stable zones, which would allow monitors to document violations [of the July 1999 Lusaka Accord]." This optimism was tempered by the reality that "there is reason to be wary of another dangerous U.N. peacekeeping operation in one of the world's most intractable war zones." It was argued, however, that if "an environment safe enough for peacekeepers can be established, the plan deserves our support." And, as was stressed in numerous prior analyses, "how to neutralize the ethnic Hutu militias that found sanctuary in eastern Congo after participating in Rwanda's genocide in 1994" was the chief problem standing in the way of achieving a peaceful settlement (*NYT*, 2000, Jan. 31: A24).

The newspaper's UN bureau chief Barbara Crossette was far less optimistic. She reported that "diplomats and United Nations officials say they see in Congo's complicated war a challenge like no other the organization has faced since the Balkans disintegrated into ethnic warfare after the collapse of European communism." It was also widely recognized that it was essential that the UN be able "to mount a credible operation in Congo [or] the organization will be in danger of repeating its experience in Somalia and Rwanda, two regional conflicts that it proved unable to bring under control." Moreover, a lot was at stake: Richard Holbrooke had told both UN officials and members of Congress "that the Congo operation may be the United Nations' last chance to prove it can get peacekeeping right" (Crossette, 2000, Jan. 31: A6).

What was in effect a mini-journal article (5,588 words), researched by an assemblage of reporters and written by Ian Fisher and Norimitsu Onishi, was published (beginning on the front page), on February 6. It referred to the Congo as perhaps "the richest patch of this planet [but] also one of the biggest battlefields in Africa's history ... '*Africa's first world war.*'" The conflict was described as a stalemated "series of related wars [three were identified], fueled by ethnic conflict, by a scramble for power and riches among people with very little of either, and by leaders with little idea of responsibility for those people" (2000, Feb. 6: I1; italics added). Motives and capabilities of all the international and major non-state actors in the conflict were evaluated, and it was noted as well that the US had been "accused of keeping the war going by failing to strongly condemn its allies, Rwanda and Uganda." Also assessed was the likely success of a proposed UN peacekeeping force of just over 5,500 troops. The conclusion was that the force was "far too small" to be very effective, with Jakkie Potgeiter of the South African-based Institute for

Strategic Studies claiming that "it's totally inadequate." According to Fisher and Onishi, "practically, the proposed deployment would probably mean battalions of soldiers placed in three strategic spots around an area roughly as big as Western Europe" (2000, Feb. 6: I10).

Also reviewed in the piece was the history of the earlier United Nations Operation in Congo (ONUC: July 1960-June 1963), which in July 1961 had a force on the ground of "almost 20,000 military personnel and 2,000 civilians," although it was noted that a force of only 4,000 had been approved initially. The authors pointed out that "as envisioned, the new peacekeeping operation in Congo will be about one-quarter that size" (Fisher and Onishi, 2000, Feb. 6: I10). Interestingly, this truly remarkable article occasioned only two letters to the editor. William Hartung, a senior fellow at the World Policy Institute, claimed that the article had understated "the role of American policy in fueling the conflict": both its long-time support for the Mobutu regime and, more recently, its transfer of "more than $125 million in armaments to governments involved in the Congo war [specifically] Rwanda, Uganda, Burundi, Angola, Namibia and Zimbabwe" (2000, Feb. 10: A30). Some weeks later, Kathryn Fuller, president of the World Wild Life Fund, stressed the devastating effects the war was having on "the already critically low populations of lowland gorillas, elephants and numerous other species" (2000, Feb. 23: IV4).

In an end-of-February editorial, the *New York Times* endorsed the UN Security Council decision "to send *a peace-monitoring mission* to Congo" as sound in principle, but stressed that the project had to "move ahead with caution." It emphasized that the force should not, and could not, enforce a peace among "unwilling combatants, nor disarm them." It should focus instead on the limited objective of "reinforcing the will" of the peace accord signers to live up the agreement. The editorial went on to weigh the risks of the operation against its benefits, and came down on the side of its benefits:

> Without effective international support for Congo's tenuous peace accord there is every likelihood of a wider war. But one may reasonably hope that the difficulties can be eased enough to create acceptable circumstances for the U.N. mission to proceed. *The U.N. must be sure, though, that it is not embarking on a futile operation, for the failed mission would be worse than no mission at all.* (*NYT,* 2000, Feb. 29: A20; italics added)

Another dimension of the complex conflict—that of the role of diamonds in sustaining it—was addressed in another long front-page news analysis article, also researched by various reporters and written by Blaine Harden. The upshot of this piece was that while the precise percentage of diamonds on the world market coming from what were termed "conflict zones" was difficult to establish, figures ranging from 3 to 10-15 percent were likely. Whatever the percentage of conflict diamonds, Congolese diamond buyer Willy Kingombi Idi pointed out the obvious: "You can't wage war without money, and diamonds are money." The importance of diamonds in the continued violence was confirmed by another diamond buyer: "What do you think is the reason for this war?" Papa Ben answered his own question. "It's only about the riches of this country" (both as quoted in Harden, 2000, Apr. 6: A1/A10).

In May, news of the capture and detention of ninety-two UN officials who were part of the peacekeeping force in Sierra Leone further dampened hopes of a successful deployment of a UN mission to the Congo. Norimitsu Onishi put the following spin on this development: "For those hoping for peace in this vast, broken country in the heart of Africa, the news ... could not have come at a worse time ... The events immediately raised doubts about peacekeeping in Congo, in particular, and Africa, in general." With the UN force in Sierra Leone numbering 11,000, Onishi claimed that "a force in Congo, to be effective, would have to number in the tens of thousands, rather than the 5,500 the United Nations is preparing to send" (2000, May 5: A1). Richard Holbrooke "acknowledged that it would be harder to persuade Congress to finance peacekeeping operations [in the Congo]," while Kofi Annan recalled the so-called "Somalia effect" generated by the killing of eighteen US troops in 1993 and offered the assessment that "after Sierra Leone, I think there's going to be very little encouragement for any [Western countries] to get involved in operations in Africa" (as quoted in Onishi, 2000, May 5: A1).

The UN mission was dealt yet another blow later in May, when Senator Judd Gregg (R-NH) "used his power as chairman of the Senate Appropriations Subcommittee to stop the State Department from transferring the [$368 million] already approved by Congress—to the United Nations for missions in Congo, East Timor, Kosovo and Sierra Leone." It was claimed that this action had "infuriated the Clinton administration and some of its allies." It was explained that "Mr. Gregg, like many of his Republican colleagues in Congress, has a low opinion of peacekeeping in particular and President Clinton's foreign policy in general" (Weiner, 2000, May 20: A1). An unnamed Clinton administration official commented that Gregg's refusal "really throws a spanner in the works ... When the U.N. sees the U.S. Congress is reluctant to pay the bills, they are less inclined to go along with U.S. leadership." Yet another American official claimed that "it undermines the capacity of the U.N. to do its job and undermines our credibility to argue that we are serious about enhancing the peacekeeping ability of the U.N." (both as quoted in Weiner, 2000, May 20: A8).

In early June the International Rescue Committee (IRC) released a study indicating that "two years of war have caused the deaths of more than 1.7 million people in eastern Congo, where people who manage to flee the fighting often die of hunger and malaria while hiding in impenetrable forests." If anything, this estimate of deaths was reported to be "conservative" (Crossette, 2000, June 9: A1).

The summer of 2000 perhaps can be seen as marking a low point in prospects for peace in the Congo, as Rwandan and Ugandan forces (supposedly on the same side) fought against each other over control of the city of Kisangani. In September Ian Fisher offered a pessimistic prognosis on the health of the Lusaka Peace Accord. Rebel leader Jean-Pierre Bemba announced: "We are at a turning point ... Is Lusaka alive or not? That is the question" (as quoted in Fisher 2000, Sept. 18: A8). The conflict was described by Fisher as "complicated ... a war rarely seen up close, and getting worse." He saw the "few surviving strands of the peace accord [unraveling, making] the United Nations' hope of stationing peacekeepers in Congo even less likely" (2000, Sept. 18: A1). Fisher claimed that "almost none of the agreement has been fulfilled. So no one with a stake in Congo—warring parties or outside nations eager for stability in central Africa—can say whether it is moving toward peace or further from it" (2000, Sept. 18: A8).

In a news analysis article, London-based financial correspondent Alan Cowell wove a critique of International Monetary Fund (IMF), World Trade Organization (WTO), and World Bank policies, pursued "at a time when the gaps between rich and poor are widening," into a review of Michela Wrong's recently published book on the Congo's long-running Mobutu dictatorship.[3] Again employing thematic framing, he pointed out that the problems associated with globalization were widely evident in Africa, but that "no single country has taken the bizarre interface of ill-fated international lending and corrupt politics to the same extremes as Congo, the former Zaire." Both the late dictator and the international financial institutions came in for their share of the blame. Moreover, while things were characterized as bad under Mobutu, there appeared to be little improvement under the government of Laurent Kabila, which was described as "a continuation of ... the history of venality" (Cowell 2000, Oct. 8: III7).

In mid-December French ambassador to the UN Jean-David Levitte indicated that he sensed "a political will in the region to move forward [and] if our partners in Africa are ready," it might be possible to send peace monitors to the contested cities of Kisangani and Mbandaka. Levitte went on to offer the opinion "that eventually peacekeepers would have to be stationed on the border between Rwanda and Congo 'where the heart of the problem lies'" (as quoted in Crossette, 2000, Dec. 15: A7).

2001: From Kabila Père to Kabila Fils and a "Glimmer of Hope"

Mid-January 2001 brought the news of the assassination of Laurent-Désiré Kabila at the hands of his bodyguards. In spite of proscriptions against speaking ill of the dead, assessments of the elder Kabila's leadership remained pervasively negative. For example, he was described by Norimitsu Onishi as having "deposed one of Africa's great dictators but then brought his country into even worse disarray." Onishi claimed that Kabila had "ruled even more harshly than the dictator from whom he said he freed the Congolese" (2001, Jan. 17: A1; A6). It was not immediately clear what impact Kabila's death would have on the "two-and-a-half-year war that has drawn in half a dozen African nations and destabilized all of central Africa [although it was pointed out that he] had long been considered the main obstacle to any diplomatic resolution to the current conflict" (Onishi, 2001, Jan. 17: A1). Kabila was also cited as the chief reason why the UN had not been able to deploy the 5,000-strong peacekeeping force that had been authorized for the Congo.

Ian Fisher and Rachel Swarns pointed out that Kabila's enemies are "aware that the uncertainty [surrounding his death] could explode into greater violence," with Zimbabwe singled out as "a key player in Congo." South African security analyst Hannelie de Beer claimed that "this Congolese government has no chance without [Zimbabwe]." As well, Richard Holbrooke "warned all foreign armies inside Congo. 'They should not seek to take advantage of the events in Kinshasa to expand their presence'" (both as quoted in Fisher and Swarns, 2001, Jan. 18: A10).

An editorial continued the condemnation of the elder Kabila's rule, claiming that he was "welcomed as a conquering hero ... in 1997 ... but like so many self-proclaimed liberators across post-colonial Africa, Mr. Kabila proved to be a tyrant himself." His death, however, was not seen as likely to "resolve Congo's myriad problems," as it was pointed out that "Mr. Kabila was not the only leader in the region blocking peace." Leaders of Angola, Namibia, Zimbabwe, Uganda and Rwanda were also singled out for mention in this regard. The editorial also offered advice regarding US foreign policy: first, that "all sides [should be urged] to exercise restraint in the perilous days ahead [and, second, that] the incoming Bush administration should refrain from embracing a new regime until it has demonstrated a commitment to peace and accountable government" (*NYT*, 2001, Jan. 18: A22). A letter from Michael West, assistant professor of African and Afro-American studies at the University of North Carolina at Chapel Hill, was perhaps the most critical of the elder Kabila: "Never in the history of postcolonial Africa has one ruler been the source of so much havoc, spread across so many countries, affecting so many people." For West, however, Kabila's death was seen to have a bright side; it "may provide a face-saving cover for some of the more reluctant combatants in Congo's imbroglio, like Zimbabwe and Namibia, to withdraw" (2001, Jan. 23: A20).

Initial framing of his appointed successor, Joseph Kabila, the deceased president's son and leader of "Congo's armed forces," was only slightly more positive. He was described by Fisher and Swarns as "a more private person and without the charisma of his father." It was also noted that "he has faced criticism for not being able to speak Lingala, the main language of Congo." Onishi and Fisher described the younger Kabila as "respected but ill prepared to lead a large country still in the grip of a 29-month war," and assessed his chances of holding on to power as doubtful. In fact, a Western diplomat was skeptical that "Joseph Kabila is in control. He's been put in as a figurehead until the real power structure turns out." According to the correspondents, "what is clear, however, is that many Congolese are getting ready to oppose the new president, secretly or openly" (2001, Jan. 21: I8).[4] A former colonel in Mobutu's army was openly derisive: "Kabila's son is nothing special. He's zero. He received his basic training in Rwanda, he goes to China for more training and comes back as a major general. You don't lead a country like Congo with that level of training. I don't think Joseph will last." On the other hand, Commander Sylvain Buki, chief of staff of the Congolese Rally for Democracy Army, described Joseph Kabila as an "honest man. He's not complicated. He is a moderate. He is a man who wanted change" (both as quoted in Onishi and Fisher, 2001, Jan. 21: I8).

An editorial published a week following the assassination contained both pessimistic and optimistic notes. It pointed out that while the presidency of Joseph Kabila "hardly represents a bright new era for that war-battered nation ... the advent of new leadership in Kinshasa, combined with a new administration in Washington, presents an opportunity for fresh thinking on Congo's ruinous war." It also reiterated an earlier assessment that a "key to untangling the warring parties is to disarm thousands of Rwandan Hutu soldiers and militiamen who fled into the eastern Congo after participating in Rwanda's genocide in 1994." Finally, commenting that "Laurent Kabila was a major obstacle to peace in

Congo," it called upon both this "friends and foes to step back and find a way to bring an end to this catastrophic war" (*NYT*, 2001, Jan. 26: A18).

An op-ed article by Michela Wrong put a different spin on the situation: that fears of a "possible fragmentation of one of Africa's largest counties" was misplaced because "Congo stopped meeting the criteria of a nation-state well before the war that led to its occupation ... by foreign armies." In her opinion, the real outcome of the "succession period [will be] to decide only who wins the right to distribute Congo's mineral resources, rather that who gets to 'rule' in any traditional sense of the word." Citing the International Crisis Group's assessment that "the restoration of territorial integrity for Congo ... 'is in no one's interest other than the Congolese's,'" she claimed that who controls Joseph Kabila is unimportant: "The unpalatable truth is that no matter who fulfills this role ... the question has long ceased being of relevance to most of Congo's inhabitants" (2001, Jan. 29: A23).

By early February, cautious optimism began to prevail over pessimism. An editorial praised the efforts of newly appointed US Secretary of State Colin Powell. Powell's meetings with Rwanda's Paul Kagame and Joseph Kabila were singled out as sending "a welcome signal that the new administration understands the gravity of Africa's multiple crises and intends to play a role in solving them." As well, a perceived even-handedness toward Rwanda and Congo was cited as an improvement over policies followed by the Clinton administration, which was judged to have been "insufficiently critical of general and widespread abuses committed by [Rwanda] and their rebel proxies." The editorial ended by putting a realistic face on the challenges facing US foreign policy: "The United States cannot end Africa's political and military conflicts, including the convulsions in Sudan, Sierra Leone, Angola and Burundi. But some creative diplomacy by General Powell can be constructive. His quick engagement with Congo is a promising start" (*NYT*, 2001, Feb. 2: A18).

Following the encouraging meeting between Joseph Kabila and Paul Kagame in Washington, the UN announced that "hoping to seize the opportunity provided by the change in leadership in Congo," it had decided to send fewer peacekeepers (about 3,000) than had been originally approved (5,537), but to send them sooner (Crossette, 2001, Feb. 13: A9). By early March, an editorial suggested that "recent developments offer tentative grounds for hope that the major belligerents may finally believe that peace is in their interest." It was also pointed out that the younger Kabila "has wisely decided to participate in talks with rival factions on the country's political future," a strategy rejected by his late father. The editorial recognized that "warlords and ethnically based militias still prey on Eastern Congo. Even so [it argued] for the first time in years citizens of Congo have reason to hope steps toward a real peace are being taken" (*NYT*, 2001, Mar. 5: A16).

In mid-April Norimitsu Onishi published an account of an interview with Joseph Kabila, who was described as "at the age of 29, not only the world's youngest president, but also the leader of Africa's most dysfunctional government." Assessments of the new president continued to be relatively positive: "So far, Mr. Kabila has made a good impression, especially in Western capitals where his father had been in the habit of making a bad one. For the first time in nearly two years, things are inching forward in Congo, a nation that had been left for dead by many until January" (Onishi, 2001, Apr. 15: I3). Onishi also identified a problem that would continue to bedevil chances for peace—the political ambitions of the Movement for the Liberation of the Congo's Jean-Pierre Bemba, who was "reportedly enraged at the warm welcome the new president has been getting abroad." Joseph Kabila's hold on power, however, was still seen to be tenuous, with "most believ[ing] that Congo's powerful allies and their Congolese representatives, chose Mr. Kabila to avoid a political and military crisis following the assassination. Whether he remains in power, the argument runs, depends on whether he serves their interests" (2001, Apr. 15: I3).

In mid-May the UN Security Council planned a trip to Africa to be led by French Ambassador Jean-David Levitte, who indicated to Barbara Crossette that he felt "that this is the moment for a concerted push on Congo." The ambassador claimed that even before the recent leadership change, the countries that had signed the 1999 Lusaka Peace Accord "have become tired of this war ... They have been trying to build an exit strategy." The assassination of the elder Kabila gave the process a push: "Against this background the new president injected a new climate, a new disposition. We have a president who is really willing to move things forward toward peace—peace inside the Congo and peace with the neighbors of the Congo." Crossette noted, however, that the UN was strapped to send peacekeepers to Africa, as there were "no more that 3,500 observers and support troops set aside for Congo, which is nearly as large as Western Europe." Ambassador Levitte asked that "if the Security Council and the U.N. as a whole were not going there, who would go?" Levitte provided the answer to his own question: "Nobody. Nobody" (as quoted in Crossette, 2001, May 16: A5).

A letter from Herman J. Cohen, who had served as assistant secretary of state for Africa from 1989 to 1993, noted positively "the growing impatience of the United States with Rwanda and Uganda" over failure to withdraw their troops from Congo. He called for additional pressure on Rwanda and Uganda in the form of a suspension of "the tens of millions in World Bank and European Union budgetary support dollars [which he claimed] has effectively financed Rwanda's and Uganda's wars in Congo since August 1998" (2001, Apr. 21: A14). An end-of-May editorial continued to push the theme of Western economic pressure to end the war. Citing "a disturbing U.N. report," it claimed that the "nearly three-year-old civil war serves the economic interests of some of the West's staunchest African allies and an array of foreign businesses." Specific countries named were Rwanda, Uganda, and Burundi, along with "some three dozen foreign businesses ... identified as having imported minerals from Congo through Uganda and Rwanda." The editorial suggested that placing "an embargo on minerals, timber, gold or diamonds shipped from states whose forces currently occupy territory in Congo—states that would not normally export large quantities of these resources—may be necessary." Pointing out that "as many as 2.5 million Congolese may have died from starvation and disease in eastern Congo [the editorial argued that] legitimate companies have no business profiting from this catastrophe" (*NYT,* 2001, May 29: A14).

In a review of ABC network's *Nightline* series on the Congo, "Heart of Darkness," written just before the events of September 11, 2001, Julie Salamon reported that Ted Koppel admitted that the program had "come late to the Congo story, in part because 'the place is distant and dangerous and not easily accessible.'" Koppel also found "Africa, particularly Congo, difficult to pin down." Salamon had no clear idea of the impact that this belated media coverage might have on American public opinion, pointing out that "times and the news business have changed ... Blanket coverage on Fox, MSNBC or even the more world-conscious CNN is unlikely. Yet as Mr. Koppel reminds us at the end of his report: 'It's not over. It continues'" (as quoted in Salamon, 2001, Sept. 6: E8).

Readers were also reminded by Michela Wrong of just how intractable the Congo conflict had been in her review of Che Guevara's book, *African Dream: The Diaries of the Revolutionary War in the Congo*, which chronicled the guerrilla leader's ill-fated mid-1960s campaign in the Kivu region of eastern Congo. She pointed out that currently, in the very same area, "in both government territory and rebel-held areas, warlords squabble over turf while taking for granted a grass-roots support they never worked to acquire. The Congolese people remain as sidelined and irrelevant to proceedings as ever" (2001, Nov. 11: VII24).

In late December, Rachel Swarns assessed the negative impact of the events of 9/11 on media coverage of the Congo: "The countries of sub-Saharan Africa have always had to fight for America's attention. Lately, most have fallen off the map. Nowhere is this clearer [than] in Congo, which has been ravaged by a three-year civil war with five foreign armies taking part." She pointed to a number of recent "setbacks, little noticed in the United States. Peace talks to lay the groundwork for a transitional government collapsed in October. In November, the United Nations reported that countries like Uganda, Rwanda and Zimbabwe were continuing to plunder Congo's riches, while relief agencies say soldiers engage in widespread looting and extortion" (2001, Dec. 23: IV4).

2002: A Deceptive "Light at the End of the Tunnel"

Just when one might have thought that things in the eastern region of Congo couldn't get much worse, in fact they did. The Mt. Nyiragongo volcano, near the city of Goma, erupted, resulting in what the Rwandan ambassador to the African Union, Pascal Ngoga, called "a catastrophic emergency." In light of the civil war that had "turned Congo into one of Africa's deadliest places," Oxfam's Rob Wilkenson described the situation as "a natural disaster on top of a conflict that has already cost millions of lives" (both quoted in Lacey, 2002, Jan. 19: A3). However, the disaster did not appear to have softened the position of Congolese Rally for Democracy forces, which were reported to be "barely tolerated by the residents of Goma." Marc Lacey noted that "the Congolese rebel ... group says it has no intention of giving up its fight" (2002, Jan. 27: IV14). Apparently, neither had the Rally's regional backer, Rwanda's Paul Kagame, who indicated that he was "not ready to withdraw his forces from Congo and that foreign diplomats urging him to do so were guilty of 'intellectual laziness' for not realizing why they were there; [namely] Congo's government had backed Rwandan militants" (AFP, 2002, Jan. 26: A6).

Beginning towards the end of February yet another round of peace talks were held in Sun City, South Africa, and, following months of false starts and wrangling, over the summer substantial progress toward resolving the international involvement in the Congo conflict was finally reported. In spite of some optimism, letter writer Jake Werner reminded readers that an enormous task of reconstruction lay ahead. He pointed out that although the immediate cause of the war could be found in the 1994 Rwandan genocide, "it might do us well to remember that this devastating war also had roots in the brutal and incompetent rule of Mobutu Sese Seko, the United States-backed dictator of Zaire." Werner asked that if and when the war finally ended, would the United States help in rebuilding the country, or "return to the business of extracting its mineral wealth at rates favorable to American corporations" (2002, July 18: A20).

An August 1 editorial claimed that the peace agreement signed between the presidents of the Congo and Rwanda "*offers the best hope yet for ending the war* [and that] the United Nations and international donors must help, pressing the countries to keep their commitments." It noted that a Rwandan troop withdrawal was linked to the often mentioned and continuing problem of what to do with the Rwandan Hutu refugees in eastern Congo. Under terms of the agreement, the Congolese government was assigned responsibility to disarm them, after which "the United Nations then brings them back to Rwanda or a third country." The editorial pointed to the obvious: "The U.N. has only 4,000 soldiers in Congo, so *more will be needed*" (*NYT*, 2002, Aug. 1: A24; italics added).

The problem of the Hutu Interahamwe occasioned an op-ed article and a responding letter to the editor. Makau Mutua, professor of law and director of the Human Rights Center at SUNY Buffalo, was less than optimistic that the war, which he described as having "deteriorated into something horribly like a free-for-all, with looting expeditions, disease and rampant famine," would be easy to bring to an end. Echoing the analysis offered by Filip Reyntjens in 1998, Muta saw the chief obstacle to peace not in the Congo, but in "the predicament of Hutu within Rwanda." Citing "the lack of democratic government in Rwanda" (an unelected minority Tutsi government under the leadership of Paul Kagame), he argued that the Hutu militias in the Congo "see the Kagame regime as bent on their permanent subjugation [and that the peace] accord will not alter that situation at all" (2002, Aug. 2: A21). Richard Sezibera, Rwandan ambassador to the United States, saw the situation differently: "The chief obstacle to peace in the Great Lakes region is the continued activity of the forces that committed genocide in Rwanda in 1994 ... The agreement between Rwanda and Congo is a breath of fresh air. We should not allow it to degenerate into farce" (2002, Aug. 9: A14).

Marc Lacey framed the new Congo peace accord as part of a continent-wide trend. In addition to positive developments in Sudan, Burundi, and Somalia, he pointed to the settlement of wars in Angola, Sierra Leone, Ethiopia, and Eritrea. John Prendergast, director of the International Crisis Group's Africa Program, added that "we seem to be in the midst of one of the ebbs of conflicts and one of the flows of peacemaking" (as quoted in Lacey, 2002, Aug. 20: A1). In November, however, Lacey identified a growing problem that in the years to come was to plague hopes for a lasting peace for the Congo: "the disparate and elusive Mai Mai [who] have marched across hundreds of miles of eastern Congo into the power vacuum left by the foreign withdrawals, waging a guerrilla campaign that the United Nations say has driven close to a million people from their homes" (2002, Nov. 21: A1).

In spite of these problems, the peace process went forward. On December 5 it was reported that "as the central African country's long civil war grinds down," the UN had authorized an additional 3,200 peacekeepers for the Congo mission, bringing the total to 8,700. It was noted, however, that at the beginning of December 2002, only 4,200 peacekeepers were actually in the country (Reuters, 2002, Dec. 5: A21). In mid-December, Rachel Swarns reported that a crucial domestic part to the peace puzzle had finally fallen into place: "Congo's government and its major rebel movements signed a peace accord ... hoping to bring an end to the war that has ravaged that country and roiled the continent for four years." She went on to note that "if peace does hold in Congo, historians may well point to this year as a turning point for several African countries rattled by seemingly relentless conflict" (2002, Dec. 18: A12). And so it appeared that at the end of 2002, with agreements on the part of regional combatants to leave the Congo, "Africa's first world war" might at last be over. Unfortunately, as we will review in the following chapter, such optimism was unfounded.

New York Times Framing of the Third Congo War

2003: Fears of "Another Rwanda" Lead to a Stronger International Response

In spite of the apparent end of regional participation in the Congo's war, *New York Times* reporting did not begin in the new year of 2003 with the same level of optimism that was seen toward the end of 2002. The reality sank in early that despite the various peace agreements signed over the previous six months, and even though the major regional combatants had withdrawn their forces, the situation on the ground in eastern Congo remained depressingly similar.

In mid-January the UN confirmed that following the withdrawal of Ugandan troops, rival factions of the Congolese Rally for Democracy (the "National" and "Liberation" militias) were fighting each other for control of the mineral-producing areas of Ituri in northeastern Congo.

In addition, inter-tribal warfare was adding to the Congo's already alarming death toll. According to Patricia Tomé, spokeswoman for the UN Congo mission, in one such massacre "'the testimony given by victims and of witnesses was of cannibalism and forced cannibalism,' including people made by rebels to eat members of their own families" (as quoted in AP, 2003, Jan. 16: A5). In April, the killing of nearly 1,000 people was reported in a massacre in the Ituri region. According to Manodje Mounoubai, a spokesman for the UN mission, this constituted the "the worst single atrocity since the start of the civil war" (as quoted in AP, 2003, Apr. 7: A6). A Western diplomat reinforced the *tribal warfare* thematic frame: "the massacre 'raises all the old demons of the past, where people kill each other with machetes on an ethnic basis'" (as quoted in Reuters, 2003, Apr. 10: A7).

In a perceptive news analysis article, Marc Lacey attempted to explain the persistence of conflict in spite of the peace agreements signed by the major combatants: "In a country of more than 50 million people speaking 700 different languages and divided into 250 ethnic groups, many of them warring ... no negotiating table is large enough to fit all the belligerent parties." He pointed out, for example, that in Ituri, "the conflict between the Hema and the Lendu, the communities involved in the massacre, has been going on for over a century" (Lacey, 2003, Apr. 9: A4). Fabienne Hara, co-director of the International Crisis Group's Africa Program, attributed the persistence of killing to differences between the nature of the conflict at the national and local levels: "Signing a national peace deal is not enough for peace to happen on the ground. That's more difficult." An unidentified aid worker from eastern Congo added to the explanation, pointing out that "right now, there are many kings with their own little jungle kingdoms ... Many of these royals have an interest in the conflict continuing and they regularly stoke the tensions that exist" (both as quoted in Lacey, 2003, Apr. 9: A4).

Lacey was also skeptical about the efficacy of an international military intervention to deal with the problem. He claimed that the UN peacekeepers already in the Congo "know the number of troops it would take to contain such a vast country—about the size of the United States east of the Mississippi—is impossibly high." For Lacey, "the ultimate answer is not one peace process but a separate peace for each little war [with true peace coming only] when each and every conflict across the land is addressed" (2003, Apr. 9: A4). Thus the Hema-Lendu conflict in Ituri was portrayed as but one piece that had to find its place in the solutions to the Congo's complex peace puzzle.

Another major problem for the Congo—the looting of its natural resources—continued unabated as well. As a result, in January the Security Council decided to extend for an additional six months the work of an expert panel that had just recommended placing "financial restrictions on 29 companies based in Congo, Belgium, Rwanda, Uganda, Zimbabwe and South Africa, and to impose a travel ban on 54 individuals, including senior officials of Congo and Zimbabwe, allegedly involved in the pillaging" (Reuters, 2003, Jan. 25: A5).

According to Adam Hochschild, author of *King Leopold's Ghost*, UN concerns over this issue were well placed.[1] In an op-ed article he claimed that "few countries have put much effort into ending this war." As to why this was the case, he explained that "Congo's current situation—Balkanized, occupied by rival armies, with no functioning central government—suits many people just fine. Some are heads of Congo's warring factions, some are political and military leaders of neighboring countries, and some are corporations dependent on the country's resources. The combination is deadly" (2003, Apr. 20: IV3). With respect to the international role in the plundering of the Congo's natural resources, Hochschild argued that an "amazing variety of corporations—large and small, American, African and European—that profit from the river of mineral wealth without having to worry about high taxes ... prefer a cash-in-suitcases economy to a highly regulated one" (2003, Apr. 20: IV3).

While getting the regional "big dogs" out of the scrap may have altered the nature of the conflict, obviously it had not ended the fighting. Whatever the cause, by mid-May the level of violence in northeast Congo had escalated to the point where it had again gained the attention of the UN Security Council. Specifically, the Council discussed "the possibility of inviting *a foreign military force* to help avert any increase in violence in the Ituri province of Democratic Republic of Congo" (Barringer, 2003, May 13: A8; italics added). We take this action on the part of the UN as de facto recognition that the international community was in fact dealing with a Third Congo War—a war with a dynamic that was quite different from the one that had preceded it—one dominated by violent non-state actors, and thus infinitely more difficult to bring under control.

France agreed to provide leadership for a proposed European intervention force, and a spokeswoman for the French-led mission commented that "'we perfectly well understand the security situation on the ground is not secure,' and that the United Nations forces present are not equipped to deal with the mounting conflict." A UN spokesman explained that the force, which was deployed in the area under the terms of the various peace agreements, is there "to monitor the peacekeeping agreement, not to restrain militias from the Hema and Lendu ethnic groups" (as quoted in Barringer, 2003, May 13: A8).

If the long history of violence in the Congo itself was not enough to prompt international attention, the spectre of the Rwandan genocide hung over Council decision making as well. Out-of-control tribal warfare clearly was a frightening reality in the region, and, according to US diplomat Richard S. Williamson, "there is no question that that dynamic lies heavy on us. And that's a good thing. It's a good thing we are all conscious of it" (as quoted in Barringer, 2003, May 13: A8).

Somini Sengupta offered an interesting explanation as to why, prior to these events, the memory of the Rwandan genocide had not been sufficient to motivate the international community into taking action to stop the Congo violence: "The problem, up to now," she argued, "has been *the absence of genocide.*" This, she claimed, was now changing in Ituri, where both Hema and Lendu tribes have "a massacre or two to its name" (2003, June 1: IV1; italics added). However, with respect to an international intervention, questions were raised regarding how many people had to die before one could consider what was occurring constituted genocide and whether genocide applied in situations "where the carnage is mutual."[2] Also problematic, unlike Rwanda and Darfur, was the fact that the Congo conflict did not easily fit into the "morality tale" of "good" vs. "evil" so useful in attracting media attention and thus generating widespread international concern (see chapter 3 of this volume). However, despite the fact that "it is very difficult to find the good guys here," a diplomat claimed "*the international community doesn't think it can afford the stain of another Rwanda*" (unnamed diplomat, as quoted in Sengupta, 2003, June 1: IV1; italics added).

On May 14 Kofi Annan reported that "France has indicated in principle that it is prepared to participate in such a force, provided there is a clear mandate, and other governments join in. So we are in touch with other governments trying to see if they will join France in such an effort" (as quoted in Barringer, 2003, May 14, A7). At this point, perhaps prompted by its embarrassing response to the Rwandan genocide, the United States added its verbal support to the effort: "This is an escalating and serious situation to which greater international attention is urgently needed" (Richard Grenell, spokesman for the American ambassador to the UN, as quoted in AP, 2003, May 17: A2).

Somini Sengupta claimed that the spike in violence in the eastern Congo should not have come as a surprise:

> The grim facts that led to the carnage here were no mystery to anyone, certainly not to members of the Security Council who sent in the peacekeepers. Troops from Uganda were pulling out of Ituri under a multinational peace deal. Rival warlords were at one another's throats. *Indeed, there was no peace to keep in Congo's northeast, certainly not by paltry force of some 300 blue-helmeted Uruguayan soldiers who were deployed with orders to guard United Nations property and to escort aid workers.* (2003, May 27: A1; italics added)

Anneke Van Woudenberg, a senior researcher with Human Rights Watch in London, agreed: "It's an abysmal response by the United Nations ... If the United Nations is serious about peacekeeping, the protection of civilians, if they are going to prevent mass killings, this is a critical test" (as quoted in Sengupta, 2003, May 27: A8). *New York Times* correspondent Nicholas Kristof expressed his concern as well: "In Congo ... 3.3

million people have died because of warfare there in the last five years ... That's half a Holocaust in a single country" (2003, May 27: A25).

By UN standards, the response to the crisis was unusually swift. By the end of May, the Security Council had voted to send a French-led European stabilization force numbering 1,400 (Operation Artemis) to Ituri. "The force, the first part of which is expected to arrive next week, would have a mandate to stabilize the situation in [the city of] Bunia and ensure the safety of the civilian population" (Barringer, 2003, May 31: A3). The Security Council resolution had authorized a three-month deployment that was scheduled to end on September 1. There was concern, however, regarding precisely what this force was prepared to do to bring the situation under control. Javier Solana, the European Union's foreign policy chief, described the mission as "an emergency 'bridging' operation designed to help fill a gap in United Nations scheduling. 'Our objective is to stabilize the situation'" (as quoted in Fuller, 2003, June 5: A5).

A *New York Times* editorial raised the possibility that the UN response might be underpowered, and, just as the UN had "betrayed Srebrenica by failing to send enough men and crippling them with restrictive rules of engagement ... today, the same thing is happening in eastern Congo." While conceding that the recently approved French-led force "is a real improvement [it was feared that it] may not be strong enough." Specifically cited was the concern that the force "will not be able to leave Bunia, the capital [while] much of the population has fled to the countryside, and massacres are occurring there." The editorial suggested that while clearly something needed to be done, any international response had to be done right:

> A strong U.N. force is just one part of the necessary response. The United States, European countries and South Africa must all increase the pressure on Congo, Uganda and Rwanda to carry out the peace accords and stop arming proxy militias. Ituri is one of the most violent and byzantine regions of a dangerous and complex war. There is no peace to keep. In such situations, peacekeepers run great risks, and the U.N. should not send them lightly. *But when genocidal massacres are occurring, the world has a duty to step in.* (NYT, 2003, May 31: A14; italics added)

The deteriorating security situation in the Ituri region also began to attract the attention of letter writers. David Hill suggested that the criteria invoked by President Bush to overthrow Iraq's Saddam Hussein— "his mass destruction of his own people"—could be applied to both North Korea and the Congo (2003, May 16: A26). Peter Bell, president and CEO of CARE, called attention to the inadequacy of the international response to what he described as "the world's most grievous humanitarian crisis," pointing out that "the international community has yet to respond adequately." He suggested that not only should the UN "act now to deploy a sizable peacekeeping force to stop the violence and clear the way for aid agencies ... the United States should vote for rapid deployment and help pay for it" (2003, May 29: A24). Jason Cone added his concerns. Characterizing the Congo as "arguably the world's most dangerous region," he asked: "How many more innocents will have to raped and murdered at the hands of thugs before President Bush opens his eyes to the horror of Congo?" (2003, June 8: IV12). In addition, issues specific to women (e.g., rape and mutilation) were addressed in two letters to the editor, both calling upon the international community to take some action to stem this developing problem. Thus, for a number of reasons, in its early stages the Third Congo War had prompted international concerns that suggested the need for a response that went well beyond the limited monitoring of a peace agreement.

The vanguard of the French-led intervention force arrived in the Congo on June 6 and began the inevitable process of "sorting out" its mission. The French force commander acknowledged that his "mission was 'sensitive and delicate and, without doubt complicated.' [But, he added] 'we have robust rules of engagement.'" Sengupta pointed out that "among the most delicate issues is whether the new multinational force can—or will—disarm the militias," while another pressing concern was whether the "force will do anything to stanch the fighting that goes on across the province, outside Bunia." With respect to the former, Colonel Daniel Vollot, commander of the existing UN force in the region, made it clear that "the force has not come with disarmament as a goal" (as quoted in Sengupta, 2003, June 7: A3). This interpretation was seconded by the French commanding general, Jean Paul Thonier, who commented that "separating the factions is not part of my mission" (as quoted in Sengupta, 2003, June 11: A3).

Nigel Pearson, medical coordinator with Medair, called such a restricted mandate "a blunder," and Somini Sengupta posed the critical question: "If Congolese militias are not disarmed or expelled, how will order be restored?" (2003, June 4: A3). A week later Pearson described the French-led mission as mere "gesture politics" (as quoted in Sengupta, 2003, June 11: A3). Toward the end of June, a *New York Times* editorial reviewed the situation, claiming that a peacekeeping force of 100,000 would be needed to expand the French-led Bunia operation "nationwide." While maintaining that peacekeeping was "not the long-term answer," it was, however, seen to be "needed in the short term" (*NYT*, 2003, June 25: A24).

Some maintained that the US had "not helped [its] credibility by its reluctance to support an expanded United Nations peacekeeping force or by its refusal to contribute troops" (Onyango-Obbo, 2003, July 12: A11). In July, however, the United States began to change its positions at least on the first of these issues. Prior to a trip to Africa, a post-9/11 President Bush distanced himself from his earlier assessment of Africa: "While [it] may be important ... it doesn't fit into the national strategic interests, as far as I can see them" (as quoted in Sengupta and Lacey, 2003, July 6: I1). The reporters added that "Africa finds itself roiled by numerous conflicts, and Mr. Bush will be pressed to beef up American involvement in peace efforts."

Perhaps sensing that the moment was right, Kofi Annan asked the Security Council to increase the size of the UN peacekeeping force in the Congo from 8,700 to 10,800. The US, which earlier had been reluctant to support an enhanced mission, now "was willing to increase troop numbers but wanted to ensure they were equipped to deal with the violence in eastern Congo" (AP, 2003, July 10: A10). By mid-July the UN was discussing sending more peacekeepers to the Congo, with "authority under Chapter VII ... which means the peacekeepers 'can use whatever force necessary' to keep the situation stable" (Barringer, 2003, July 16: A6). By the end of the month, an additional force, bringing the total to 10,800 and operating with a Chapter VII mandate, had been approved.

In late July and early August three articles appeared that dealt broadly with strategies and tactics of peacekeeping. In the first, Felicity Barringer explored changes in the way in which UN peacekeeping operated. As "classical" peacekeeping was originally conceived, UN troops "were likely to be the first force on the ground, after combatants had agreed to step back." Conditions, however, were seen to have changed: "Military action is needed more quickly than a United Nations blue-helmeted force can be authorized and deployed. In these knotted conflicts, ad hoc multinational forces have taken the lead, with the United Nations' blessing, and they have been led by developed countries—the British in Sierra Leone and the French in the Ivory Coast" (Barringer, 2003, July 20: IV4).

Barringer went on to examine the implications of this trend that saw "the countries with the most robust economies ... paying most of the bills." David Rudd, president of the Canadian Institute for Strategic Studies, commented that "it is all well and good to support an operation financially [but] if you subscribe to the notion of some form of global community, this demands an equitable sharing of the risks." Her article ended by introducing the admittedly controversial notion of *privatizing peacekeeping*. Citing the work of the Brookings Institution's P.W. Singer, she explained that privatization would involve tapping the resources of "the growing industry of private military firms ... to protect humanitarian aid workers or to intervene 'whenever recalcitrant local parties break peace agreements or threaten the operation.'" It was noted that "they could even take over the whole operation, as a coalition of private security companies offered to do in the Congo, for $100 million or more" (both as quoted in Barringer, 2003, July 20: IV4).[3]

Long-time UN official Brian Urquhart agreed "on the need for a speedy response to critical situations." However, he offered quite a different solution—that of a long-sought-after UN rapid reaction force: "From a purely practical point of view, a highly trained rapid reaction force, permanently at the disposal of the Security Council, would be the most efficient way of spearheading international efforts to deal with the Liberias of the future." Urquhart acknowledged that the "idea is heresy in some circles in Washington [but that] amid the desperate appeals for help from victims of anarchy and civil war, surely it deserves renewed consideration" (2003, Aug. 7: A23).

In an article focused mainly on the situation in Liberia and the role of Charles Taylor in the violence there, Marc Lacey assessed the trend that saw Africa adopting "a new activist approach toward its trouble spots and its troublemakers." While the term "African solutions to African problems" was not used, Lacey argued that, in addition to Liberia, where the efforts of the Economic Community of West African States (ECOWAS) were cited positively, "Africans are taking the lead in the peace efforts under way in Congo, Burundi, Somalia and Sudan" (Lacey, 2003, Aug. 12: A8).

Interestingly, the withdrawal of the French-led peacekeeping force in September was not reported, nor was there any assessment of the overall effectiveness of its mission. As 2003 moved from fall into winter, pessimism competed with optimism in *New York Times* Congo reporting. Pessimism stemmed from the persistence of violence. In early October, twenty-three bodies (later revised to sixty-five), reported to be "Hema killed by Lendu [were discovered] in a village northwest of Bunia" (Reuters, 2003, Oct. 7: A9). This was followed a few days later by reports that sixteen bodies, reported to be Hutu militia from Burundi, were found by UN forces in South Kivu Province (Reuters, 2003, Oct. 11). And in November, another very troubling issue surfaced: Christiane Berthiaume of the UN's World Food Program reported that "never before have we found as many victims of rape in conflict situations as we are discovering now" (as quoted in AP, 2003, Nov. 6: A6). Unfortunately, the problem of rape was to get even worse in coming years.

Over the same period, however, reporting contained more than a ray of optimism. In late October Marc Lacey commented that "after a calamitous war, Congo is at a fragile point of healing, with a whiff of hope now detectable in the humid air here." This, however, was tempered by the assessment that "beyond the capital ... many Congolese are still running for their lives. Despite the supposed cessation of hostilities, massacres continue in the remote reaches of eastern Congo, where United Nations peacekeepers deployed there, now numbering more than 10,000, always appear one step behind the latest killings" (Lacey, 2003, Oct. 21: A1). These massacres were referred to by William Swing, head of the UN Congo Mission, as "the dying gasps of a spent war" (as quoted in Lacey, 2003, Oct. 21: A1). Reporting for the year ended on November 7 with the appraisal that the US would continue to support "the peace agreement that has brought an end to decades of war in Congo [and that] the country might be one day stable enough to draw the foreign investment to develop its resources, including diamonds and cobalt" (Holmes, 2003, Nov. 7: W7).

2004: Continued Massacres, Rebel Attacks, and Allegations of Sexual Abuse by UN Troops

In spite of Mr. Swing's optimistic assessment, *New York Times* reporting from the Congo in early 2004 did not reflect such optimism. It began with a report that perhaps as many as one hundred people had been killed when "armed fighters attacked several passenger boats in Congo's lawless northeast" (Reuters, 2004, Jan. 24: A6). A UN mission sent to investigate the massacre was also fired upon, forcing the abandonment of the operation (Reuters, 2004, Feb. 5: A4). In addition, it was reported that UN World Food Program workers "*were uncovering rape on a horrific scale* as the peace process allowed them to move deeper into rebel-held regions" (AFP, 2004, Jan. 27: A11; italics added). Putting Congo's crisis into a world perspective, Kamel Morjane, UN Assistant High Commissioner for Refugees, claimed that the Congo and Sudan ranked first in seriousness, followed by Colombia (Forero, 2004, Feb. 5: A6).

In mid-February the first death of a UN peacekeeper was reported—a Kenyan army major had been shot in an ambush of a UN convoy on a road fourteen miles north of Bunia. According to Somini Sengupta, "the killing ... sent a chill through the United Nations mission here and raised new questions about the adequacy of the roughly 5,000 peacekeepers stationed here in Ituri Province, the sprawling eastern swath of Congo thick with gold—and rival gunmen all too willing to fight for it" (2004, Feb. 14: A7).[4]

Two issues were to dominate coverage over the remainder of the year: first, an escalation in Hutu-Tutsi tribal violence that threatened to bring Rwandan troops back into the Congo as combatants, and later, allegations of sexual abuse on the part of UN peacekeepers.

In early June, a new name entered the list of combatants, and it was one that would dominate coverage in years to come: Brigadier General Laurent Nkunda, referred to in a "World Briefing" as a "renegade commander." Nkunda, a former Tutsi rebel leader who had been supported by Rwanda, captured the city of Bukavu, an important trading centre on the Rwandan border. It was reported that the UN's 800-strong contingent of troops in Bukavu did nothing to stop the fighting, resulting in protest riots in Kisangani, where "residents set fire to six United Nations vehicles and an office" (AP, 2004, June 3: A6). The UN's response to these protests resulted in two deaths. UN spokesman Hamadoun Touré claimed that "our security people were overwhelmed ... They had to open fire to calm down the situation" (as quoted in Lacey, 2004, June 4: A8). The Congolese government accused Rwanda of "helping the former rebel soldiers [but Rwanda] denied responsibility" (Sengupta, 2004, June 7: A3).

The situation was clearly deteriorating. Agence France-Presse reported that the threat of a major war in eastern Congo had sent 30,000 refugees fleeing across the border to Burundi (AFP, 2004, June 21: A3). By mid-August the violence in eastern Congo had spilled over into Burundi, where some 180 Banyamulenge (Congolese Tutsi) refugees were killed by a Burundian Hutu rebel faction that claimed the targeted camp was being used as a base to attack them (AP, 2004, Aug. 15: I10).

In early October the UN responded by increasing "the peacekeeping force in Congo by 5,900 troops and police officers—less than half the amount requested by ... Kofi Anan" (AP, 2004, Oct. 2: A4). In November, Reuters reported that UN forces were joining Congolese military patrols in eastern Congo. These operations were described "as a dress rehearsal for larger operations aimed at restoring order in the east, where thousands of Hutu fighters from neighboring Rwanda have ignored calls for them to disarm and return home" (2004, Nov. 11: A9). The joint mission strategy did not appear effective as in early December the UN mission cited evidence "indicating that Rwandan troops had crossed the border into Congo" (Wines, 2004, Dec. 3: A6). With the Congo death toll now estimated by the International Rescue Committee (IRC) to stand at 3.8 million (Lacey, 2004, Dec. 19), toward the end of the year hundreds of thousands of additional refugees were reported fleeing from advancing rebel troops (AP, 2004, Dec. 20: A11).

Toward the end of November an issue arose that was to continue to plague the Congo mission throughout its deployment—serious allegations of sexual abuse on the part of UN peacekeepers. *New York Times* UN correspondent Warren Hoge filed the initial report, along with the following preliminary response by Kofi Anan: "This is a shameful thing for me to have to say and I am absolutely outraged by it ... My attitude toward sexual exploitation and abuse is one of zero tolerance, with no exception" (as quoted in Hoge, 2004, Nov. 20: A6). This report was followed up about a month later in a front-page story by Marc Lacey wherein it was reported that the UN was in fact dealing with "150 allegations of sexual abuse committed by United Nations peacekeepers stationed in Congo ... These allegations ... include sex with underage partners, sex with prostitutes and rape. A confidential report ... says the exploitation 'appears to be significant, widespread and ongoing'" (as quoted in Lacey, 2004, Dec. 18: 1, 10).

Allegations of sexual abuse led to two letters to the editor, each taking a different position. The first, by International Rescue Committee (IRC) Director Dr. Richard Brennan, argued that in spite of the obvious setback caused by the sex abuse scandal, "stark humanitarian needs should lead us to reform and strengthen, not disband, the peacekeeping contingent" (2004, Dec. 21: A28). Larry Vigon, who described himself as "a fervent supporter and defender of the United Nations," disagreed, arguing that "when United Nations peacekeepers charged with protecting the most defenseless and helpless members of the Congolese society become involved in the sexual exploitation and abuse of young girls, one must ask whether the United Nations is worth defending" (2004, Dec. 24: A18).

2005: UN Peacekeeping Efforts Remain under Attack

As was the case with the previous year, 2005 was not kind to UN peacekeeping operations in the Congo. Charges of sexual abuse, as well as a perceived inability to curb widespread tribal violence, continued to give grief to the mission, contributing to a widespread feeling at the UN "that a big change is necessary for the institution to regain its footing and restore its name" (Hoge, 2005, Feb. 28: A3).

January began with a report that "sexual abuse of girls by United Nations peacekeepers in Congo has continued despite recent revelations of past incidents and preventive measures ... put in place." UN investigator Barbara Dixon concluded that "the problem was and continues to be widespread" (as quoted in Hoge, 2005, Jan. 8: A7). Toward the end of March, a UN report "recommended ... that offending soldiers and their commanders be punished by their home countries, that payments made to them be recovered and put into a fund for victims and that the United Nations make compliance with these measures a condition for taking part in its missions" (Hoge, 2005, March 25: A8). In June, "for the first time [the Security Council condemned] sexual abuse among peacekeepers, after being told that ... members ignored such exploitation for decades, fearing exposure of their soldiers' wrongdoing" (Reuters, 2005, June 1: A9).

The UN's peacekeeping operations on the ground did not fare much better. By the end of February the Congo mission had grown in size to become the UN's largest peacekeeping operation worldwide (numbering about 16,000), with 4,800 troops deployed in Ituri (Lacey, 2005, Feb. 26: A6). However, at the same time, nine UN peacekeepers were killed and mutilated in Ituri in an assault that was described as "the worst attack in the six years of the mission." It was reported as well that "more than 70,000 people had fled their homes and settled in camps scattered throughout the region" and that it was the mission of the UN peacekeepers who had been killed to protect one of those camps. Johannes Wedenig, head of UNICEF's operations in Ituri, acknowledged that "the situation has been deteriorating over the last two months" (as quoted in Lacey, 2005, Feb. 26: A6).

In early March the UN forces counter-attacked, killing up to fifty Lendu militiamen suspected in the earlier killing and mutilation of UN peacekeepers. In the report UN officials claimed that "since 1999, fighting between Hema and Lendu militias has killed more than 50,000 and forced 500,000 to flee their homes." The French chief of staff of the UN forces in Congo, General Jean-François Collot d'Escury, stated that the UN force "would 'keep putting pressure on the ground until those militia are dismantled entirely'" (as quoted in AP, 2005, Mar. 3: A11). Marc Lacey reported that "revenge killings between rival tribes, the Hema and Lendu, have turned Ituri into one of Congo's most volatile regions," and a UN official conceded that "we don't have access to most of the people. They're hiding and we don't have any idea of what is happening to them" (Modibo Traore, as quoted in Lacey, 2005, Mar. 6: 13). By mid-March, Jan Egeland, UN Undersecretary for Humanitarian Affairs and Emergency Relief, had elevated the conflict in the Congo to "*the world's worst current crisis*, outstripping that in the Darfur region of Sudan [adding that] *it is beyond belief that the world is not paying more attention*" (as quoted in Reuters, 2005, Mar. 17: A6; italics added).

In a late-May front-page story, Marc Lacey reported significant changes in UN peacekeeping tactics: "Burdened by its inability to stave off mass killings in Rwanda in 1994 and by failed missions in Bosnia and Somalia [the UN] is allowing its peacekeepers to mount some of the most aggressive operations in its history." These tactics included the use of attack helicopters and hut-by-hut searches for weapons (Lacey, 2005,

May 23: A1). According to David Harland, an official in the UN's Department of Peacekeeping Operations, "the ghost of Rwanda lies very heavily over how the UN and the Security Council have chosen to deal with Ituri" (as quoted in Lacey, 2005, May 23: A1). It was noted, however, that UN officials still considered a peacekeeping force that at the time numbered 16,500 to be inadequate for the task at hand.

In a July 3 article in the *New York Times Magazine*, contributing editor James Traub offered an extremely worrying mid-year appraisal of the situation in the Congo, describing the country as "a state in name only ... on life support, attended around the clock by aid organizations, international bankers, diplomats and, above all, by a vast U.N. civilian and military operation costing $1 billion a year" (2005, July 3: VI35). Although the UN's peacekeeping record came in for criticism (the failure to defend Bukavu was likened to Srebrenica), for Traub the Congo's problems were not primarily related to lack of military security—its problems ran deeper: "While we may know how to stand up to warlords and militias, even if the U.N. has trouble mustering the force needed to do the job, *we don't really know what it means to 'intervene' against a political culture that is corrupt, mendacious and self-perpetuating*" (2005, July 3: VI35; italics added). Traub was clearly not impressed with President Joseph Kabila, whom he described as "a feckless character," nor with the upcoming elections that were likely to cost several hundred million dollars. With respect to these elections, MONUC's Special Representative, Ross Mountain, commented sarcastically that "normally you can get a dictator cheaper than that" (as quoted in Traub, 2005, July 3: VI38). Traub's solution to the Congo's problems, however, was not without controversy:

> If we believe that in the post-9/11 world we can no longer afford to let failed states fester, then we plainly owe it to ourselves to stop the Congolese political class from preying on its people and to shape the nascent institutions of state in such a way as to give legitimate economic and political activity a decent shot at survival. Is that, in fact, a prescription for some kind of benevolent imperialism? If so, then bring it on. (2005, July 3: VI39)

Despite Traub's opinion that UN forces had the ability to deal with tribal miscreants, over the final six months of 2005 there were continued reports of massacres, and in December a new group was identified as contributing to the chaos—Uganda's Lord's Resistance Army (LRA).[5] This organization was described as "a guerrilla group that is notorious for kidnapping, raping and maiming thousands of children [and] threatening the stability of three countries, Uganda, Congo and Sudan."

According to Jan Egeland, "more is currently at stake in terms of lives saved or lost in Africa than on any other continent ... We must recognize that too many of these humanitarian crises result from a total absence of peace and security ... Humanitarian aid cannot be an alibi for unwillingness to address the root causes of conflict" (as quoted in Hoge, 2005, Dec. 20: A5).

Nor could the UN seem to escape the continuing impact of the sex abuse scandal. In mid-October, a report by the advocacy group Refugees International concluded that in spite of new procedures devised to deal with sexual abuse on the part of UN peacekeepers, these "measures are not being put into force because of a deep-seated culture of tolerating sexual exploitation" (Hoge, 2005, Oct. 19: A5).

The Refugees International report prompted only the third *New York Times* editorial since the beginning of the Third Congo War, and the first since June 2003. The critical editorial, headlined "The Worse U.N. Scandal," claimed that after almost a year after allegations of sexual abuse had first surfaced, "far too little has been done to end the culture of impunity, exploitation and sexual chauvinism that permits them to go on." Member states were seen as bearing primary responsibility for the abuses, and the editorial proposed that "the clearest possible message needs to be sent at every level that sexual abuse will not be tolerated, that individual offenders will be prosecuted and punished, and that countries that fail to impose discipline will no longer be allowed to take part in peacekeeping missions" (*NYT*, 2005, Oct. 24: A20). In a letter to the editor, Undersecretary General for Peacekeeping Operations, Jean-Marie Guéhenno, disputed the editorial's allegations that the organization had done "far too little" to deal with the problem of sex abuse, claiming that "our strategy of prevention, enforcement and remediation ... is starting to have a real impact" (2005, Oct. 29: A18). While this might well have been the case, there is little doubt that, along with its failure to adequately control the violence in eastern Congo, the sex abuse scandal contributed to an undermining of the UN's reputation as an effective and responsible humanitarian actor (see Kristof, 2006, May 16).

2006: Increased Media Attention, Focused Primarily on Presidential Elections

Congo coverage in 2006 began in January with an Associated Press story on an article published in the British medical journal *Lancet* that claimed that 38,000 people were dying each month in the Congo, mainly due to "easily treatable conditions like diarrhea and respiratory infections." It reported that a total of "nearly four million people" had died between

1998 and 2004 as "an indirect result of years of fighting that has brought on a collapse of public health services." The Congo's minister of information dismissed the report, claiming that "these figures are very exaggerated. All over the world, people die of disease. It's not just Congo" (Henri Mova, as quoted in AP, 2006, Jan. 7: A3).

Regrettably, violence in the Congo was far from over. Towards the end of the month there was a report of an LRA ambush that killed eight UN peacekeepers in a four-hour gun battle (AP, 2006, Jan. 24: A8). Jan Egeland continued to push for a greater international response, claiming that "too few leaders understand that four million people have died and many more can die unless we put it right." Egeland attributed the difficulty in getting the international community more involved in the Congo to the fact that the Congo "was seen as hopeless by many potential donors" (as quoted in Reuters, 2006, Feb. 13: A3).

March saw the beginning of an International Criminal Court (ICC) prosecution of Congolese warlord Thomas Lubanga Dyilo, "founder and leader of ... one of the most dangerous militias in the Congo's northeastern Ituri district." The militia leader was "accused of conscripting and enlisting children under the age of 15 [some as young as 7] into armed groups and using them in hostilities" (Luis Moreno-Ocampo, as quoted in Simons, 2006, Mar. 19: I10). According to Moreno-Ocampo, "Mr. Lubanga's hearing was only the start of cases linked to the years of militia violence in Ituri, which has killed thousands and produced more that 600,000 refugees." In addition, a Human Rights Watch report cited Rwanda and Uganda as having supported Congolese militias for their own economic gain (Simons, 2006, Mar. 21: A6), a charge that was to resurface in future reportage.

Beginning in late March presidential elections dominated media coverage. Marc Lacey led off the pre-election analysis, reporting that the Congo, "battered by almost unimaginable civil strife, is approaching its first nationwide elections in nearly half a century with a mixture of optimism and outright fear" (2006, Mar. 26: I10). The UN peacekeeping force, described as being "in the country and available should violence break out," was seen as playing a key role in the elections. As well, "a separate European Union force of about 400 soldiers is due here before the vote to act as a rapid response force [and] an additional 1,000 or so European troops will be on standby outside the country" (Lacey, 2006, Mar. 26: I10). UN election official Ross Mountain claimed that "compared to the Congo, Iraq's elections were a walk in the park" (as quoted in Lacey, 2006, Mar. 26: I10), and the Carter Center's Colin Stewart described them "as challenging and complicated an election as anything we have seen" (as quoted in Polgreen, 2006, July 1: A1).[6]

In previewing the election, Lydia Polgreen offered a cogent explanation of what the transition from the Second to the Third Congo War had meant for the Congo:

> At the end of the [second] war, the country was carved up by the warring parties to secure peace, with the strongest militias getting top posts in the transitional government and autonomy to rule the areas they controlled. The militias were to disband and be reorganized into a national army.
>
> In reality, the fighting never stopped completely, and some militias have refused to disarm or join the army. Other forces, like the Hutu militias who fled to Congo from Rwanda after committing genocide in 1994, continue to wreak havoc across the countryside. (Polgreen, 2006, July 1: A8)

General Laurent Nkunda was identified as a "potential spoiler," and an International Crisis Group (ICG) report concluded with the assessment that "the logic of the ballot has not yet replaced the logic of the gun ... It has merely become an appendix to it" (as quoted in Polgreen, 2006, July 1: A8). This appraisal was given some credence by a rebel attack that resulted in the recapture of the town of Tchei from Congolese and UN forces that had taken the town in May. A Reuters report claimed that the recapture of Tchei "hand[ed] the world body and the government a major military setback" (2006, July 5: A4).

The UN peacekeeping mission's reputation was dealt yet another blow in an op-ed piece by television journalist Aidan Hartley, who claimed that "not only has [MONUC, described as "an ill-equipped third-world army"] failed to stop the killing, its troops have even been party to some of the violence against civilians whom they were deployed to protect" (2006, July 28: A29). Hartley, on assignment for Britain's Channel 4, accompanied UN forces to the eastern Congo village of Kazana and described a seven-hour mortar barrage, as well as the use of machine guns and rocket-propelled grenades by UN troops in support of the Congolese Army, which he characterized as "the worst abuser of human rights in the country today." According to Hartley, following the battle,

> among the well-tended gardens and thatched huts, we mostly observed signs of civilian life brutally interrupted, with pools of blood alongside half-cooked meals. And after the fighting stopped, as the peacekeepers stood idly by, Congolese troops set every house on fire. When I complained to the Congolese commander, he said, "I can't control my soldiers." (2006, July 28: A29)

In a responding letter to the editor, the UN's Chief of Mission in the Congo, William Swing, claimed that Hartley's picture of Kazana as a peaceful village was inaccurate, citing "no fewer that 19 firefights and attacks originating from militia groups using Kazana as an operational base." Swing also addressed the more general problem of the UN supporting the Congolese Army:

> While it is legitimate to ask the extent to which United Nations peacekeepers should work with an army composed of belligerent forces, the alternative is even less palatable: hostile militias continuing to inflict unbridled violence on a vulnerable civilian population. [He added that] without international support, training, mentoring and monitoring, the Congolese Army could become an equal danger. (2006, Aug. 4: A16)

In October, a *New York Times* editorial focused attention on another particularly troublesome aspect of the Congo tragedy—the use of child soldiers. Citing the ICC prosecution of Congolese warlord Thomas Lubanga Dyilo, the editorial pointed out that as of 2003 "around 30 percent of militia fighters were children." The editorial praised the work of UNICEF and Save the Children for efforts at rehabilitation, and that of the ICC for first establishing rape "as one of the most serious international crimes [thus changing] legal standards and practice worldwide [and] now drawing attention to another, widespread, yet widely ignored, horror" (*NYT*, 2006, Oct. 12: A28). In a letter to the editor, Janet Kim, founder of the Advocacy Lab, offered one of the rarely reported connections between Africa's problems and US foreign policy, pointing out that since 2001 "the United States has supplied substantial military assistance (arms, training or both) to 22 of 26 countries identified as using child soldiers" (2006, Oct. 19: A26).

Nor were the problems of abuse at the hands of the Congolese Army a matter of history. In late November Reuters reported that UN investigators had uncovered a mass grave with thirty bodies at a Congolese Army camp in eastern Congo. The victims were said to have been killed in late August or early September. According to UN spokesperson Kemal Saiki, "apparently these people were executed ... Among them are women and children" (as quoted in Reuters, 2006, Nov. 25: A5). Suspected in the killings was the First Brigade of the Congolese Army, described as "made up of members of a range of rebel and government factions who fought in Congo's War from 1998 to 2003." Despite the cited need to do so, there was an obvious price to be paid by UN peacekeepers for working with the Congolese Army.

2007: Media Advocacy amid Allegations of Horrific Rape and Intensified Fighting

In mid-January, claiming they had not been paid year-end bonuses, Congolese Army troops in Bunia rioted, fired weapons, and engaged in looting and rape. UN troops managed to halt their move on the city, arresting twenty-four soldiers. According to a Reuters report, "the fledgling army is badly paid, operates in appalling conditions and is the worst rights abuser in the country" (2007, Jan. 13: A4).

Following a 1,200-mile cross-country trip, Jeffrey Gettleman's post-2006 election assessment presented a pessimistic take on the situation: standing in the way of progress were "Congo-size obstacles," chiefly neglect and corruption that were "not going away" (Gettleman, 2007, Mar. 28: A1). As an example, he pointed to "the disappearance of millions of dollars meant for the disarmament of militias. In 2004, Western donors gave Congo more than $200 million to get 330,000 militiamen out of the killing business [by providing a salary of] $25 and job retraining." After assisting but a fraction of the total number for which it was intended, "the money suddenly ran out." According to a top UN official in the Congo, Ahmed Shariff, "the money got stolen" (as quoted in Gettleman, 2007, Mar. 28: A11).

Parts of eastern Congo remained clearly beyond the control of the Congolese government, with whatever rule as might exist there exercised by Laurent Nkunda. Nkunda, who was described as "a Tutsi nationalist, and with Hutu death squads roaming the countryside ... sees himself as all that stands between Congolese Tutsis and genocide." Nkunda claimed that "Tutsis who were killed in Rwanda were my friends ... I cannot accept it here" (as quoted in Gettleman, 2007, Mar. 28: A11). It was noted, however, that "Congolese officials continue to accuse Mr. Nkunda of war crimes, including massacring prisoners of war."

In June, the editorial pages of the *New York Times* began to advocate for greater international involvement in the Congo. Beginning on June 12, an editorial pointed out that the Congo conflict had "taken more than three million lives in the last nine years." Moreover, "thousands of people are still dying as violence once again flares in the east ... where government troops and rebels continue their ruthless war of attrition." While the UN peacekeeping force was given credit "for reducing the fighting," it was pointed out that the force has "also been accused of smuggling gold, sexually abusing minors and deliberately killing militia members under its custody. [In addition,] the organization has a poor record of seeing that the guilty are appropriately punished." Primary responsibility for making improvements to the situation was seen to rest with the Congolese government as well as the international community; both needed to work to achieve "better governance, including a healthy, independent judiciary and better disciplined security forces ... Until that happens, the death toll will continue to rise" (*NYT*, 2007, June 12: A22). The editorial appeared just prior to a trip to Africa by op-ed columnist Nicholas Kristof.

Unlike *New York Times* reporting on the contemporary conflict in Darfur, until June of 2007, when four of Nicholas Kristof's articles appeared as products of his trip, op-ed articles had not formed a major part of its reporting on the Congo.[7] In the first article, datelined "on the Rwanda-Burundi Border," Kristof called attention to "the vast human cost when we in the West allow conflicts to fester in forgotten parts of the world." He told readers that since the Rwandan genocide began in 1994, at least 5 million people have died in the Great Lakes region [and that] in the Congo, those deaths are still piling up." Kristof stressed the importance of early intervention in Third World conflicts; specifically the need for "Western military assistance in squashing rebellions, genocides and civil wars, or protecting good governments from insurrections." He noted that "the average civil war cost $64 billion, yet could be suppressed in its early stages for very modest sums." As an example, Kristof pointed to Sierra Leone, where a British military intervention "ended a savage civil war and was enthusiastically welcomed by local people" (Kristof, 2007, June 14: A31).[8]

Kristof's second article recounted an interview with Laurent Nkunda, whom he described as "a smart and charismatic man with a university education [and] a devout Pentecostal." In the interview, Nkunda claimed "I'm not a warlord ... I'm a liberator of the people." Kristof commented, "That's the problem: So are they all." Reiterating earlier comments by the UN's Jan Egeland, Kristof focused major attention on the lack of media coverage of the Congo's woes: "*Probably no slaughter has gotten fewer column inches—or fewer television minutes—per million deaths. So even after all that suffering, Congo still hasn't risen to a prominent place on the international agenda*" (2007, June 18: A19; italics added).

Kristof's third op-ed piece explained how death in the bush worked— it told of a personal encounter with a woman dying from "a deadly mixture of war and poverty." Kristof noted that "even in the 21st century, wars like Congo's—the most lethal conflict since World War II—kill the old-fashioned way, by starving people or exposing them to disease." For Kristof, "the way to help Congo isn't to take individual starving people to the hospital but to work to end the war—yet instead the war is heating up again here, *in part because Congo is off the world's radar*" (2007, June 21: A23; italics added).

In his final article based on the trip, Kristof again stressed the need to draw international attention to the conflict in the Congo: "*This war staggers on in part because the suffering here hasn't registered on the international conscience*, and because it has been allowed to fester and continue" (2007, June 25: A19). He ended by noting that

> there is no simple solution to the conflict, but we can lean on Rwanda to stop supporting its proxy force in eastern Congo, and also work harder to repatriate Hutus who have destabilized Congo since they fled here after the genocide in 1994. We can push a peace process. We can support the U.N. peacekeepers. We can help with the reform and training of Congo's security forces. *And a six-hour visit by Condi Rice would help put the crisis on the map.* (2007, June 25: A19; italics added)

As was the case with his articles on Darfur, Kristof's advocacy for international action did promote a response from readers, but unlike Darfur, only one letter to the editor appeared. Edwin Andrews praised Kristof "for bringing attention to the conflict in the Congo, the world's most horrific since World War II [noting that] it's about time that the world paid attention to this terrible display of humanity ... We should all be outraged at what has happened to innocent Congolese this past decade, and *we must demand that the actions suggested by Mr. Kristof be carried out*" (2007, June 28: A20; italics added).

However, it was not until October, when a front-page story by Jeffrey Gettleman detailed an epidemic of horrific rapes in eastern Congo, that letter writers were again exercised to take up the pen. This time they did so in significant numbers, and without exception their letters called for more international action. Gettleman claimed that

> Eastern Congo is going through another one of its convulsions of violence, and this time it seems that women are being systematically attacked on a scale never before seen here.
>
> According to the United Nations, 27,000 sexual assaults were reported in South Kivu Province alone, and that may be just a fraction of the total number across the country. (2007, Oct. 7: I1)

John Holmes, UN Undersecretary General for Humanitarian Affairs, termed the sexual violence in Congo as "the worst in the world ... The sheer numbers, the wholesale brutality, the culture of impunity—it's appalling." Researcher Alexandra Bilak offered that "it's gone beyond conflict ... Brutality toward women had become almost normal." According to Canadian aid worker André Bourque, "sexual violence in Congo reaches a level never reached anywhere else. It's even worse than in Rwanda during the genocide" (all as quoted in Gettleman, 2007, Oct. 7: I1, I11). It was noted that "the attacks go on despite the presence of the largest United Nations peacekeeping force in the world, with more than 17,000 troops."

A week later, five letters to the editor were published, all demanding a far greater international response than seen previously. For example, Ty Kipling called for a re-examination of "our resignation to this situation and find an actual solution, rather than continue to aid the exploitation of women through desensitivity" (2007, Oct. 14: IV11). Documentary filmmaker Lisa Jackson took aim at what she saw as a lack of *New York Times* attention to the Congo: "Finally the paper of record has acknowledged on its front page the unimaginable horrors being visited on the women and girls of the Democratic Republic of Congo." She cited a UN report calling what was happening to women in the Congo as "beyond rape," and asked, "How far beyond the beyond must this go before an outraged world responds?" (2007, Oct. 14: IV11).[9] Alyoscia D'Onofrio, regional director for the International Rescue Committee in the Congo, reported that the organization had "helped more that 40,000 survivors of sexual violence" in the DRC. She added that "the international community has a role to play in stopping the impunity and holding the perpetrators accountable for the havoc they wreak. We must act to end it" (2007, Oct. 14: IV11).

Toward the end of October heavy fighting was again reported "between the Congolese Army and Laurent Nkunda ... who has accused the Congolese Army of helping the Hutu militias, which the army denies." Adding to the confusion, "the Mai-Mai entered the equation." Described as "a huge force of loosely organized Congolese militiamen, [they] jumped into the fight on the side of the government, saying Mr. Nkunda is a warlord—and not even a Congolese one at that" (Gettleman, 2007, Oct. 25: A3). With more than 750,000 people displaced in eastern Congo, UN spokeswoman Sylvie van den Wildenberg described the situation as "a catastrophe ... All these people are running, and no one seems to know where to go" (as quoted in Gettleman, 2007, Oct. 25: A3).

Mid-November brought the encouraging news that Congo and Rwanda had come to an agreement. The Congo agreed "to disarm Rwandan Hutu rebels on its soil." For its part, Rwanda "agreed to seal [its] border with Congo and ensure that illegal armed groups, particularly a Tutsi insurgency led by Laurent Nkunda ... did not receive cross-border support" (Reuters, 2007, Nov. 12: A9).

In December, however, fighting intensified in what was described in a front-page story by Lydia Polgreen as "a major confrontation between the Congolese Army and a renegade general [Laurent Nkunda]." This fighting was seen as "plunging the country back toward war, threatening to undermine the fledgling democratic state and set off a new regional conflict on a scale not seen here in years" (Polgreen, 2007, Dec. 13: A1). According to Anneke Van Woudenberg, the problem was that "the fundamental issues that led to the Congo war have never really been dealt with ... We are seeing the results of that now" (as quoted in Polgreen, 2007, Dec. 13: A1).

Understandably, the population in eastern Congo was not happy with developments. Lydia Polgreen reported that "the fight against General Nkunda has pushed Congo to the brink of a new civil war" and noted "frustration at the United Nations peacekeeping force and dozens of aid organizations." According to Polgreen, "many Congolese want the United Nations peacekeepers to intervene more forcefully and fight beside the Congolese Army against the rebel forces of Laurent Nkunda." A refugee from the town of Sake complained, "Why is [MONUC] here, if not to fight these people who make us suffer? ... Why don't they help us get peace?" (Mwenge Biroto, as quoted in Polgreen, 2007, Dec. 16: I35).

Polgreen explained in detail the complex linkage between the Rwandan genocide in 1994 and the "seemingly endless conflict that drew in neighboring countries and killed as many as four million people"; the Hutu Interahamwe were never repatriated to Rwanda and now were fighting alongside the Congolese Army against Nkunda's forces. In Polgreen's view, the key to peace in eastern Congo remained the removal of the Hutu militias, and she reported that a peace conference to accomplish this had been planned before the end of December (Polgreen, 2007, Dec. 19: A14). In spite of this development, Reuters reported an increase in abductions of children to be used as fighters. According to Save the Children spokesperson Hussein Mursal, "the situation in eastern Democratic Republic of Congo is catastrophic ... Fighters from all sides are using children as frontline fodder" (as quoted in Reuters, 2007, Dec. 25: A4). It was reported that in addition to heavy fighting between the Congolese Army and General Nkunda in North Kivu province, "a host of other armed groups, including traditional Mai-Mai militiamen and Rwandan Hutu rebels, also roam Congo's eastern provinces."

2008: A Peace Agreement Runs Afoul of "The Legacy of Rwanda" and General Nkunda

In early January 2008 a UN report confirmed prior reports that the Congolese Army was committing acts of violence, including the summary execution of civilians and the use of "excessive force during clashes with the militia last year." Congolese Defense Minister Chikez Diemu responded that "there are means of dealing with such serious issues, and not through the media" (as quoted in AP, 2008, Jan. 6: A6).

At the same time, the peace talks promised in December got under way in Goma amid renewed fears of "a 'Balkanization' of the vast African country." In preparation for the talks, "the government announced the suspension of military operations against Mr. Nkunda's rebels." Nkunda's demands centred on the removal of the Rwandan Hutu Interahamwe and called "for the return of around 46,000 Tutsi refugees forced into exile by violence" (AFP, 2008, Jan. 7: A10).

A front-page story by Lydia Polgreen recounted yet again the origins of the Congo Civil War in the Rwandan genocide of 1994, the flight of the Hutu Interahamwe to the Congo, and their targeting of Congolese Tutsi in eastern Congo. This material put into context the efforts of General Nkunda to protect the Banyamulenge. The critical question centred on whether Nkunda had overreacted to the threat. According to a report by the International Crisis Group, the answer was that he had: "In response to the cumulative deaths of fewer than 20 Tutsi over the past two years, Nkunda has launched offensives that have killed over 100 persons and displaced hundreds of thousands … While Nkunda has defended the Tutsi minority in North Kivu, he has become a potential danger to the community's security as a whole" (as quoted in Polgreen, 2008, Jan. 10: A10). However, Polgreen reminded readers of the fragile state of security for Tutsis in the Great Lakes region of Africa: "Rwanda's history is a powerful touch stone for Congo's Tutsi. Similar disparities—a small group controlling considerable wealth and influence, amid a powerful sense of grievance from the majority—helped create the conditions that led to the genocide in Rwanda in 1994" (2008, Jan. 10: A10).

On January 22 Polgreen reported what appeared to be a landmark agreement between the Congolese government and General Nkunda to end the fighting in eastern Congo. Under that agreement both rebel troops and the Congolese Army were to withdraw from the positions they held, and a UN peacekeeping force would "establish a buffer zone" between them. Nkunda's forces were to be "granted amnesty on insurrection charges" but could be held accountable for "war crimes and crimes against humanity." Foreshadowing greater problems later in the year, it was noted that "the future of General Nkunda, one of the thorniest issues in eastern Congo, was left out of the negotiations" (Polgreen, 2008, Jan. 22: A3).

A day later, Polgreen reported on an International Crisis Group mortality survey that indicated that in spite of the formal ending of the Second Congo War in 2002, "the rate at which people are dying in the country remains virtually unchanged." As well, the survey reported a new figure of 5.4 million Congolese as having died since the beginning of the Second Congo War in 1998. The ICG's Richard Brennan cautioned that "the Congo is still enduring a crisis of huge proportions ... *The international engagement has to be sustained and committed for years to come*" (as quoted in Polgreen, 2008, Jan. 23: A8; italics added).

UN peacekeeping operations continued to garner criticism. In April 2008 allegations surfaced that not only UN peacekeepers, but French troops sent to Congo in the summer of 2003 as a part of the EU stabilization force were accused of torturing a Congolese civilian (Polgreen, 2008, Apr. 3). Further, on May 23, Matthias Basanisi, who had been deputy chief investigator with the UN Offices of Internal Oversight Services in the Congo from 2005 to 2007, took issue with a UN report on an investigation into illegal activities on the part of Pakistani peacekeepers—namely, allegations of "gold smuggling and arms trafficking." The report found that "there was little to warrant prosecution or further investigation." However, Basanisi claimed that he had found evidence "that senior officers of the Pakistani contingent secretly returned seized weapons to two warlords in exchange for gold, and that the Pakistani peacekeepers tipped off two warlords about plans ... to arrest them" (2008, May 23: A25). The UN mission in the Congo received yet another black eye in August with the release of a report indicating "that Indian peacekeepers may have engaged 'in sexual exploitation and abuse.'" Secretary-General Ban Ki-moon was reported to have been "deeply troubled" (as quoted in Schneider, 2008, Aug. 13: A8).

On June 25, what was to be the final Nicholas Kristof op-ed article dealing with the Congo in our study period appeared. Written prior to a UN Security Council special session on sexual violence, it dealt with the issue of rape as a weapon of war. Kristof identified two reasons for using rape as part of a military strategy: First, "mass rape is very effective militarily. [It is less risky and less costly] to terrorize civilians sympathetic to a rival group and drive them away." Second, "mass rape attracts less international scrutiny than piles of bodies do, because the issue is indelicate and the victims are usually too ashamed to speak up" (Kristof, 2008, June 15: IV14).

The *New York Times* did not report the August collapse of the peace agreement between the Congolese government and General Nkunda. However, on October 15, a Reuters "World News Briefing" recounted the effects of this collapse: 100,000 people had fled the fighting in North Kivu Province. In addition, Reuters reported the displacement of an additional 50,000 people in Ituri due to fighting between the Congolese Army and the LRA (2008, Oct. 15). This report was the first in what was, over the next two and a half months, the most intensive reporting of the Congo conflict since the outbreak of Lendu-Hema atrocities in 2003; from October 15 to the end of the year a total of thirty-eight items of content appeared in the newspaper.

In the first of these, Jeffrey Gettleman refocused attention on the issue of rape, commenting that "the recent surge of fighting between the Congolese government and rebel groups" and "the sheer number of armed groups spread over thousands of miles of thickly forested territory ... [make] it incredibly difficult to protect civilians" (2008, Oct. 8: A14).

The renewed fighting dealt another serious blow to the reputation of UN peacekeeping efforts in the region. It was reported that "hundreds of furious protesters hurled rocks at a United Nations compound ... in frustration that peacekeepers had not halted the rebel advance through the countryside." UNICEF's Jaya Murthy explained that "the population is not happy with the U.N. ... They feel they are not protected. They are getting extremely angry" (as quoted in Gettleman and MacFarquhar, 2008, Oct. 28: A6). Alan Doss, the Secretary-General's representative in the Congo, said he "understood the civilian frustration." However, he said: "we cannot have a soldier behind every tree, in every field, on every road and in every market; it is impossible" (as quoted in Gettleman and MacFarquhar, 2008, Oct. 29: A8). At the same time, the recently appointed Spanish general commanding the peacekeeping operation in the region "abruptly resigned." While his resignation was officially attributed to "personal reasons," it was reported that General Díaz de Villegas y Herrería "had criticized the lack of a coherent strategy, the lack of a mandate and the lack of resources needed to get the peacekeeping job done" (Gettleman and MacFarquhar, 2008, Oct. 28: A6).

On the last day of October, Gettleman reported good news from Goma indicating that "the crisis seemed to be easing," although no one seemed to know why General Nkunda "stopped on the outskirts of Goma and decided to call a cease-fire" rather than capturing the city that he was clearly in a position to take. The Congolese government accused Nkunda of "trying to carve out a buffer zone between Rwanda and Congo [and of] being a front man for Tutsi-led Rwanda" (2008, Oct. 31: A12). Whatever truth lay in these allegations, the result for the civilian population was more devastation: "No food. No shelter. Pounding rain. Sick babies" (Gettleman et al., 2008, Nov. 1: A9).

At this point the renewed fighting again caught the eye of the European Union. This time, however, a British Foreign Office spokesperson indicated that the EU "would send troops to Congo only as a last resort if the existing United Nations force needed to be reinforced and diplomatic peace efforts failed" (Reuters, 2008, Nov. 2: I14). Jeffrey Gettleman also reported on the possible involvement of African states. Citing the propensity for neighbours to become involved in Congo's troubles, he began a news analysis piece on the Congo with the words "when Congo shakes, Africa trembles," and Belgian Professor Koen Vlassenroot assessed "the political damage [from the renewed fighting as] enormous" (as quoted in Gettleman, 2008, Nov. 3: A6). Among the problems revealed were the "fecklessness of the Congolese government" and the less-than-stellar performance of the UN peacekeeping mission: "Not only were the peacekeepers unable to stop the rebels' advance ... but they were unable to protect civilians, which is their mandate" (2008, Nov. 3: A6). John Prendergast, now associated with Project Enough, offered a devastating appraisal of UN efforts: "It is remarkable that 14 years after the genocide in Rwanda, U.N. peacekeeping remains as ineffectual at protecting civilians as it was then. This, despite all the rhetoric about the responsibility to protect and never again. Empty slogans for the people of Central Africa" (as quoted in Gettleman, 2008, Nov. 3: A6).

At the UN, Ban Ki-moon offered "to mediate a cease-fire," and both Joseph Kabila and Paul Kagame were reported to have "expressed support for the idea of meeting to hammer out a solution" (MacFarquhar, 2008, Nov. 4: A13). The meeting began a few days later in Nairobi, Kenya. However, "conspicuously absent was the man who started the crisis in the first place: Laurent Nkunda, who has threatened to take over all of Congo." Explaining Nkunda's absence, UN Mission Head in the Congo, Alan Doss, indicated that "Mr. Nkunda was not invited" (as quoted in Gettleman, 2008, Nov. 8: A11).

Amid allegations that both Rwandan and Angolan troops had re-entered the fray, at the end of the meeting "African leaders ... signed a multipronged agreement calling for an immediate end to the conflict." And, in what can only be interpreted as a lack of confidence in the ability of the UN to control the situation, "they said that if United Nations peacekeepers could not protect civilians from senseless killing, African peacekeepers would be sent to the front lines." Nkunda's rebels, however, were unimpressed. Spokesperson Bertrand Bisimwa commented that "the only way for us to resolve this is to sit down and talk with the Congolese government," something the Congolese government had refused to do (as quoted in Gettleman, 2008, Nov. 8: A11). In early December, Reuters reported that the Congolese government and General Nkunda's representatives would in fact meet to "formalize a cease-fire and discuss a peace process" (2008, Dec. 6: A8).

In mid-November the penultimate *New York Times* editorial on the Congo in our study period appeared. While blame for the crisis was spread widely (among presidents Kabila and Kagame, as well as General Nkunda), it was the UN Security Council that came in for the major blast of criticism: "More international peacekeepers and aid are urgently needed, but the United Nations Security Council is shamefully failing to act ... The situation merits the extra 3,000 forces that United Nations officials are begging Security Council members to provide. The Council has been mulling the issue for a month and not acting." While unfortunate moral lapses on the part of UN peacekeepers were acknowledged, the editorial pointed out that "they have helped control the violence," and citing a Council on Foreign Relations Report, it described the mission as "'the single most important factor preventing the full collapse of state authority' in the region." The editorial ended with the charge that "the international community failed to stop Rwanda's genocide" [or to honour the promise] ... "not to let it happen again." It ended with the question, "Has the world forgotten so quickly?" (NYT, 2008, Nov. 13: A36).

International action was not long in coming. A few days later it was reported that France was "circulating a draft resolution ... that would temporarily authorize an additional 3,085 troops and police officers" for the Congo mission (NYT, 2008, Nov. 18: A11). A few days later Jeffrey Gettleman reported that the Security Council had indeed authorized an additional 3,000 peacekeepers, bringing the total force in the Congo "to more than 20,000" (2008, Nov. 21: A14), a number close to ONUC's complement in the early 1960s (see chapter 2 of this volume).

In mid-November Gettleman began a series of on-the-ground news reports from eastern Congo. In the first of these he noted that the ceasefire was reported to be holding but cautioned that "the longer the instability continues ... the more dysfunctional and confusing life [in eastern Congo] gets ... Nobody, it seems, is in charge." He also noted a change in the character of the conflict, describing it as "broader and more focused politically, with [Gen. Nkunda] talking at times of marching to the capital and toppling the government" (2008, Nov. 19: A6). However, a second report claimed that it was not clear that Nkunda had "the professional rank and file to get him to higher office" (Gettleman, 2008, Nov. 20: A16). The final story in the series dealt with the tribal Mai-Mai militias, described as "the third piece to eastern Congo's violent puzzle." According to Gettleman, the degree of Mai-Mai influence was "questionable." However, over "the past few weeks they have emerged as spoilers, fighting on when the other armed groups have agreed to stop." He noted that, as usual, "Congolese civilians have been the victim of most of these skirmishes" (Gettleman, 2008. Nov. 21: A14).

Toward the end of the month, a new rebel offensive was reported, directed "at driving some 1,500 Hutu militiamen out of Congo," many of whom were thought to have fled Rwanda following the 1994 genocide

(AP, 2008, Nov. 27: A11). Although not specifically linked to this offensive, a delayed report recounted a November rebel-perpetrated massacre in the small eastern Congo town of Kiwanja. Although the killings of some 150 people went on for twenty-four hours, a contingent of UN peacekeepers "less than a mile away ... said they had no idea that the killings were taking place until it was all over." It was explained that "the peacekeepers were short of equipment and men [and] had no intelligence capabilities or even an interpreter who could speak the necessary languages." Lydia Polgreen cited the episode as "a textbook example of the continuing failure of the world's largest peacekeeping force, which has a mandate to protect the Congolese people from brutality" (2008, Dec. 11: A1). Anneke Van Woudenberg called the incident "a disaster for everyone ... The people were betrayed not just by rebels who committed terrible war crimes against them but by the international community that failed to protect them" (as quoted in Polgreen, 2008, Dec. 11: A21).

The year ended with an intense probing of the regional dimensions of the conflict. Commenting "that behind any rebellion with legs is usually a meddling neighbor," Jeffrey Gettleman focused on Rwanda's continuing role in the Congo, arguing that "whether the rebellion ... explodes into another full-fledged war, and drags a large chunk of central Africa with it, seems likely to depend on the involvement of Rwanda, Congo's tiny but disproportionately mighty neighbor." Gettleman pointed to the "long and bloody history here" and cited growing evidence "that Rwanda is meddling again in Congo's troubles," mainly by supporting General Nkunda's Tutsi rebel forces. According to Gettleman, "there seems to be a reinvigorated sense of the longstanding brotherhood between the Congolese rebels, who are mostly ethnic Tutsi, and the Tutsi-led government of Rwanda, which has supported these same rebels in the past" (2008, Dec. 4: A6).

At mid-month, Lydia Polgreen cited a UN report that explicitly described the war as "a complex proxy struggle between [Congo and Rwanda] with each using armed forces based in the area to pursue political, financial and security objectives in a region ravaged by conflict." Not only was Rwanda charged with supporting General Nkunda, the Congolese government was accused of "collaborating with the Hutu militia that is led by the authors of the Rwandan genocide" (2008, Dec. 13: A5). Jason Stearns, coordinator of the group producing the report, claimed "It's obvious that Rwandan authorities and Congolese authorities are aware of support provided to rebel groups [but] they haven't done anything to bring it to an end" (as quoted in Polgreen, 2008, Dec. 13: A5). The Rwandan government rejected the report, "describing it as inaccurate and biased" (Reuters, 2008: Dec. 17: A8).

In an op-ed article, former State Department official Herman J. Cohen addressed the implications of the previously discussed report, calling "the conflict in eastern Congo ... as much a surrogate war between Congo and neighboring Rwanda as an internal ethnic insurgency." Moreover, he saw "the only way to end a war that has caused five million deaths and forced millions to flee their homes [lay in addressing] the conflict's international dimensions." Specifically, Cohen claimed that "the failure of international diplomacy [was] related to the economic roots of the problem"—namely, Rwanda's "effective control of Congo's eastern provinces of North and South Kivu": "Having controlled the Kivu provinces for 12 years, Rwanda will not relinquish access to resources that constitute a significant percentage of its gross national product. At the same time, Congo's government is within its rights to take control of the resources there for the benefit of the Congolese people" (Cohen, 2008, Dec, 16: A37).[10]

The final editorial dealing with Congo issues focused on genocide, noting "that it is hard to contemplate man's capacity for inhumanity without feeling despair and paralysis." It called attention to a report on genocide by Madeleine Albright and William Cohen that placed an emphasis on the *Responsibility to Prevent* over the *Responsibility to React*: "The goal is to engage leaders, institutions and civil society in affected communities urgently, and at an early stage when talk and other help may defuse the situation." The Obama administration was counselled to "seriously consider the report's policy recommendations" before it had to react to yet another outbreak of mass killing (*NYT*, 2008, Dec. 16: A36).

On December 20, Lydia Polgreen addressed the political ambitions of General Nkunda, who was described as having "pushed the nation to its most dangerous precipice in years." Polgreen recounted the transition from "a local insurgency aimed at redressing the grievances of a Tutsi minority that felt threatened [into] a rebellion with a broad set of aims that include the removal of President Joseph Kabila, who was elected in 2006 after more than 40 year of tyranny and war" (2008, Dec. 20: A1). The portrayal of Nkunda was generally critical. He had been accused of numerous human rights abuses, and the possibility he "could be a leading figure [in a move to oust President Kabila] is a chilling thought for many Congolese" (Polgreen, 2008, Dec. 20: A16).

While Nkunda continued to remain a problem, year-end progress was cited in dealing with another of Congo's troublemakers, LRA leader Joseph Kony. It was reported that Uganda, Congo, and South Sudan had launched an offensive against the Lord's Resistance Army in Congo, and Congo's Foreign Minister, Alexis Thambe Mwamba, indicated that "he expected to be 'totally rid' of the rebels within days" (as quoted in Reuters, 2008, Dec. 27: A8). As in 2002, advances in bringing peace to the Congo yet again fell short, and we will attempt to bring readers up to date on developments in the Congo in the Postscript to the book.

Media Coverage of the Congo Wars: An Overall Assessment

Before we begin our overall evaluation of US media coverage of the Congo it is important to reiterate that agenda-setting theory maintains that media effects are not immediate. Elizabeth Perse tells us that "agenda setting is not an effect that occurs after a single exposure to the news. Instead, salience emerges in the public's mind because of consistent coverage of certain issues over a period of time" (2001: 99; see also Salwen, 1988). In this study we were primarily interested in two such cumulative effects: First, was media coverage sufficient to place the Congo conflict on the agenda of US foreign policy decision makers? And, following this, was it sufficient to keep it on that agenda over the long duration of the conflict? Second, we wanted to compare television and newspaper coverage to discover how well they performed their "alerting" and "evaluation" functions. Finally, we wanted to compare and contrast Congo coverage with that accorded the conflict in Darfur over the same time period, especially with respect to whether such coverage could be seen as having supported a military intervention on the part of the international community.

Television and Newspaper Coverage Compared

As the previous three chapters have told us, television and newspaper performances with respect to both alerting American audiences to the crisis and evaluating its meaning and impact differed widely. Thus in addressing questions of adequacy of performance in these areas, we must first discuss key differences between the two media as conveyors of news and shapers of public opinion.

In a relatively early comparison of newspaper and television news, William Gormley saw the two media as more complementary than competitive. In identifying their different capacities and strengths, he saw television as holding the advantage in providing timely coverage, while newspapers were better able to deal with a story in depth and at length. Overall, television stories were judged to be "superficial," sometimes serving as little more than "teasers" for a more in-depth newspaper treatment (1976: 96–111).

Canadian media theorist Marshall McLuhan looked at deeper dissimilarities, arguing that different forms of media *do* follow different paths of organizing experience, knowing, and understanding. Print organizes reality into discrete and uniform causal relations, whereas a television viewer is forced to add information to complete the message or image (Carey, 1967). In McLuhan's words, print is "hot"—it does not leave much to be filled in or completed because it extends one single sense in "high definition" (McLuhan, 1964: 22–23). Television, on the other hand, is "cool"; for McLuhan this means a TV image is "low definition" and does not provide detailed information about subjects (317). If one form of media dominates coverage, we might then expect the audience's perception of the story to reflect this. Print seemingly provides clarity and uniformity to the portrayal of individuals and descriptions of events. But in seeking to complete the image, the TV viewer may only be frustrated if, as was the case with the Congo, the story itself is inherently complex and confusing. Contrary to more recent research on television and advocacy (see the views of Kimberly Gross below), McLuhan notes paradoxically that television demands audience participation, yet it does not "excite, agitate or arouse" (337).

In their examination of US media coverage of Darfur, Abdel Salam Sidahmed and colleagues saw variations between the two media differently:

> Television and newspapers each have their own unique style of presentation, which to some extent also influences the nature of the information they lay before the public. With its graphic visual component, television is emotive and high impact, but its standard newscasts at least have few analytical or advocacy elements. Television newscasts contain no equivalent of the op-ed article, or the editorial, or the letter-to-the-editor, but might be said to be comparable to newspaper front and inside news pages. (Sidahmed, Soderlund, and Briggs, 2010: 93)

Perse argues that "although some argue that television's visuals add information that newspapers cannot furnish … most research confirms television's limited effectiveness in transmitting information" (2001: 95). In spite of this, Doris Graber (2005) confirms that television news remains the major source of political news for Americans, and it is reasonable to assume that this is the case more broadly.

Kimberly Gross focuses attention on the emotional impact of television, telling us that "emotional appeals matter. Those seeking to influence opinion and frame political issues to their advantage certainly seem to believe that appeals to emotion aid them in their attempts to gain public support" (2008: 109). Newspapers operate in the cognitive sphere of influence, and she maintains that both affective and cognitive framing effects are important in influencing public opinion on issues of public policy. Finally, Sidahmed and colleagues conclude that while "strictly speaking ... television and print are not directly comparable, with respect to [crisis coverage] their relative performance may nonetheless be assessed on two key components: how well each 'alerted' the American public to the crisis, and how they 'evaluated' the various options for international intervention" (2010: 93).

Quantitative Indicators of Coverage in the New York Times

In the case of the Congo, the difference in the volume between newspaper and television coverage can only be described as huge—a total of 89 stories aired on three television networks over the nearly twelve-year study period from 1997 through 2008, as opposed to 819 items of content published over the same period in the *New York Times*.[1] It is difficult to imagine a greater difference in performance on the part of major media organizations. In fact, we have concluded that with respect to the Congo, television news cannot be considered to have contributed in any meaningful way to either the "alerting" role, where one might have expected at least a reasonable effort, or the "evaluative" role, where less could have been expected due to the conflict's complexity and difficulty in covering it (see discussion in chapter 3).

However, the same conclusion does not apply with respect to newspaper coverage. While even in terms of "quick hit" coverage, television news failed the American people with respect to an important story, the *New York Times* did consistently better on both "alerting" and "evaluation" dimensions. Newspaper coverage did fall off significantly following the end of the Second Congo War in 2002, (totals of 515 vs. 304 items for the two conflicts); however, it seems clear that any reasonably dedicated reader of the international pages of the newspaper would have been aware of the conflict and its severity. Moreover, from reporting by Howard French, Raymond Bonner, James McKinley Jr., Donald McNeil Jr., and Barbara Crossette early in the conflict, continuing with pieces from Norimitsu Onishi, Someni Sengupta, Steven Lacey, Warren Hoge, and Ian Fisher, to the contributions of Nicholas Kristof, Lydia Polgreen, and Jeffrey Gettleman, not to mention op-ed pieces by knowledgeable writers such as Adam Hochschild and Michela Wrong, *New York Times* readers would also have come away with a more than adequate appreciation of the complex nature of the conflict and the difficulties entailed in bringing it under control.

As can be seen from table 6.1a, in 2002 (its leanest year of coverage of the Second Congo War), the *New York Times* ran one more story than aired on the three television networks combined over the duration of that conflict. The overall comparison over the six-year period 1997–2002 stands at 515 stories vs. 59. Moreover, if we examine this newspaper coverage closely we see that in spite of the fact that our 1997 sample covered only seven and a half months, it was the fall of Mobutu Sese Seko and his replacement by Laurent Kabila in that year that proved to be the biggest Congo story overall. However, in 1998, when the Second Congo War began, and continuing over the next four years, total newspaper coverage did decline, with the exception of 2001, when Laurent Kabila's assassination drew considerable press attention. As mentioned, a low of 60 stories appeared in 2002.

Data also show that over time the percentage of inside-page news stories declined in favour of coverage contained in one-paragraph "World News Briefings." This trend was especially noticeable in 2002, the final year of Africa's first world war, when "World News Briefings" accounted for almost half (47 percent) and inside-page news made up about one-third of total content. In contrast, at the beginning of the war in 1998 "World News Briefings" provided only 12 percent of total content, while inside-page news stories accounted for just over 50 percent. Editorials and op-ed/news analysis articles peaked in 1997 and 2001 (for editorials 4 and 6 percent respectively, and for opinion articles 7 percent in both years). The first year of the study also saw by far the highest percentage of front-page stories (14 percent) as well as most letters to the editor (9 percent).

Due largely to the start of major international peacekeeping operations in the late spring of 2003, what became known as the Third Congo War also received a good deal of press attention in its first year. As shown in table 6.1b, the years 2005 and 2007 recorded the fewest stories (N=34 and N=35), while 2004, 2006, and 2008 all featured between 50 and 60 items of content.

Differences in content type in coverage of the two Congo wars were not great, the most noticeable difference being a slight decrease in inside-news stories in favour of "World News Briefings," combined with a

Media Coverage: An Overall Assessment

TABLE 6.1a
New York Times Coverage of the Second Congo War, by Type of Content, by Year

	1997	1998	1999	2000	2001	2002	Total
	N=110	N=96	N=81	N=78	N=90	N=60	N=515
	N/%	N/%	N/%	N/%	N/%	N/%	N/%
Front page	15/14%	5/5%	2/3%	6/8%	3/3%	2/3%	33/6%
Inside page	56/51	50/52	34/42	34/44	34/38	19/32	227/44
World Briefs	13/12	20/21	38/47	26/33	38/42	28/47	163/32
Editorials	4/4	3/3	1/1	2/3	5/6	1/2	16/3
Articles	8/7	6/6	4/5	2/3	6/7	3/5	29/6
Letters	10/9	6/6	1/1	2/3	2/2	2/3	23/4
Other	4/4	6/6	1/1	6/8	2/2	5/8	24/5
Total	110/101%	96/99%	81/100%	78/102%	90/100%	60/100%	515/100%

TABLE 6.1b
New York Times Coverage of the Third Congo War, by Type of Content, by Year

	2003	2004	2005	2006	2007	2008	Total
	N=77	N=51	N=34	N=50	N=35	N=57	N=304
	N/%	N/%	N/%	N/%	N/%	N/%	N/%
Front page	3/4%	2/4%	1/3%	3/6%	2/6%	5/9%	16/5%
Inside page	30/39	21/41	10/29	20/40	10/29	25/44	116/38
World Briefs	24/31	23/45	13/38	17/34	9/26	18/32	104/34
Editorials	3/4	0/0	1/3	1/2	1/3	2/4	8/3
Articles	6/8	0/0	2/6	3/6	4/11	4/7	19/6
Letters	6/8	2/4	2/6	2/4	6/17	0/0	18/6
Other	5/6	3/6	5/15	4/8	3/9	3/5	23/8
Total	77/100%	51/100%	34/100%	50/100%	35/101%	57/101%	304/100%

slightly higher percentage of letters to the editor during the Third Congo War.

With respect to datelines, as shown in table 6.2a, just over 60 percent of *New York Times* coverage of the Second Congo War originated from African locations. The United States and the United Nations were the origin of just over 10 percent of material each, with the US total peaking at 19 percent in 1997 and the UN's at 29 percent in 2000.

As was the case with type of content, differences in origin of content were not especially noticeable with respect to coverage of the Second and Third Congo Wars; the most important of these was that there

TABLE 6.2a
New York Times Coverage of the Second Congo War, by Dateline, by Year

	1997	1998	1999	2000	2001	2002	Total
	N=110 N/%	N=96 N/%	N=81 N/%	N=78 N/%	N=90 N/%	N=60 N/%	N=515 N/%
Africa	69/63%	69/72%	65/80%	30/39%	46/51%	34/57%	313/61%
US	21/19	14/15	2/2	6/8	10/11	6/10	59/11
UN	14/13	4/4	4/5	23/29	14/16	5/8	64/12
Europe	5/5	2/2	0/0	5/6	4/4	2/3	18/3
Other/Unk	1/1	7/7	10/12	14/18	16/18	13/22	61/12
Total	110/101%	96/100%	81/99%	78/100%	90/100%	60/100%	515/99%

TABLE 6.2b
New York Times Coverage of the Third Congo War, by Dateline, by Year

	2003	2004	2005	2006	2007	2008	Total
	N=77 N/%	N=51 N/%	N=34 N/%	N=50 N/%	N=35 N/%	N=57 N/%	N=304 N/%
Africa	45/60%	34/67%	14/41%	38/76%	18/51%	35/61%	184/61%
US	10/13	3/6	3/9	3/6	10/29	6/11	35/12
UN	11/14	5/10	9/26	0/0	0/0	4/7	29/10
Europe	3/4	6/12	1/3	5/10	4/11	8/14	27/9
Other/Unk	8/10	3/6	7/20	4/8	3/9	4/7	29/10
Total	77/101%	51/101%	34/99%	50/100%	35/100%	57/100%	304/102%

were relatively more stories originating from Europe in the latter—an increase from 3 to 9 percent (see table 6.2b). This was due to French/European Union leadership in a brief emergency stabilization mission (Operation Artemis) and the International Criminal Court (ICC) prosecution of a Congolese warlord for war crimes. Largely as a result of coverage of the ICC case, European datelines in 2008 exceeded those from both the US and the UN: 14 percent versus 11 percent and 7 percent respectively.

As reviewed in chapter 2, a UN peace-monitoring mission (MONUC) had been authorized and was deployed fairly early in the Second Congo War. However, its numbers were relatively small and it operated under a "classic" Chapter VI peacekeeping mandate. Since there was "no peace to keep" in the Congo until 2003, MONUC did not become involved in major operations on the ground until after the international combatants had withdrawn their forces, leaving the eastern part of the country prey to less disciplined warring groups.

However, in the spring of 2003, when regional involvement in the conflict declined and it became primarily a matter of localized militia warfare, France was called upon to lead a European stabilization force into Bunia, a city in the Ituri region of northeastern Congo. As well, over that summer, the UN authorized additional peacekeepers for MONUC, bringing the total UN force in the Congo to over 10,000 troops, now equipped with a Chapter VII mandate to deal more effectively with the persistent violence perpetrated by proxy and locally generated militias, among others. During the Third Congo War these developments led to increased media attention on UN peacekeeping activities.

Table 6.3 shows the extent to which *New York Times* reporting tended either to *support* or *discourage* international intervention in the Congo.[2] In 2003, 21 stories addressed the efficacy of intervention, and among these, an impressive two-thirds were judged to have been supportive of such efforts, while one-third were seen to have been discouraging. As time went on and UN peacekeepers actually took to the field, the distribution of this evaluation shifted quickly and significantly. By 2004, the escalation in violence in eastern Congo, and especially the failure of the UN force to protect the city of Bukavu (coupled with the emerging scandal focused on sexual abuse by UN peacekeepers), resulted in only 13 percent of 15 stories dealing with peacekeeping being judged as supportive, while fully 87 percent were seen as discouraging. In 2005, 10 stories expressed a judgment on the efficacy of intervention one way or another, and of those that did, a strong percentage (80 percent) were also seen as critical or discouraging. In 2006, among the same number of intervention-evaluating stories, 30 percent offered support and 70 percent discouragement with respect to international efforts to deal with the violence.

Yet another dramatic turn around in evaluation of peacekeeping began in the summer of 2007 when Nicholas Kristof's series of op-ed pieces called attention to the devastating impact of the continuing fighting in eastern Congo. The Kristof articles, followed by Jeffrey Gettleman's October front-page story on the use of rape to terrorize the Congolese population, prompted letter writers to call for a more forceful international response than had been the case earlier. In total, 19 items offered evaluations on intervention, and of these, 58 percent were judged supportive of intervention as opposed to 42 percent seen as discouraging. However, 2008 saw a return to the pattern set in 2004, and this continued in 2005 and 2006: 18 stories offered some evaluation, and of these 28 percent showed support for intervention, while 72 percent offered discouraging

TABLE 6.3
Number and Percent of Intervention-Supporting and -Discouraging Items during the Third Congo War, by Year

2003	2004	2005	2006	2007	2008
N=21	N=15	N=10	N=10	N=19	N=18
SUP DIS	SUP DIS	SUP DIS	SUP DIS	SUP DIS	SUP DIS
67% 33%	13% 87%	20% 80%	30% 70%	58% 42%	28% 72%

views. What is apparent is that after MONUC took to the field in 2003, with the exception of 2007 (the only year when the newspaper adopted an advocacy role) *New York Times* reporting was not supportive of UN peacekeeping activities.

Congo and Darfur Coverage Compared

Gérard Prunier (2009) has called our attention to the gap between media attention paid to conflicts in Darfur and that devoted to the Congo, with Darfur getting the lion's share of coverage.[3] Prunier is correct in pointing out a gap in media interest, but our study shows neither television nor print coverage reaching the 5-to-1 ratio cited by Prunier, though television news came close. For television, the difference over the five years between 2003 and 2007 (during which we were able to do a head-to-head comparison between the two conflicts) stands at 72 stories for Darfur compared with 21 stories for the Congo, slightly higher than a 4-to-1 ratio. For the *New York Times*, the gap is far less pronounced, as we found just over twice the number of items dealing with Darfur (N=615) as for the Congo (N=304).

There were, however, other fairly significant differences in the treatment accorded the two crises (see table 6.4). If we compare coverage of Darfur against coverage of the two Congo wars, we find that a greater percentage of Congo coverage received front-page placement—(6 percent vs. 2 percent), while for Darfur, editorials accounted for a slightly greater percentage of material than seen for the Congo—(5 percent vs. 3 percent). However, the truly important differences between Darfur and Congo coverage are seen in the use of op-ed pieces and letters to the editor—(17 percent Darfur vs. Congo 6 percent for op-ed articles and 20 percent Darfur vs. 5 percent Congo for letters). In total, what may be seen as "primary influence-generating content" accounted for about 45 percent of Darfur material as opposed to only 20 percent for the Congo, with almost all of that Darfur content calling for the international

Media Coverage: An Overall Assessment

TABLE 6.4
Percentage of New York Times Darfur and Congo Coverage, by Type of Content

	Darfur*	2nd Congo War	3rd Congo War
Front-page stories	2%	6%	5%
Editorials	5	3	3
Op-ed/news analysis pieces	17	6	6
Letters to the editor	20	4	6

Figures do not add to 100 percent.
*The Darfur sample consists of the first four months of each year.[4]

community to take some action over and above verbal condemnation of the Sudanese government.

With respect to the origins of media coverage of the two conflicts, big differences again are apparent. First, only 25 percent of Darfur content originated from African locations, while for the Congo, African-originated content accounted for just over 60 percent. This no doubt relates at least in part to the effectiveness of the Sudanese government's efforts to restrict journalists from entering the country, much less the conflict zone in Darfur (Bacon, 2004, Sept./Oct.). Moreover, data in table 6.5 tell us that unlike Darfur, where slightly more than 40 percent of material originated in the United States, the world's superpower was largely "missing in action" with respect to stories on the Congo, with US datelines accounting for just over 10 percent of content. Especially scarce among US-originated content were stories emanating from Washington. Most of those which did emerge from the nation's capital were associated with the fall of Mobutu and the best way to approach the Congo's new leader, Laurent Kabila. US officials are well schooled in how to use media effectively; this suggests a lack of US government involvement in the Congo once Africa's world war started in 1998, as well as little interest in changing that position when the conflict shifted primarily to civil violence in eastern Congo in 2003. In contrast, both the president and secretary of state were engaged on Darfur.

The percentage of material written by *Times* reporters on the Second Congo War exceeded that for Darfur by 2 percent. However, during the Third Congo War (which paralleled in time the conflict in Darfur), home-grown material on that conflict dropped by more than 10 percent behind Darfur. This decline in coverage by *New York Times* reporters was matched by an increase in the percentage of wire service material in Congo coverage, which accounted for 38 percent of total content.

TABLE 6.5
Percentage of New York Times Darfur and Congo Coverage, by Dateline

	Darfur*	2nd Congo War	3rd Congo War
Africa	25%	61%	61%
US	41	11	12
UN	12	12	10
Europe	4	3	9

Figures do not add to 100 percent.
*The Darfur sample consists of the first four months of each year.

The really big difference between Darfur and Congo, however, is found in the percentage of material generated by letter writers: 20 percent of Darfur content, as opposed to only 6 percent of Third Congo War content, was provided by those writing to express their opinions to the newspaper (see table 6.6). This is significant in terms of an international response, for as Sidahmed and colleagues noted in their analysis of *New York Times* coverage of Darfur, advocacy for international intervention originated largely from op-ed articles, which in turn generated popular concern that was reflected in letters to the editor. This can be seen as the first step in the process of awakening public opinion, which leads to a possible "CNN effect" (Sidahmed et al., 2010: 99–100). Simply put, the advocacy/public-opinion-generating process so central to Darfur coverage was not duplicated in the newspaper's coverage of the Congo, save for one year, 2007.

Why Was Congo "Neglected" Relative to Darfur?

The Complex Character and Long-Running Duration of the Congo Conflict

As we pointed out in chapter 3, the conflict in Dafur fit extremely well into the simple, two-sided, "good" versus "evil" frame so attractive to television news and amenable to strategies of mobilizing public opinion. This was not the case with the Congo.[5] As much of the preceding has shown, the Congo situation did not fit into any standard frame that would be immediately meaningful to readers. As Tony Iltis observed, "in fact, this brutal multi-sided conflict, involving shifting alliances between a bewildering array of armed factions as well as both government and opposition forces from seven neighboring countries, is the product of continual Western intervention since the 1880s" (Iltis, 2008, Nov. 7). In addition to the *intractable conflict* and *Western responsibility* frames seen in the quote, others that were frequently used included

Media Coverage: An Overall Assessment

TABLE 6.6
Percentage of New York Times Darfur and Congo Coverage, by Source of Content

	Darfur*	2nd Congo War	3rd Congo War
Newspaper staff	61%	63%	50%
Wire services	13	30	38
Letter writers	20	5	6

Figures do not add to 100 percent.
*The Darfur sample consists of the first four months of each year.

tribal/ethnic warfare, Rwandan genocide, proxy forces, poor leadership, and *corporate/national greed.* The problem is that each of these frames could be applied to explain one, or perhaps two, dimensions of the conflict at different times in its evolution, but none had the capacity to explain all of the dimensions, all of the time. Moreover, none was immediately understandable to the general public, as the US government did little to clarify its own interpretation of the conflict, while both President Bush and Secretary of State Powell did so with respect to Darfur.

While US network television news never seemed comfortable with the complexity of the Congo, as shown in chapters 4 and 5, overall the *New York Times* did a credible job of sorting out and explaining the various dimensions of the conflict. Especially significant is that virtually from the beginning to the end of our study, newspaper reporting emphasized that the failure to deal with the issue of the Rwandan Hutu Interahamwe remaining in the Congo was central to both the initiation and the persistence of the conflict.

Further, let us not forget that the term *news* implies that something *new* is happening (see Livingston, 1996: 77-78). In that media capacity to report is not unlimited, how much coverage can one reasonably expect of a conflict that is drawn out and in which there is little day-to-day change? Should we expect continuing reports of chaos and death in the Congo to replace stories on important new developments, both elsewhere in the world and at home?

In contrast to the Congo, and also the civil wars in southern Sudan, where conflict was endemic and Moeller's concept of "compassion fatigue" likewise came into play (Livingston, 1996), the conflict in Darfur sprang onto the scene unexpectedly. It projected a sense of immediacy about stopping the marauding Janjaweed militias, especially after the American president and secretary of state used the term *genocide* to describe what was occurring there. Note, for example, Amanda Grzyb's assessment of how the conflict in Darfur was framed in a way that encouraged an international intervention: "The situation in Darfur appears to be strikingly simple: civilians are being systematically raped, massacred, and forcibly driven from their homes by their own government, and the world has a moral (and, some say, legal) responsibility to intervene and stop these atrocities" (2009b: 66). Contrast this with Robert Kaplan's description of hopelessness in the situation in Sierra Leone in the early 1990s: "the withering away of central governments, the rise of tribal and regional domains, the unchecked spread of disease, and the growing pervasiveness of war" (2000: 9). The situation in the Congo fit the latter picture far better than the former. As bad as the Congo was, there was no dramatic change in the level of the violence after 2003, just a depressing continuation of the killings that had gone on before, month after month, year after year—a situation that could easily appear to be beyond help, even from a well-intentioned international community.

Differing Perceptions on the Need for UN Intervention

The perceived need for UN involvement in the two conflicts also differed. Beginning a good six years before the Darfur insurgency in 2003, the Second Congo War appeared at least to involve primarily regional combatants. The UN took action relatively early, first in authorizing a "classic" peacekeeping force in 1999, and then waiting for the combatants to signal that they needed help in disengaging their armies. Over the fall of 2002, a combination of fatigue and diplomacy succeeded in ending the fighting by regional forces. Thus, for a significant part of the Congo conflict, the need for the UN "to step up and do something" (an issue at the heart of the Darfur debate and which prompted citizen mobilization) was not a pressing concern. That a UN peacekeeping mission had been authorized and a small number of peacekeepers deployed to the Congo meant that at least an effort was being made to deal with the problem. The question of whether the right call had been made in characterizing the war as inter-state was not a topic of discussion.

Ironically, what happened was that the neighbouring states fighting in the Congo largely withdrew their forces to their own borders at the end of 2002. This meant that a conventional Chapter VI *peace-monitoring* force deployed between rival national armies was not needed, yet the conflict continued, perhaps unexpectedly. Unfortunately, what the Congo needed in 2003 was a Chapter VII *peace enforcement* mission to establish and maintain a peace among warring tribal, rogue, and proxy militias, tasks that MONUC in its classic peacekeeping configuration was ill equipped to handle. The EU's Operation Artemis filled the immediate need, and the transition from Chapter VI to Chapter VII was in fact made relatively quickly over the summer of 2003. In short, the Congo did not need demands that the UN become involved, a key issue with citizen mobilization in Darfur. It already was.

Radical Islam and the Arab World versus the West

The events of September 11, 2001, dramatically raised the profile of Islam as a factor in world politics, especially with respect to Africa, described by President Clinton's Assistant Secretary of State for African Affairs Susan Rice as "unfortunately the world's soft underbelly for global terrorism." She argued further it was of great concern "that some of Islam's most radical and anti-American adherents are increasingly active from South Africa to Sudan, from Nigeria to Algeria" (as quoted in Herbst and Mills, 2003: 26). Even prior to 9/11, Francis Deng noted "the American view of the Sudan as an Arab or Middle Eastern story, emphasizing Sudan's involvement in terrorism" (Livingston, 1996: 74).

In the context of the linkage between internal conflict and its international consequences, Sudan of course is a part of the Muslim world, and although both African and Arab sides in the Darfur conflict were in fact Muslim, in a post-9/11 context, Darfur could be seen as a conflict where "bad" Arab militias were attacking "good" African farmers.[6] As Roger Howard, the author of a recent book on Western intervention explained: "In Darfur the fighting is portrayed as a war between black Africans, rightly or wrongly regarded as the victims, and 'Arabs,' widely regarded as the perpetrators of the killings. In practice these neat racial categories are highly indistinct, but it is through such a prism that the conflict is generally viewed" (Howard, 2007, May 16; see also Howard, 2006). Lobby groups and other interested parties—both on the left (such as Hollywood celebrities) and on the right (including American Evangelical Christians who long had a presence in Southern Sudan), plus neo-conservative journalists and policy makers—also took up the cause of Darfur as it fit into their world-view paradigms, thus giving the conflict greater attention (Howard, 2006; Crilly, 2010; see also blogs by Beckett, Crilly, Jones, Moore, and Zuckerman). Howard's observations regarding the motivations of at least some of these interest groups are instructive:

> It is not hard to imagine why some in the west have found this perception so alluring, for there are numerous people who want to portray "the Arabs" in these terms. In the United States and elsewhere those who have spearheaded the case for foreign intervention in Darfur are largely the people who regard the Arabs as the root cause of the Israel-Palestine dispute. From this viewpoint, the events in Darfur form just one part of a much wider picture of Arab malice and cruelty. (2007, May 16)

Further, the growing military insurgency in Iraq, as well as Osama bin Laden's call to protect Islam and Darfur from possible Western intervention, gave that conflict a post-9/11 "War on Terror" dimension (Slackman, 2006, Apr. 24). For example, the respected African historian Mahmood Mamdani of Columbia University viewed the extensive media focus on Darfur in these terms: "I think it is about linking Darfur with the larger war on terror by portraying and framing the perpetrators of violence in Darfur as Arabs" (as quoted in Khadr, 2008, July 21). In this respect, the Congo was quite different as there was no Islamist/terrorist threat to fuel international interest in the conflict.

Lack of Knowledge about Africa and Negative Images of the Congo

Beverley Hawk has pointed out that among many sources of information on Africa available to Americans, none is more important than mass media. She argues that "it is to the media that individuals look to be informed. The media hold responsibility for the interpretation of the events they report, and their interpretations, in turn, define the understanding of the events by readers and viewers." But she maintains that African stories are "different from other foreign relations stories" in that "there is little common understanding between Africans and Americans to provide context for interpretation." For Hawk, the result has been that "the image of Africa in the American mind ... is worse than incomplete, it is inaccurate" (1992: 3-5). Bosah Ebo concurs: "American news media have shaped the American image of Africa as a most unpleasant part of the world ... The underlying point is that Africa has no redeeming value to Americans or Western societies" (1992: 15). Curtis Keim points to the consequences of these Western inaccuracies with respect to Rwanda, for instance:

> Ethnic consequences played a large role, but not "age-old" ethnicity. This ethnicity was created and maintained in modern times. And it was not the kind of ethnicity that Americans think of when they use the terms of *tribal war* or *ethic war*. Not only do Hutus and Tutsis share the same language and culture but their relationships are mediated by modern institutions such as states with armies, identity cards, state-run newspapers and radio, cash-crop markets, and for the Hutus, a secret hate-radio station. Moreover, there has been considerable regional and urban-rural tension *among* Hutu. [Thus] to mistake the Rwandan civil war for a stereotypical "tribal" war is very dangerous because it causes us to misperceive what really happened. (1999: 106)

Charles Quist-Adade made the additional point that Western media images of Africa have not changed since the days of "early explorers, colonial masters and missionaries ... The Western media ... emphasize the message that Africans cannot govern themselves; that the continent 'is still stuck in its primitive, bloodthirsty past,' that nations have wasted the 'golden opportunity' to build civilized statehood after attaining political independence" (2001: 97-98).

In a historical review of images specific to the Congo, Kevin Dunn argues as well that popular negative images in the Western world have remained consistent over the past hundred years and this has had unfortunate consequences. He cites as an example that early in 2002, ABC News ran a series of reports on the Congo under the title "Heart of Darkness." According to Dunn,

> considering the Congo inherently chaotic and irrational ... guarantees that events that occur there will lack political rationale. By employing the label "Heart of Darkness," ABC News attempted to make the events in central Africa comprehensible to their viewers by drawing on *a tradition that frames that part of the world through a lens of primitivism, backwardness, and irrationality.* (2003: 5; italics added)

Dunn argues that the persistence of these images fed into the media's fall-back frame, *intractable conflict,* thus discouraging a more robust intervention on the part of the West (2003: 141).[7]

Lack of US Government Interest in the Congo

Once the Cold War had ended it was generally felt that, with the exception of France, the West had largely lost interest in Africa. For example, in reference to Somalia, Ali Mazrui commented that "during the Cold War the strategic value of Somalia to the superpowers was inflated ... When the Cold War ended, the strategic value of Somalia plunged like the stock market prices on Wall Street at the start of the Great Depression ... No one cared enough to help prevent its disintegration" (1997: 9). Also, as noted by Simon Massey in an article on the aborted Operation Assurance in 1996, "there is strong evidence that Africa sits very low on America's list of priorities, [and] in contrast to France's highly interventionist policy, British armed intervention following the east-of-Suez withdrawal has been highly infrequent and limited" (1998, Feb. 15: 10, 11; see also Martin, 2000; Jones, 2001).

Moreover, scholarly accounts of post-Cold War US foreign policy toward Africa, especially as they relate to conflict suppression, generally have not been favourable. President George Bush the elder's intervention in Somalia in late 1992, which in the following year turned into an absolute debacle for President Clinton, seriously dampened any enthusiasm that might have existed for further African interventions (see Soderlund et al., 2008: chaps. 3 and 5). Joseph Opala notes the impact of the failure of intervention in Somalia on President Clinton's subsequent policy timidity in confronting African violence:

> Every president has difficulty in crafting a responsible Africa policy. Our traditional stance of America as a force for good in the world runs headlong into that continent of more than fifty nations, many wracked by instability and endemic violence ... But President Clinton has gone far beyond the usual hypocrisy ... By making public relations his priority goal in two cases of mass murder [Rwanda and Sierra Leone] he crossed a deadly line—the line between standing by while mass murders do their work, and giving aid and support to those very murderers. He took US Africa policy to a terrible place it had never been before. (Opala, 2000, Apr. 24)

Jeffrey Herbst and Greg Mills assess the causes of the Clinton administration's policy failures in Africa differently, arguing that they resulted from doing "more of the same, just with more energy." Thus despite having "devoted extraordinary attention to Sub-Saharan Africa," the overall result of Clinton's policies was failure (2003: 38).

As was noted in chapter 5, President George Bush the younger had come to power with the view that African problems occupied a low priority in terms of "the national strategic interests" (see Sengupta and Lacey, 2003, July 6: I1). The events of 9/11, however, were perception-changing to the point where Herbst and Mills described Bush as "surprisingly attentive to the needs of the continent" and speculated that he "may be on his way to becoming the US president to be most engaged with Sub-Saharan Africa" (2003: 34). In 2002, under the aegis of a new National Security Strategy, the Bush administration sought "to develop ties with a small number of prominent countries [Ethiopia, Kenya, Nigeria, and South Africa] in order to engage Africa in a low-cost but effective way" (Herbst and Mills, 2003: 36). As Robert Rotberg has argued, because "failed states are hospitable to and harbor non-state actors—warlords and terrorists—understanding the dynamics of nation-state failure is central to the war against terrorism" (2002: 85). No doubt as a consequence, over the summer of 2003, the US began to cautiously back the establishment of a UN peacekeeping force to bring the violence in the Congo under control (Barringer, 2003, July 16).

One of the most useful contributions to understanding the connections between mass media and foreign policy is Lance Bennett's theory of *indexing*. Indexing posits that US media coverage of an issue will increase when foreign policy elites are split on an issue and make this disagreement public (1990; see also Bennett, Lawrence, and Livingston,

2007). In the case of the Congo, not only was no policy split evident among elites, Herbst and Mills argue that a *policy consensus* was in fact passed on from the Clinton to the Bush administration—a policy consensus described as "support for the sovereignty and territorial integrity of the Congo" (Susan Rice, as quoted in Herbst and Mill, 2003: 39). This, in Herbst and Mills's judgement, happened "despite the fact that it is obvious that the DRC has no territorial integrity, has not been an integral unit for many years, and will not for many more to come" (2003: 39).

Nor, with respect to the atrocities in Darfur, did US foreign policy elites appear divided on the need to pressure the Sudanese government to stop the violence, although there were some differences over the extent and means to exert such pressure.[8] The conflict also engaged President Bush and his administration, at least at the rhetorical level, as both the president and secretary of state characterized Sudanese government actions in Darfur as meeting the criteria of genocide, a major change from President Clinton's reluctance to do this with respect to a much clearer case in Rwanda ten years earlier. Moreover, the lack of a more robust Western response to atrocities in Darfur was stressed not only by Kofi Annan, but by Nicholas D. Kristof, one of the *New York Times* premier columnists, who, in the op-ed pages of the newspaper, relentlessly pushed the American president to do more, especially in light of the fact that genocide had been determined to be occurring (see Sidahmed et al., 2010: 99-100).

Not only were US contributions to UN Congo peacekeeping minimal during the Bush administration, interestingly, not much more was expected on the part of the Obama administration.[9] As noted by Bruce Jones and Michael O'Hanlon, "it is unlikely the U.S. ground forces will be in a position to consider even a modest role in a new [Congo mission] until 2011. As such, direct American involvement on the ground in Congo seems implausible. Unfortunately, without such American leadership, the world is unlikely to want to do more itself" (2009, Apr. 29).[10]

Reduced Media Budgets, Attrition in Reporting Staffs, and Competing Crises

Since at least 2000 media industries in the US have been hemorrhaging jobs. According to a report in 2006 there have been a total of "nearly 72,000 job cuts since June 2000," including cuts at all the media outlets studied for this research, the *New York Times* not excepted (I Want Media, 2006). Another report by the consulting firm Challenger, Gray and Christmas pegged industry layoffs in 2008 at 28,083, "the highest since 43,420 staffers were let go in 2001 following the bursting of the dot.com bubble" (Szalai, 2009, Jan. 7). The Pew Center's "Project for Excellence in Journalism" cited further cutbacks in personnel in 2009, with ABC experiencing the hardest hit—"as high as 27% of the news division." News was grim for CBS as well. Newspapers, by far the largest employers of journalists, also experienced cutbacks: "Roughly 13,500 jobs for full-time, newsroom professionals disappeared [over the period 2007-2009] the total falling from 55,000 to 41,500 ... This means that newsrooms have shrunk by ... just under 27% since the beginning of the decade" (Pew Project for Excellence in Journalism, 2010).

A loss of personnel of this magnitude cannot but have consequences, for as Ginia Bellafante has reminded us, "shrinking budgets at news outlets across the country mean that many atrocities in far corners of the globe receive diminished attention" (2008, Apr. 8). In fact, the decline in the number of foreign news bureaus maintained by US newspapers and television networks accelerated in the 1990s and continued into the first decade of the new century. In the 1980s the three major US television networks each maintained about fifteen foreign bureaus; today there are about half that many among them. From 2002 to 2008, the number of correspondents sent abroad by American newspapers on a permanent assignment also declined from 188 to 141 (Constable, 2007).

Management justifications for closing foreign bureaus include the facts that improved air connections enable roving journalists to be "parachuted" into far-flung places (Gorney, 2002: 15), that amateur reporting on the internet competes with professional journalism (Hamilton and Jenner, 2004), and that freelancers and stringers provide local flavour and content (Adams and Ovide, 2009). But the rationale for shutting foreign bureaus is just as likely to be tied to costs of operation. The cost of maintaining a single foreign correspondent is cited to be at least $250,000 per year (Russo, 2010).[11]

Despite the cuts to foreign bureaus over the past twenty years, international news is still available to those who seek it out.[12] In the context of our study, the pertinent questions are whether a story like that of the Congo will be covered by the new breed of foreign correspondent, and, if so, whether the mainstream media and audiences be interested in picking up their material.[13] And, for whatever the reasons, as we have pointed out, the Congo did not fare especially well in competition for newspaper attention in comparison with Darfur. The same was true for television news, where from between 2003 and 2007, ABC, CBS, and NBC ran a total of 72 stories on Darfur as opposed to 22 on the Congo. Of course Darfur was not the only competitor for scarce media resources. As noted, Afghanistan and Iraq were huge recipients of media attention; the Asian tsunami and the Haitian intervention in 2004, and Kenyan election violence in 2008 competed for stretched media attention as well (see Sidahmed et al., 2010: 98-99).

Lack of Celebrity Activism

What has been termed "celebrity diplomacy" in the literature has a mixed reputation. Some believe it to be valuable in the resolution of conflict; others strongly doubt it (for a range of views see Alleyne, 2005; Cooper, 2008; Austin, 2009, May 11; Vallely, 2009, Jan. 17; Chouliaraki, 2011). While it is not our intention to enter into this debate here, it is nonetheless clear that celebrities do attract media attention (especially television cameras). Moreover, NGOs have learned to cultivate, and recruit, celebrities to advance their humanitarian causes (Barratt, 2005; Hilsum, 2007), as has the UN itself (Alleyne, 2005; Cooper, 2008; Wheeler, 2011). The difference that recognized stars like George Clooney and Mia Farrow were able to make in getting television cameras into refugee camps on the Darfur-Chad border were obvious to all. It resulted in emotional video footage which could hardly fail to invoke demands of corrective action (see Crilly, 2010). Nothing equivalent was evident in television coverage of the Congo, save NBC reporter Ann Curry's memorable visit to a hospital that cared for rape victims in eastern Congo. Though not normally thought of as celebrities, reporters focusing on human-impact situations in conflict zones could also stimulate emotive reactions. But this is not likely to be a priority for them (and in Curry's case, it came only in 2008, relatively late in the day), and is likely to be more reinforcing than motivating, especially when international intervention is already under way.[14]

Conclusion

Our assessments regarding the overall impact of media coverage of international responses to humanitarian crises will be addressed in the Conclusion to the book. However, we will answer the question here as to why the Congo failed to elicit the same attention as afforded Darfur. While there are a variety of determinants of media performance, we suggest that these will combine in different ways for different situations, and it would be a mistake to expect (or even to want) too much uniformity. Nonetheless, we believe that the principal reason that the American media, and particularly television, devoted less attention to the Congo than to Darfur was the long-running nature and very real complexity of the former situation. As noted by former American ambassador to Sudan Donald Petterson, referencing the Sudanese civil war, "something awful happens and then maybe [media] will cover it. But a sustained story is difficult when the war goes on year after year" (as quoted in Livingston, 1996: 78).

For the Congo, no one was sure how to sort it all out or knew what should be done about it, much less by whom. To some extent, that remains true today. A contentious presidential election held in November 2011 raised speculation of a renewal of widespread violence, and this in turn spurred a resurgence of media interest (see, for example, editorials in the *Globe and Mail,* Nov. 11, and the *Windsor Star,* Nov. 21), but this too has passed. The reality is that low-intensity violence has persisted in the Congo for so long that it constitutes a "new normal." Because there is little *new* that can be said about it, and given the cost and danger involved in reporting, "non-newsworthiness" is a good excuse for the media to let the Congo slip quietly onto the back burner and remain there.

Peacekeeping in the Age of R2P

Introduction

As its subtitle indicates, this book addresses two major issues: media coverage of the Congo wars (dealt with in chapters 3 through 6 and to be addressed further in the Conclusion) and the UN response to these conflicts (reviewed in chapter 2). In this chapter we will expand on this second point to determine directions for the future of UN peacekeeping. As a number of commentators have noted, there is no shortage of humanitarian crises to which the international community will be called upon to respond in the coming years. In the pages that follow we will offer our analysis of what we see to be the cutting-edge issues that have emerged for peacekeeping/peace enforcement in the twenty-first century.

Context: The ICISS Report

With the publication of the Report of the International Commission on Intervention and State Sovereignty (ICISS) in September 2001, the debate over when *international humanitarian intervention* is permissible in an international system that is firmly based on the principle of *state sovereignty* entered a new phase. The commission's report, which was first endorsed by the UN General Assembly in 2005 and later by the Security Council in 2006, in effect reframed the issue from a focus on "the right of humanitarian intervention" to one which emphasized the "responsibility to protect" (R2P) individuals who fell into harm's way within the borders of their own states. The commission's co-chairs explained that the key issue of state sovereignty could be diffused if states were considered to have primary responsibility to protect their citizens from serious harm, but if they were unable or unwilling to provide such protection, that responsibility would then pass into the hands of the international community (Evans and Sahnoun, 2002: 101–2). As commission member Ramesh Thakur has expressed it, R2P "encapsulates the element of international solidarity, [refocusing] the international searchlight back onto the duty to protect the villager from murder, the woman from rape and the child from starvation and being orphaned" (Thakur, 2010: 12).

In elaborating the concept, the report identified three distinct elements as falling under the general rubric of R2P:

A. *The responsibility to prevent:* to address both the root causes and direct causes of international conflict and other man-made crises putting populations at risk.

B. *The responsibility to react:* to respond to situations of compelling human need with appropriate actions, which might include coercive measures like sanctions and international prosecutions, and in extreme cases military intervention.

C. *The responsibility to rebuild:* to provide, particularly after a military intervention, full assistance with recovery, reconstruction, and reconciliation, addressing the causes of the harm the intervention was designed to halt or avert. (ICISS, 2001, XI; emphasis in original)

Appearing in the immediate aftermath of the catastrophic events of 9/11, and not receiving UN endorsement until four years later, R2P was a standard which existed for only part of the Congo wars. In addition, as chapters 4, 5, and 6 reveal, "Responsibility to Protect" language was not prominent in the limited media calls for international involvement in the Congo, even after the R2P report had been given official approval. It will be recalled that this was also the case with respect to the concurrent crisis in Darfur (Sidahmed, Soderlund, and Briggs, 2010: 102). Some of the sentiments expressed by reporters and op-ed and editorial writers, however, were consistent with R2P principles, even if these were not specifically mentioned. It must be recognized as well that R2P was never without its critics (see for example Rieff, 2002; Belloni, 2007; de Waal, 2007; Janssen, 2008; MacArthur, 2008), or those who simply seemed unsure what to make of it. Media, on the whole, appear largely to have fallen into the second category. Nonetheless, there is no doubt that the

ICISS report changed the norms of humanitarian intervention. At the very least, like the Universal Declaration of Human Rights, the Genocide Convention, and other such documents before it, it provides an internationally approved standard by which efforts (or the lack thereof) to protect ordinary people from atrocities can be judged.

Roughly a decade into the Congo's existence as an independent state, Jean-Claude Willame described its political system as based on *patrimonialism*, which he defined as "a system of rule incorporating three fundamental and related elements: appropriation of public offices as the elite's prime source of status, prestige, and reward; political fragmentation through the development of relationships based on primordial and personal loyalties; and the use of private armies, militias, and mercenaries as chief instruments of rule" (1972: 2).

Willame's assessment proved to be prophetic: under Mobutu Sese Seko's thirty-two years of misrule, these elements contributed to a set of problems that are deep-seated and exist at every level of analysis—local, national, regional, and international. In this sense the Congo meets all the characteristics identified by Edward Azar in his description of "protracted social conflict" (1990: passim). As was explained in chapter 2, in the mid-1990s these problems of governance were compounded by the intrusion of regional violence, resulting in a quintessential manmade "complex humanitarian emergency" characterized by large-scale loss of life, displacement of people, disease, starvation and malnutrition, mutilation, and sexual violence (see Natsios, 1996b; Klugman, 1999). We also submit that international responses to the conflict (especially those by its peacekeeping missions), have yielded far less than desired outcomes in terms of mitigation. What follows therefore is an attempt to consider the three principal elements of R2P in light of experiences in the Congo as well as other humanitarian crises to which the international community has been called upon to respond over the past two decades.

The Responsibility to Prevent

The ICISS report emphasizes that *"[p]revention is the single most important dimension of the responsibility to protect: prevention options should always be exhausted before intervention is contemplated and more commitment and resources must be devoted to it"* (ICISS, 2001: XI; emphasis in original). No one is likely to quarrel with this basic principle. It is a modern statement of the old adage "an ounce of prevention is worth a pound of cure." Numerous writers have asserted that it is easier, and cheaper, to deal with deteriorating political situations early rather than after animosities have become entrenched, parties have resorted to violence to resolve their differences, and what Filip Reyntjens has described as "entrepreneurs of insecurity" are able to exploit the situation for their own advantage (2009: 283). There are, however, a number of practical difficulties with the operationalization of the principle of prevention.

The most obvious of these is how to identify situations in which a humanitarian disaster may be in the making. As the ICISS report itself acknowledged (2001: 20–22), the general conditions that may produce political instability and the possibility of violence are reasonably well known. At the same time, these conditions are extremely widespread in the world, and it is another matter entirely to predict which of them is likely to produce intolerable violations of human rights and therefore merits a concentrated application of scarce resources. As Ramesh Thakur has put it, the question is "how to prioritize. Not all crises turn unto catastrophes, and we lack theoretical knowledge to determine in advance which will do so" (2010: 11). For example, identifying dictators who have passed their "expiration date" is not especially difficult; unfortunately, as Sebastian von Einsidel cautions, predicting the events that trigger their often bloody downfalls is notoriously problematic (2005: 22–24).

When a high-risk situation has been identified and there is a desire to prevent it from erupting into a humanitarian catastrophe, a second problem is how to determine what tools are appropriate and effective, and when they should be applied. The answer that springs most readily to mind—that it depends on the specific circumstances—is true enough, but not very helpful. Take, for example, a hypothetical case—that of Zimbabwe. Since achieving independence under Robert Mugabe, Zimbabwe has gone from being one of the most prosperous and promising states in Africa, to being "a nation whose economy is in tatters, where poverty and unemployment are endemic, and political strife and repression commonplace" (BBC, 2010, Nov. 11). According to the Heritage Foundation's 2011 Index of Economic Freedom, Zimbabwe is now "one of the poorest countries in the world" (Heritage Foundation, 2011). Sources also report death threats, arbitrary arrests, and youth militias loyal to the governing regime "'running amok' in poor townships" (*Guardian*, 2011, Feb. 3). It is true that no large-scale massacres have yet occurred, but it seems reasonable to suggest that common people are under considerable risk from a government that is primarily concerned with remaining in power. This is precisely the kind of situation where significant violence could easily erupt, and thus a candidate for preventive measures. But how much and what kind?

In fact, the international community has not been oblivious to the Zimbabwe situation. The International Crisis Group has repeatedly drawn attention to abuses committed there (see, for example, Kagwanja and Lamberti, 2005, Apr. 21), and both the UN, through the office of the Secretary-General, and individual states have applied diplomatic and economic pressures to induce reforms. These efforts have met with some limited success. In 2009 Mugabe was forced to agree to the formation of a transitional government in partnership with the opposition Movement for Democratic Change, although only portions of the agreement have so far been implemented (International Crisis Group, 2010, Mar. 3). It is not entirely obvious what more can or should be done beyond maintaining the type of pressures which have already been put in place.

The Zimbabwe case is by no means unique. Considerable efforts by the international community are frequently made with the objective of preventing disastrous explosions in world trouble spots. Although it is impossible to verify, some of these efforts may well have averted catastrophes. But failures, on the other hand, are not always the result of insufficient effort or resources. One of the great ironies of recent peace-management history is that the Rwandan genocide was, arguably, an indirect result of prevention efforts in that country. Fears that long-standing Tutsi-Hutu animosities might lead to a yet another bloodbath led to international pressures to conclude the Arusha Agreement aimed at power sharing between the two groups. It was the unacceptability of that outcome to those who controlled the government that precipitated the launching of the genocide (see Soderlund et al., 2008, chapter 5). This is not to say that those well-intentioned efforts at bringing about political compromise should not have been made, or that the Rwandan tragedy would not have occurred without them, but merely to underline that the ease with which humanitarian disasters can be prevented should not be exaggerated.[1]

In 2011, the world was keeping a wary eye on Sudan for reasons not too dissimilar from those in Rwanda. Sudan suffered a two-phased civil war between north and south which stretched over nearly forty years, was responsible for the deaths of some 2.5 million people, and concluded (after intense international pressure) only in 2005 with a peace agreement that provided for a referendum in the south on an option for separation. Authorities had long been apprehensive about what might occur if the vote favoured severing ties with the north. For example, in May 2010, US National Intelligence Director Admiral Dennis Blair indicated that "of all the countries at risk of experiencing a widespread massacre in the next five years, 'a new mass killing is most likely to occur in southern Sudan'" (as quoted in Sheridan, 2010, May 13: A8; see also Johnson,

2007). The outcome of the vote in January 2011 was close to 99 percent in favour of secession. The Sudanese government agreed to accept the results of the referendum, and independence of the Republic of South Sudan occurred on July 9, 2011, although not without some last-minute jitters when in May the Sudanese army invaded and occupied the disputed region of Abyei. Many issues between the north and south remain unresolved (including the status of Abyei). Violence has also flared up in neighbouring Southern Kordofan, where Nuba peoples in pursuit of greater autonomy have been attacked by Sudanese aircraft (Gettleman, 2011, July 4), and in Blue Nile, where in September 2011 President Omar al-Bashir was forced to declare a state of emergency (BBC, 2011, Sept. 2). There is no doubt that both UN agencies as well as interested governments (especially the United States) pressured both sides to continue to negotiate in good faith in an effort to prevent what Admiral Blair had feared (see Sheridan, 2010, Dec. 30). While independence was achieved without major violence, thus registering a success for "responsibility to prevent," problems for South Sudan as well as Sudan are far from over.[2]

For the Congo, efforts were also made to deflect the danger from the massive flood of Rwandan Hutus into the Congo following the Rwandan Patriotic Front's assumption of power in Kigali in the summer of 1994. As was shown in our analysis of the aborted Operation Assurance in 1996, the danger was probably underestimated (or its real nature misunderstood), but it cannot be said that it was ignored by the world at large.

Two things should also be remembered about humanitarian crises: First, the interpretation of them (as well as their resolution) may differ among states, and thus the effectiveness of pressures for restraint and accommodation of differences are accordingly reduced. This was the case with respect to Darfur, where Western pressures in one direction were at least partly counterbalanced by Chinese pressures of a different kind (Sidahmed et al., 2010). Second, calculating how much pressure to apply to whom, in what manner and at what time, is not without its difficulties. There is no simple or blanket formula which can be applied; finding the right strategy is not just a matter of applying more effort or more resources.

Prevention of international humanitarian disasters is, from a variety of viewpoints, an uncertain and difficult undertaking, and when prevention fails, it is not always due to a lack of commitment on the part of the international community. In general, most international actors will always prefer to prevent the escalation of conflicts to the point that forceful interventions might be called for—which are costly, uncertain in result, and often thankless—though they will of course not always agree on particular strategies. In this sense, the R2P report's call for prevention is a bit like preaching to the choir: a useful reinforcement, perhaps, but not likely to bring new converts to the faith.

The Responsibility to React

The ICISS report is on stronger ground with respect to the "responsibility to react," not least because its language seeks to replace permissiveness with obligation. Obviously, however, this is not without its problems either. Perhaps key to understanding where intervention stands under R2P is the reality, noted by Laura Neack, that participation in UN peacekeeping operations is voluntary (1995: 182). And, while R2P introduced the language of "responsibility," it did not extend the authority of the UN to compel members to contribute to intervention missions. Thus any reaction on the part of the UN still depends on the voluntary participation of member states, and missions undertaken since the adoption of R2P demonstrate the continuing problem of unenthusiastic responses by the international community to calls for help.

Among other problems are questions of when the international community should take action, and what kind of action is most appropriate. With respect to the first issue, it is often suggested that violence in which innocent people are among the principal victims should be addressed early, and certainly before it reaches a "tipping point" where it has become a way of life and/or a source of income for its perpetrators, as has happened in the eastern Congo and perhaps also in Darfur (Autesserre, 2010; Marlow and Akkad, 2010, Dec. 7).[3] The quick (less than two weeks) UN response to problems in the Congo in 1960 probably averted a full-scale civil war at the point when that country won independence from Belgium (see chapter 2 of this volume). On the other hand, some have argued that the failure to quickly address violence in Somalia in 1991 following the overthrow of Said Barre set the scene for the chaos that followed (see Sahnoun, 1994). Similarly, General (now Senator) Roméo Dallaire has maintained that had he been allowed to take more assertive action when he detected signs of impending bloodshed in Rwanda, the genocide might have been averted or at least mitigated and the chain of continuing disasters which have followed in the Great Lakes region could have been avoided (see Dallaire, 2003). It has also been suggested that had the problem of the Hutu Interahamwe refugees in the Congo been dealt with more adequately earlier on, Rwanda would not have seen the need to invade, and Africa's first world war might have been avoided (see Jones, 2001: 140–41).

None of these assertions is self-evident or beyond challenge. With respect to Rwanda, for instance—and with every sympathy for the acute distress General Dallaire experienced at being forced to stand by while unimaginable slaughter occurred all around him—to have authorized Dallaire's peace-monitoring mission to take forceful action against government agents on the basis of suspicion and unsubstantiated information would have violated his mandate and undermined the very basis on which such missions must operate (see Dallaire, 2003; Soderlund et al., 2008, for details). It would also have placed his small and ill-equipped UN force firmly on the Tutsi side of the conflict, but without adequate means to exercise more than minimum interference in the well-planned and -executed country-wide campaign of genocide. There were, in other words, many more issues involved than simply one of timing.

In the case of Somalia, it is true that "the international community responded slowly to the growing humanitarian disaster" (Soderlund et al., 2008: 48). Said Barre was chased from the capital in January 1990, and it was not until a year later that the UN passed its first resolution on the chaotic situation which developed as a result. It should be noted, however, that during this time a number of neighbouring states, including Ethiopia, Eritrea, and Djibouti, undertook to mediate among the warring factions (Soderlund et al., 2008: 48-49; see also Sahnoun, 1994: 9-10). From the point of view of the larger international community, therefore, it was not unreasonable to await the results of these efforts before considering more comprehensive actions, especially as the exact nature of the situation was both unclear and frequently changing. Moreover, it was equally unclear what could be done about it, beyond urging the various parties to come to a peaceful settlement. Jeffrey Clark has charged that the UN "dithered" during this period (1993: 115). It probably did, but there was good reason for dithering, and in any case it may be doubted that the dispatch of even a robust peace force in 1990 or 1991 would have worked any wonders.

To contrast unfavourably the hesitant reaction to post-1994 Congo difficulties with the swift launch of ONUC in 1960 is also misleading. In 1960 the UN was reacting to a direct request from the recently established government for aid in resisting an alleged aggression by Belgium. The situation thus appeared clear and the task apparently simple, though as we pointed out this was far from the reality that confronted ONUC once it deployed. Such clarity was not the case after 1994, but neither was international reaction unduly delayed. As indicated in chapter 2, the assumption at that time (emphasized by numerous humanitarian agencies) was that the primary need was to arrange the return of the Hutu refugees to Rwanda. Attention was given fairly quickly to that objective, including the authorization of an international force to assist in the process. When the bulk of the refugees returned "voluntarily," there was no immediate rationale for such action and much to be said against it, as any such action could not avoid being seen as interference favourable to the discredited government of Mobutu Sese Seko. Moreover, at the time, the chaotic situation which was to develop had yet to manifest itself, and while its development might have been anticipated, fears and suspicions could reasonably be dealt with only by employing diplomatic means. It is important to reiterate that diplomatic means are reactions too, and it should be recalled that the R2P report cautions that "less intrusive and coercive measures should always be considered before more coercive and intrusive ones are applied" (2001: 29).

In fact there is good reason for such caution. As Alan Kuperman and others have argued, if it is assumed that intervention means using forceful methods (an all too frequent assumption), then "a 'moral responsibility' to intervene" constitutes an invitation to dissident groups everywhere to embark on insurrections in the expectation that the international community will come to their rescue (Kuperman, 2006: 18). Tonny Brems Knudsen, for instance, contends that the Kosovo Albanians courted Serbian reprisals in 1999 with precisely this expectation (Knudsen, 2006: 317). While military intervention clearly cannot be the default response to atrocities, the fact remains that there are "cases of violence which so genuinely 'shock the conscience of mankind,' or which present such clear and present danger to international security that they require coercive military intervention" (ICISS, 2001: 31). Kuperman correctly refers to this as a "moral dilemma."

Unfortunately, moral dilemmas do not lend themselves to formulaic, or universally satisfying, solutions. Probably the best that can be suggested with respect to intolerable atrocities in the international community is that a balance be sought between the need to minimize human suffering as much as possible, and the reality that if that means military action, an entirely new set of problems will be created, in both the short and long terms.

This is particularly true with respect to Africa, which, because of the confluence of a myriad of conflict-producing factors, has been especially prone to internal political violence (see Misra, 2008: chap. 1). The civil wars which occur, moreover, are of a new kind. Amalendu Misra maintains that "because of the presence of multiple and often competing leaderships there is rarely a commonly defined goal ... [A] significant portion of participants participates ... either to eke out a living or make personal gain ... The new civil wars, thus, are not only perverse but sometimes operate within an illogical paradigm," characterized by refugees, disease, environmental degradation, weapons smuggling, human trafficking, banditry, and terrorism, and in which the civilian to combatant casualty ratio is 9:1 compared with 1:9 at the time of the First World War (Misra, 2008: 4-5). In cases such as these, Kaplan maintains that "war and crime become indistinguishable," leading to situations where "the old rules of state warfare [no longer] apply" (2000: 47-49). To complicate matters, Young points out that such situations "inevitably become internationalized. Of the 16 protracted internal wars in Africa in the 1990s, only one (Senegal) has been resolved by internal negotiation" (2006: 324).

In extremely messy circumstances of this kind, it is practically impossible for any international force to intervene impartially, or with the clear and unambiguous objectives and the straightforward rules of engagement that are frequently called for. UN peacekeepers in situations like the Congo may be impartial in the sense that they are more or less indifferent as to which party to the conflict should emerge victorious, but they are not, and cannot be, impartial with respect to the methods employed by the parties when these impact on the human rights of ordinary people. Moreover, as has been pointed out, even if they do not actively engage in combat, as ECOWAS forces did in Liberia in 1990 (see Soderlund et al., 2008: chap. 2), their very presence will alter the balance of existing forces and thus constitute a new factor to which those forces will have to adjust. To a greater or lesser extent, that adjustment will create a situation different from that which existed when the peacekeepers arrived. Some combatant groups (as again occurred in the Liberian case) may seek to use international interveners for their own ends; and for all of them, the presence of peacekeepers will almost certainly create opportunities or difficulties which did not previously exist. It is therefore difficult to know in advance precisely what UN contingents will need to do, or what is expedient for them to do, once they are in place or what resources will be needed for the task.

On the issue of resources some suggest that it would be better to overestimate possible needs rather than the reverse, and that the UN has instead habitually operated on a minimalist basis. For instance, respected Canadian historian J.L. Granatstein has charged that the Congo operation "is underfunded and undersupplied, and has been neither competent militarily nor effective in halting the violence that is estimated to have killed more than five million Congolese since 1999" (Granatstein, 2010, Apr. 7: A17). There certainly were occasions, as in Bukavu in 2004 and Goma in 2008, when MONUC did not have sufficient forces in place to deal with the situations which developed, but these were in part the result of previous deployment decisions. More important, it is by no means clear that even a force of twice MONUC's already large size would have been able to prevent such occurrences somewhere or other—any clear-thinking "rebel" leader, after all, will choose to move against points of weakness wherever they are to be found. Every effort should always be made to ensure that peacekeeping operations are not "underfunded and undersupplied" (and this is especially true for those which operate under a Chapter VII "peace-enforcement" mandate), but these calculations are not easy and are subject to both practical and political constraints. As is well known, recruiting troops for peacekeeping missions is not usually easy, and convincing the principal economic supporters of the UN to assume the costs of forces of unlimited size appears to lie beyond reasonable possibility.[4]

Apart from the issue of resources alone, the likelihood that peacekeepers will be forced to operate in a landscape of shifting sand suggests that there is a need for both flexibility and decisiveness of command. Lise Morje Howard has suggested that the success of UN peacekeeping depends on two types of what she terms "organizational learning": "First-level learning" refers to "within-mission" adaptations to conditions on the ground, while "second-level learning" takes place at UN headquarters between peacekeeping missions (2008: 14-15). She maintains that the first of these is the most important; it is measured by four indicators: the extent to which it is possible to "(1) gather and organize information; (2) coordinate among different divisions of the peacekeeping mission; (3) engage the organization with its post-conflict war environment; and (4) exercise leadership in such a way that the organization commands authority from all actors, even during crises" (16). While it may be supposed that it is not necessary to score 100 percent on each of these dimensions in order for an operation to be judged a success, taken together they still suggest that there is little chance of earning that accolade outside of those situations in which hostilities have already ceased and peacekeepers have mainly a monitoring and reporting role. Unfortunately, these are not the situations for which there is the greatest need for international intervention. Still, Howard's indicators are useful in that they establish a sort of Platonic ideal at which would-be interveners should aim. The practical difficulties, however, should not be underestimated. Establishing adequate intelligence contingents within peacekeeping operations has frequently been difficult, for instance, because participating countries detect a fine line between gathering information and spying in such situations, and peacekeepers see charges of the latter as destructive of relations with the conflicting parties (for Canadian positions on this issue, see Spooner, 2009: passim).

For a number of reasons "coordination" within and between peacekeeping units is even more difficult. In the first place, UN headquarters has traditionally, and understandably, sought to maintain overall political control over missions operating in its name, and this means that force commanders have limited freedom of decision making (see, for example, MacKenzie, 1993, and Dallaire, 2003). More important, given that UN missions are made up of contingents from many countries (UNMIS, the mission to the southern Sudan, is perhaps an extreme example with contingents from sixty-one countries), many different military and cultural traditions are involved. This means that coordination is problematic at the best of times. This is doubly true when it is remembered that few national governments are prepared to place their nationals entirely under the control of a foreign, UN-appointed force commander. Contingent commanders thus normally maintain close communications with their own defence departments, and it is the latter which have the final word with respect to what those units may or may not do (see chapter 2 of this volume; Neack, 1995; Spooner, 2009). UN missions consequently nearly always suffer from unity-of-command problems, and this is not likely to change.

One possible solution to this is to have a single nation take the lead in such endeavours. This worked well in the Australian-led mission to East Timor in 1999 and, in a more limited context, the French-led Operation Artemis in the Congo in 2003, but these were far less complex and altogether more finite situations than the broader and larger Somalia-, Liberia-, Angola- or Congo-type crises with which the UN must so often deal. These could only be led by one of the principal, mainly Western, powers. Quite apart from the latter's willingness to make such a military and financial commitment, they would be open to charges of imperialism and self-interest if they did so. It is something which is simply not feasible except in very special and time-limited circumstances. The bottom line is that humanitarian international interventions, when they occur, will remain messy and inefficient affairs, and their "success" partial at best.

Some fault the "political will" of the international community and of the rich and powerful in particular (see our discussion in the Conclusion). Despite the theoretical adoption of "new norms" under R2P, lack of national interests, aversion to costs (especially those involving lives), and perhaps to some extent a dismissive attitude toward more "primitive" parts of the world, continue to be of significance. Sir Kiernan Pendergast, former UN undersecretary for public relations, makes a telling point:

> We don't mean it when we say that we're not going to accept other Rwandas, further Rwandas. But I never thought we didn't mean it. And that's a very—it's a very sad conclusion, but I don't think there's any evidence to

sustain the view that we did mean it. We might have meant it in a kind of, you know, a level of general indignation. But when it comes to accepting the consequences of that, we don't. (as quoted in PBS, 2007, Nov. 20)

The fact is, humanitarian intervention of the military kind, even in the most egregious circumstances, can never be an absolute obligation. There will always be a calculation of costs and a balancing of many relevant factors, including estimates of whether such action can reasonably be expected to improve or rectify the situation. There is nothing reprehensible about this, or unnatural, or even un-humanitarian. Sacrificing oneself for others may be a noble deed, but it should not be a moral requirement, and it would arguably be *im*moral for governments to engage in activities which they believe would imperil the security or well-being of the populations they represent.

How much, and what kind, of cost is bearable, short of complete self-sacrifice, is variable and depends in part on public attitudes. This is where, as the ICISS recognized, the mass media come into the picture. People's attitudes, we contend, are formed largely by the information presented by the media outlets to which they are exposed. Part of that information will be generated by their own governments, but some will also come from other sources. If there is a preponderance of information which emphasizes the unacceptability of horrors occurring in a particular country, publics at large are likely to adopt the same position, and government leaders (who are themselves not immune to accounts of human horror) may be inclined to accept the greater costs of "doing something" than would otherwise be the case. Media, in other words, can help to "push" governments, and by extension the international community, toward doing the "honourable thing" when humanitarian disasters occur.[5] However, the international community will not always do so, partly because when disaster comes piled upon disaster, "intervention fatigue" sets in, a point made by Ramesh Thakur in his review of *Mobilizing the Will to Intervene* by Frank Chalk, Roméo Dallaire, and colleagues (Thakur, 2010).

When people make declarations such as "we can't accept further Rwandas," they *are* expressing a "general indignation," or a moral determination to combat "man's inhumanity to man," and they are not necessarily being hypocritical. They *do mean it*, but it is naive to assume that as a result the need for assessments and judgments and calculations of costs and probabilities of success can be ignored when the next humanitarian crisis arises. Because of documents like *The Responsibility to Protect*, there is, we would contend, a greater acceptance of the international obligation to respond to human tragedy in the world than ever before in history. One would hope that it is less likely that situations like that in the Congo could occur today without some international reaction, but whether that reaction will, or should, take the form of military intervention must depend on the circumstances and the judgments of world leaders. Those judgments, it goes without saying, will not always be wise or correct, but they cannot be escaped.

The Responsibility to Rebuild

In the words of the R2P report,

> the responsibility to protect implies the responsibility not just to prevent and react, but to follow through and rebuild. This means that if military intervention action is taken ... there should be a genuine commitment to helping to build a durable peace, and promoting good governance and sustainable development. Conditions of public safety and order have to be reconstituted by international agents acting in partnership with local authorities, with the goal of progressively transferring to them authority and responsibility to rebuild. (ICISS, 2001: 39)

Few would dispute the logic of that statement, but neither can it be denied that it constitutes a barrier to deciding to intervene militarily in the first place. Clearly the responsibility to rebuild means that any such commitment will be a long and costly one. With respect to the Congo, as early as 2002 Georges Nzongola-Ntalaja warned of difficulties that lay ahead:

> The establishment of a lasting peace in the Great Lakes Region is a long process. It involves the demobilization and disarmament of thousands of combatants, including boys, and their reconversion to civilian life; the rehabilitation of millions of people whose lives have been disrupted as a result of the war and its devastation; and the reconstruction of the physical infrastructure of production needed to improve their lives. Although a cease-fire agreement and the cessation of hostilities are essential to any peace process, only a comprehensive political settlement can address the root causes of the war and propose the solution likely to prevent the recurrence of violent conflict in the future. (2002b: 109)

Some seven years later, Reyntjens likewise saw the reconstruction of the failed Congolese state as a "colossal task [due to] the extent of state decay, the sheer size of the country, the degree of fragmentation, and indeed the nature of the political leadership and of the political culture more generally" (2009: 284).

MONUC/MONUSCO has attempted to rebuild—especially in regard to the demobilization of "rebel" forces, their reintroduction into civilian life, or their incorporation into a more professionalized national army—but thus far without obvious success. Specifically, in eastern Congo the UN has never been able to establish what could reasonably be called a stable, peaceful situation. Among the problems peacekeepers have faced (as outlined in chapter 2) are the slow progress in the development of an adequately remunerated and disciplined national force, and, in particular, the attractiveness of the eastern Congo's mineral riches to everyone from local independent operators, to remnants of the Hutu Interahamwe, to external opportunists like the Lord's Resistance Army, to officers of the national army. The last, Geoffrey York has recently observed, "[collude] with Hutu rebels ... to extort and loot the local population" (2010, Dec. 3: A18) and, it might be added, do not hesitate to engage in rape or other atrocities in the process.

One radical solution that has been offered for this problem is the establishment of complete international control over the eastern provinces of the Congo. Jeffrey Herbst and Greg Mills determined relatively early in the conflict that there was little hope of major progress toward peace without such a measure:

> To play a constructive role in promoting peace in the DRC, it will be necessary to tear up the old rule book. The international community should say, plainly and simply, that the DRC is not a sovereign state ... Given that there is no hope of Kinshasa issuing a credible promise of protecting Rwanda's and Uganda's interests in eastern DRC (it may not have the physical capacity to do so even if it wanted to), some kind of security zone in eastern DRC might have to be established. (2003: 73)

Today, Rwanda and Uganda may be less directly involved than was earlier the case (though this could easily be reversed again), but the problem is scarcely less severe for that reason. In a similar vein, James Traub has written that it might be time to consider "benevolent imperialism" (2005, July 3: V139). Amalendu Misra, however, has wondered how external actors can introduce values and ideals such as democracy and good governance by "using benevolent autocracy" (2008: 90).

There would be unquestionable advantages to what would amount to an international occupation of eastern Congo, as it would ensure that the mines there operated for the benefit of the national government, and, most important, deprive others of the opportunity to exploit resources and thus reduce the incentive to engage in violence. There are, moreover, some at least partial precedents for such a move. In 1999 the UN

Transition Mission in East Timor (UNTAET) took temporary control of the territory until appropriate local authorities were ready to take over. In the same year the UN Interim Administration Mission in Kosovo (UNMIK) was created to do essentially the same following NATO efforts to curtail Serbian ethnic cleansing in that area. Success, however, has been problematic. Kosovo has suffered wholesale disintegration since the UN's departure, and in 2006 the UN had to send a new peacekeeping force (UNMIT) to East Timor to deal with renewed violence and instability (see UN 2007).

Jarat Chopra has pointed out that in the case of East Timor UNTAET was presented with "conditions of success that are rarely available to peace keeping missions. The belligerent power [Indonesia] had completely withdrawn, and an effective multilateral force could credibly guarantee internal and external security" (2000: 28). The same might be said for UNMIK. In both cases, not only had hostilities ended, but the territory that needed to be controlled was minuscule in size compared with even the eastern portion of the Congo. Nevertheless, the fact that attempting to establish an international administration for eastern Congo would be a far larger and more difficult undertaking does not in itself render the idea unworthy of consideration.

But there are significant difficulties. First and foremost, Herbst and Mills's suggestion that the DRC "plainly and simply" be declared non-sovereign is clearly a non-starter. Few members of the United Nations would agree to something which would change the basis upon which international affairs are conducted to a greater extent than the tweaking of sovereignty conducted by the authors of R2P. It might be possible, however, to negotiate permission for such an operation with the Kinshasa government. Admittedly, this is not now very likely, but it is an approach which has not so far been tried, and it could, if implemented, be of benefit to Kabila's regime as well as to the development of peacekeeping repertoires. While the strategy is perhaps moot as far as the Congo is concerned, it does seem to us a possibility that should be kept in mind in future difficult peacekeeping operations.

We also need to remember that most civil violence takes place in states that are "failing" or that in fact have already "failed," which means that over time they have lost their capacity not only to govern, but also to provide essential services to their populations (see Zartman, 1995; Mazrui, 1995; Rotberg, 2002; Young, 2006). Hence, the deceptively easy solution of "a return to normal conditions" following an intervention is hardly a desired outcome. Moreover, as the case of Haiti in particular demonstrates, restoring effective governance following military interventions in failed states is measured in decades, not in years or months.[6]

The lesson here is that states that are contemplating a military intervention, as well as those organizations pushing for them to do so, had better be prepared for a long stay once the violence that necessitated the intervention has been brought under control.

Conclusion

That there will be future occasions which call for international intervention is all but certain, and if MONUC/MONUSCO demonstrates anything it is that some kind of new approach to man-made humanitarian crises is badly needed.[7] It is true that more than ten years of international effort in the Congo, however flawed it may have been, will undoubtedly leave the country better off than it might otherwise have been. But the cost in Congolese lives has been unacceptably high, and at this stage the future of the country is still precarious.[8] Based on arguments offered above, this is probably all that could reasonably have been hoped for, but for most observers the outcome to date is unlikely to produce any sense of satisfaction. There is still much work to be done to bring a modest degree of safety and security to many of the peoples of the world. Toward this goal we see R2P as a positive step in the right direction, even though it has clearly not a provided a solution. R2P has begun the process of re-thinking the principles of international responsibility for the protection of people in harm's way—over and above the responsibility for states to do so—a process that we hope will continue and deepen.

Conclusion: The Impact of Mass Media on "The Will to Intervene"

According to the so-called "CNN effect," what appears in the media, and especially on television, has a major, if not determining effect in getting governments to respond to faraway humanitarian disasters. A good deal of effort has gone into trying to assess the validity of this theory. Most assessments of the deterministic claims for the CNN effect have ranged from skeptical to dismissive (see Livingston and Eachus, 1995; Jakobsen, 1996; Minear, Scott, and Weiss, 1996; Natsiois, 1996a; Livingston, 1997; Mermin, 1997; Livingston and Eachus, 1999; Robinson, 2002. This, however, is not to say that media have no impact at all.

In *International Crises and Intervention*, a study that surveyed ten major Third World humanitarian crises of the 1990s, Walter Soderlund and colleagues found a relatively strong Spearman Rank Order Correlation (+.79) between volume of media coverage (the media "alert") and the strength of the international response. The correlation was somewhat stronger (+.81) for the eight African crises included in the study (2008: 272–73).[1] The authors concluded that

> the alerting function clearly is of some importance. And, while this by no means constitutes a wholesale endorsement of the CNN effect, it does appear to indicate that in the overall mix of factors leading to an international intervention, *the international community is more likely to respond to a serious crisis in a country of marginal strategic or economic importance if the mainstream media are effective in alerting the population to the crisis.* (2008: 279–80; italics in the original)

David Rieff agrees, pointing out that during the 1990s it was precisely those conflicts that garnered significant media attention that received robust international responses (2003: 38–42).

Governments, at least democratic governments, do listen to their publics, and it may reasonably be argued that a high volume of media attention to a particular event or situation will ensure public and, more important, government awareness of it. But in reality government awareness of international crises is likely to precede extensive media attention; government information sources are simply more extensive than those available to media organizations. As a result, it may be a government (or a specific agency within it) that alerts the media to a crisis as much as or more than the reverse. This would be particularly true if there is division within the government concerning the appropriate response to events and if it is thought useful to test the temper of public opinion by issuing statements concerning the matter. However, a government that is united behind a policy response may also be interested in seeing whether there is adequate support (both domestic and international) for that course of action and, if support is wanting, attempt to "shape" public opinion in a desired direction. While governments respond in one way or another to media/public pressure, it must be recognized that media are conduits that governments routinely use to inform, consult, and persuade their publics with respect to issues of the day. Indeed, the "need to persuade" may have a significant impact on the amount of media coverage an issue or situation receives, as well as on how it is framed. The relationship between media and governments is a symbiotic one, and influence can run in both directions, often at the same time.

It is often assumed, however, that the relationship is far more direct and unidirectional: that a "failure to report" on the part of the media is a major contributing factor to the international community's "failure to respond" to a humanitarian crisis. Our study shows that the media, television in particular, did not provide a steady stream of news from the Congo, much less any discussion of a possible response called for by Washington. This finding is consistent with the "failure to report" argument (for the case of Rwanda, see Thompson, 2007b; for Darfur, see Grzyb, 2009b).[2]

Although there is no agreed-upon definition of "failure to report" or "failure to respond," there is considerable evidence that it is not always a lack of reporting or knowledge about a situation that inhibits a response. For instance, during the height of the genocide in Rwanda (April to June 1994), the combined television and newspaper coverage of the disaster was the third highest of the ten major humanitarian crises of the 1990s studied (Soderlund et al., 2008).[3] There is also evidence that the Clinton administration was well aware of the horrendous events occurring in Rwanda, but was paralyzed by the possibility of "another Somalia" (Power, 2002: 354-57), especially in light of up-coming elections where it was feared Republicans would use US involvement to their advantage (Caplan, 2009: 32-33). Accordingly, it is difficult to conclude in this instance that the failure to respond was due to lack of reporting or to lack of government awareness.

Darfur is a more complicated case, mainly because there were significant differences in the volume of television as against newspaper coverage. In the four months prior to the authorization of a UN interventionary force to join African Union peacekeepers in 2007, only eight stories were aired on the ABC, CBS, and NBC networks' prime-time news programs. The *New York Times*, in contrast, ran fifty-seven stories during the same period (Sidahmed, Soderlund, and Briggs, 2010: 61, 96). In addition, as was pointed out in chapter 6, there was strong framing favourable to the African Darfurians and active encouragement of intervention on their behalf by both electronic and print media. The picture is therefore somewhat mixed, but Sidahmed and colleagues concluded that "data from neither television nor newspaper treatment [of Darfur] provide solid evidence that media can be held responsible for the slow and tentative response of the international community" (Sidahmed et al., 2010: 102; see also Caplan, 2009: 35).

Frank Chalk, Roméo Dallaire, and colleagues, however, maintain that media support and citizen advocacy are essential components for creating the "will to intervene" on the part of the international community in far-off humanitarian disasters. Working under the auspices of Concordia University's Montreal Institute for Genocide and Human Rights Studies, they carried out extensive research which resulted in the report entitled *Mobilizing the Will to Intervene: Leadership and Action to Prevent Mass Atrocities*. It argues that

> *the failure of civil society and the news media to exert sustained pressure on the Canadian and American governments has been a central obstacle to preventing mass atrocities* [because] politicians often cannot be relied upon to act of their own volition. Rather a vocal and broad-based constituency must emerge with the ability to advocate the case for governmental action in a persuasive manner. (2010: 47; italics added)

The "civil society" referred to is defined as being composed of "individuals, organizations and community groups that are non-state and non-commercial"—including NGOs such as Amnesty International, Oxfam, and the like—and, on the national level, charitable foundations, and student, senior, and veterans groups, among others. Under the leadership of the International Coalition for the Responsibility to Protect, the report calls for greater cooperation between national and grassroots groups (Chalk and Dallaire et al., 2010: 47–48).

The report does not examine in detail specific connections between media and civil society groups in the formation of public opinion (agenda setting and framing). Its policy recommendations focus heavily on what Canadian and American governments should do, largely in terms of improving structures to deal with genocide and assorted mass atrocitities.[4] However, the report emphasizes the importance of media in creating both an *active* effect (by pushing intervention) and a *passive* effect (by not creating political costs for inaction):

> The "fourth estate"—the news media—exerts a powerful influence on government. The "CNN effect" is credited with persuading the U.S. and Canadian governments to intervene in Somalia in 1992, Bosnia in 1995, and Eastern Zaire in 1996. Policy experts argue that the process of "policy by media," or formulating policy in response to media coverage, is a contemporary phenomenon that arises from the government's sensitivity of media coverage. While news media reports influence policy, the inverse is also true: *an absence of reporting on mass atrocities in a particular country removes the pressure on the American and Canadian governments to act on their "responsibility to protect."* (Chalk and Dallaire et al., 2010: 48; italics added)

The latter is of course in line with the ICISS identification of the need for a "political cost" to governments that are guilty of policy inaction, and the key role of mass media in creating that cost (ICISS, 2001: 7).

The Congo conflict was characterized by *passive* effects stemming from media inattention: coverage was not voluminous, and there was little framing of stories that could be seen as advocating international involvement. Indeed, the conflict was framed as "intractable," and UN peacekeeping efforts were generally criticized, thus providing little encouragement that additional international intervention would likely be effective. Beginning in 2005, both UN Undersecretary for Humanitarian Affairs and Emergency Relief Jan Egeland and *New York Times* columnist Nicholas Kristof recognized the negative consequences of media neglect (see chapter 5 of this volume), but their concerns seemed to have had little impact on either media behaviour or government policy.

While the linkages between media inattention and lack of international response may appear to be straightforward, they require closer examination from a number of points of view. In the first place, we need

Conclusion

to consider what constitutes "inaction." There is little doubt, for instance, that occurrences of mass atrocities, gross human rights violations, or significant violent unrest anywhere in the world will be a cause for concern in the capitals of the major powers, both for humanitarian and more material reasons. In all such instances there will almost certainly be a variety of "diplomatic actions" by governments such as those of the United States, France, Britain, and Canada, as well as by the United Nations and/or other international organizations. These diplomatic actions are designed in the first instance to prevent crises from developing and, following that, to mitigate them after they have begun. Many of these efforts will not be publicly known, but they are no less real.

Second, to use the word "inaction" implies that no forceful, compulsive (i.e., military) intervention has been taken, or if it has, that it has not been effective. Yet as the ICISS report itself acknowledges, the use of force should always be a last resort, and most people would agree that force is seldom the most appropriate method of dealing with political and social problems. Touched as we may be by the suffering of our fellow human beings, "forceful action" on their behalf can never be automatic or instantaneous. This is the case because it is infinitely better for people to solve their own problems (if that is possible), and because if the use of force were automatic and inevitable, as argued in the previous chapter, this would constitute an open invitation to the many dissident groups of the world to instigate situations that would bring them external aid for their particular, and not necessarily justified, objectives.

Third, "inaction" or slowness to act, even in dire humanitarian crises, therefore, may reflect genuine uncertainty about the nature of the situation on the ground, or about what can and should be done, rather than an unwillingness to come to the aid of the population at risk. Media personnel, moreover, are just as likely to experience these uncertainties as are those serving in government (for journalists covering Rwanda in 1994, see Chaon 2007; Hilsum, 2007).

Finally, the ability to intervene effectively without causing still more serious problems, and at acceptable costs, must also be a part of the decision-making process. Judgments about when these conditions may be met will inevitably differ from case to case, and there will never be absolute certainty that the right decision was made. The "will to intervene" is clearly important, as some crises will demand nothing less than a resort to force, but it does not seem either logical or useful to reduce a complex problem to a single dimension. This is not to suggest that mass media, or public opinion, are unimportant in the struggle to deal with the world's calamities, for surely they are. But it is probably better to think of these as components of the overall decision-making process than as driving or determining forces.

As the preceding analysis has shown, American mass media over the course of twelve years did relatively little to "push" the international community to halt the horrific atrocities in the Congo. But we cannot say that the Congo was "forgotten." While the *New York Times*'s coverage was not extensive, in our judgment it was well informed and steady enough to have kept the matter before the public eye—at least before the eye of the attentive public that plays an important role in the shaping of public opinion on a crisis that was remote from people's everyday lives and by its very longevity projected a sense of permanence.

It is difficult, if not impossible, to establish a priori the appropriate threshold by which to judge the adequacy of media coverage of humanitarian crises. It is perhaps even more important to acknowledge that conflict resolution will not necessarily benefit from international involvement, especially a peace-enforcement type of intervention (see discussion in chapter 7 of this volume). That being the case, it is essential to continue the debate of these issues, to encourage widespread attention to inhumanity, and to formulate more adequate international responses.

We believe that understanding the Congo conflict and the international response to it requires careful consideration of the role of the media. Only through such examinations can evidence-based conclusions be reached about media influence in general. It is also helpful to understand how the unique set of circumstances that brought disaster to that country, coupled with the largely ineffective international response, have affected the development of responsibility to protect-based conflict management strategies more broadly. On this point our research is clear: if the success of R2P depends on substantial mass media coverage of protracted, low-intensity wars in far-off lands, a new strategy is clearly needed. Moreover, there is some urgency in finding one. As the oppressions and rebellions across the Arab world in 2011 indicate, it is unlikely that there will be any shortage of unstable situations and large-scale loss of life in the foreseeable future. And it would be naive to believe that these will not involve the international community, however unwilling that involvement might be.

Postscript: An Update on Events

The Arrest of General Laurent Nkunda and a Rwanda-Congo Rapprochement

By the end of January 2009, the "Nkunda problem" had been addressed. Nkunda's military and political downfall came in a series of rapid developments. First, on January 12, Lydia Polgreen reported a split between General Nkunda and his chief of staff, Jean Bosco Ntaganda. While Nkunda dismissed the seriousness of the defection, Polgreen claimed that "it creates the first cracks in the invincible image General Nkunda has cultivated" (2009, Jan. 12: A5). The second bit of bad news for General Nkunda was contained in a "World Briefing" by Jeffrey Gettleman on January 21, namely that Rwandan military units had crossed the border to participate in a joint offensive with the Congolese army "against a Hutu militia that has been terrorizing eastern Congo for years." The UN reported that "the Rwandans crossed the border near Goma and were working as 'advisors' for the Congolese troops" (2009, Jan. 21: A12).

The final event in the switch in Rwanda's loyalty from Nkunda to the Congolese government was completed a few days later with the report of the general's arrest in Rwanda by Rwandan officials. Jeffrey Gettleman indicated that the change in fortunes for Nkunda signalled the strengthening of "the hand of the Congolese government, militarily and politically, right when the government seemed about to implode." The arrest also provided hope "that the proxy war between Rwanda and Congo is finally drawing to a close." A member of Congo's Parliament, Kikaya bin Karubi, indicated that "General Nkunda's arrest 'could be the beginning of the end of all the misery'" (as quoted in Gettleman, 2009, Jan. 24: A6).[1]

The arrest of General Nkunda was indeed a significant step in a long process of bringing some semblance of peace to eastern Congo (Lemarchand, 2009: 121–22). However, the rapprochement with Rwanda came with costs for President Kabila. Josh Kron reported that in 2006, critical electoral support had come from eastern Congo, Kabila's home region and where his popularity stemmed from "his nationalistic and confrontational stance against Rwanda … But in 2009, Mr. Kabila invited Rwandan troops into Congolese territory to help root our Rwandan rebels in the areas in exchange for renewed diplomatic relations [and this led] many in eastern Congo to believe that Mr. Kabila had betrayed them" (Kron, 2011, Nov. 10: A9). Whatever the case, the problem-filled relationship between Rwanda and the Democratic Republic of the Congo makes any prediction of future cooperation between the two extremely uncertain.

Intermittent, low-level violence in the region has indeed continued in the wake of twelve years of devastating conflict (see York, 2010, Mar. 27: F1). At the centre of the Congo's security problems is the failure of state institutions. René Lemarchand, for example, argues that "the state in the DRC is effectively non-existent—it lacks the capacity to resolve conflict. Without an efficient and neutral constabulary, a reliable police force, a functioning judiciary, a legislative assembly that actually legislates, and an executive that enforces the law, conflict resolution is left to the whims of the same groups perpetrating the violence" (2009: 125).

Additionally, Project Enough's John Prendergast points out that the current conflict in the Congo is "not really a war [but] a business based on violence."[2] Specifically, he argues that

> there are numerous armed groups and commercial actors—Congolese, Rwandan, and Ugandan—that have positioned themselves for the spoils of a deliberately lawless, accountability-free, unstable, highly profitable mafia-style economy … Armed groups use terrifying tactics such as mass rape and village burning to intimidate civilians into providing cheap labor for the elaborate extortion racket … And until this logic of unaccountable, violent, illegal mineral extraction changes, all the peacekeepers and peacemakers in the world will have very little impact of the levels of violence there. (Prendergast, 2010, Feb. 26)

While U.S. legislation curtailing the importation of minerals from the eastern Congo war zone was said to be having "a positive effect," there were unintended negative side effects. According to critics, "the new obligations have merely resulted in a de facto ban on mineral exports from eastern Congo, blowing a further hole in the region's already fragile economy" (Willis, 2011, Sept. 19).

The November 2011 Elections

The presidential (11 candidates) and legislative elections (19,000 candidates running for 500 parliamentary seats) in the Congo in November 2011 appeared every bit as challenging as those held in 2006 (*Windsor Star*, 2011, Nov. 21). President Kabila was widely predicted to win the presidency, due in large part to a change in the electoral system which substituted a "first-past-the-post" system for the former 50-percent-plus requirement, thus negating the need for a run-off election. In the absence of a dominant opposition candidate, the system was seen as virtually guaranteeing the election of the incumbent (AP, 2011, Nov. 9). Congo expert Jason Stearns, however, still predicted that "'the election will be very close' ... with 'a high probability of violence'" (as quoted in Kron, 2011, Nov. 10: A9).

Problems of violence in the eastern region have continued. The remnants of the Hutu leadership of the 1994 Rwandan genocide—the Democratic Forces For the Liberation of Rwanda [FDLR]—stood at the "top of the list ... [of] ... rebel groups that continue to harass inhabitants," a list that included the Mai-Mai militias, and former Chief of Staff for Laurent Nkunda, Bosco Ntaganda. Although the last was wanted by the ICC for war crimes, he was reported serving as a general in the Congolese army (Willis, 2011, Sept. 19).[3] Congolese peacemaker Henri Ladyi also warned that Congolese militias were reorganizing in anticipation of the election: "The election motivates many people and many armed groups to go back to using guns as a way to gain power ... The numbers are increasing and many ex-combatants are going back to the bush now: violence is what they know." Ladyi attributed the Congo's difficulties to a lack of a reconciliation process: "We should have learned from every other African country—Liberia, South Africa, Rwanda—who put in place a reconciliation process after conflict. We did not succeed in the DRC, and these leaders who are in power also don't admit what their role was, so people do not trust them" (as quoted in McVeigh, 2011, Oct. 29).

In addition to problems in the eastern region, there were signs that politically inspired violence had spread to areas that had previously been relatively calm. In the capital, Kinshasa, "there were violent clashes between government and opposition supporters ... An opposition television station was among a number of buildings to be burnt to the ground on September 5th." Fears were also expressed that the election could result in "a post-election stand-off similar to that in the Ivory Coast."[4]

Asked about "the likelihood of prolonged violence," Richard Zink, EU ambassador to the DRC, was non-committal: "History doesn't repeat itself, there are many potential outcomes" (as quoted in Willis, 2011, Sept. 19).

Toward the end of October, the *Globe and Mail*'s Africa bureau chief, Geoffrey York, offered an even more dire picture of conditions: "One of Africa's biggest and most unstable countries is sliding toward a resurgence of armed conflict as a crucial election campaign is increasingly tainted by fraud allegations and violent clashes." President Joseph Kabila's chief opponent was 79-year-old Étienne Tshisekedi, who, along with the president's late father, had been a political opponent of Mobutu Sese Seko. York pointed to concerns

> that Mr. Kabila will not permit a free election. Police have disrupted or halted many of the opposition rallies with brutal tactics. Four consecutive rallies by Mr. Tshisekedi's party have turned into violent battles with police, who have fired tear gas and beaten and arrested opposition supporters. Regardless of who wins the election, many observers expect the losers to take to the streets, sparking a new war. (York, 2011, Oct. 26: A19)

Following a trip to the Congo, Canadian policy analyst Glenys Babcock offered an equally pessimistic assessment of the situation: "There will be violence following the election ... The possibilities range from a few deaths to all-out war, depending on the outcome of the election." Liberal Member of Parliament John McKay criticized the Canadian government for neglecting Africa: "Canada is prepared to engage in a very robust fashion in a military mission like Libya, but it's far less robust when it comes to aid and diplomacy" (both as quoted in York, 2011, Oct. 26: A19).

November saw the election take a bizarre turn, even for the Congo. In a pre-election television interview, Étienne Tshisekedi further muddied the waters by proclaiming himself "Head of State" immediately. Claiming that "Kabila no longer represents anyone but his wife," he dismissed the need for elections as "the majority of people was with him." He went on to urge his supporters "everywhere in the country to go to the prisons, to break down the doors and to liberate my supporters." He added that as president, "I'm ordering prison guards not to resist" (as quoted in Stearns, 2011, Nov. 8).

In Toronto, Tshisekedi's unusual approach to democratic governance occasioned a critical editorial in the *Globe and Mail* that argued the move "has damaged democracy in Africa's most underachieving country" ... Democracy demands a respect for whatever democratic freedoms do exist. Instead, Mr. Tshisekedi abused those freedoms, saying ... 'We don't need to wait for elections ... From this day forward I am the head of state of the DRC.'" The editorial further noted the incongruities between his dismissal of elections and his views expressed in a June 2011 visit to Toronto: "'To take power, we don't rely on the guns, but the ballot boxes'; [in addition, he promised to] ... 'restore the rule of law.'" Nonetheless, the editorial was not complimentary to incumbent president Joseph Kabila, who was described as "no saint." It reported that the UN documented "188 human-rights violations related to the elections, with dozens of attacks on Mr. Tshisekedi's supporters by government forces" (as quoted in *Globe and Mail*, 2011, Nov. 11: A18).

The Election and Post-Election Developments

Although President Kabila won the late November election with a reported 49 percent of the vote, his opponent, who gained 32 percent, "immediately disputed the result and declared himself president. 'I consider these results a real provocation of the Congolese people ... As a consequence ... I consider myself, from today, the elected president of the Democratic Republic of Congo.'" UN Secretary-General Ban Ki-moon urged "all candidates and their supporters to exercise restraint and refrain from any acts of violence, provocation and incitement to violence" (both as quoted in Smith, 2011, Dec. 9). The Carter Center agreed with Mr. Tshisekedi's evaluation, stating the election results "'lack credibility' [and] international observers fear[ed] that there could be further violence if the current stalemate lingers into the coming weeks" (Pflanz, 2011, Dec. 11).

The election and its outcome did indeed spark intermittent violent protests, with at least eighteen deaths reported immediately after the results were announced (Smith, 2011, Dec. 9). Although the major crisis predicted by many did not occur, in early January Col. Rick Fawcett, the senior Canadian serving in the Congo, indicated that "it's unclear whether the worst of the post-elections violence in the country has passed." He indicated that "there's still a lot of tension out there" (as quoted in Levitz, 2012, Jan. 3). As was the case previously, in early 2012 the eastern area continued to be the scene of low-intensity conflict (BBC, 2012, Jan. 10).

As of February 22, 2012, it was reported that President Kabila was still seeking a rapprochement with his electoral opponent: "Information Minister Lambert Mende told a news conference that the door for dialogue with opposition leader Etienne Tshisekedi remains open" (Congo News Agency, 2010, Feb. 22).

Appendix: Descriptive Language

Mobutu Sese Seko

Positive

- "[The United States] saw [Mobutu] as a man who could hold the country together to avoid pieces falling off, which would create opportunities for the Soviets and their friends to play around"
- viewed as a counter-weight to Soviet influence in Africa

Negative

- Africa's longest-ruling dictator/ruled this country for three decades/dictatorship controlled this country for more than thirty years
- former dictator
- hated
- Swiss agreed to freeze Mobutu's assets/Swiss froze Mobutu's assets/Swiss authorities froze his bank accounts
- lived like a king in his luxurious palace while most the 44 million people suffered in poverty
- his assets are believed by some to be in excess of 4 billion
- stole money/robbed and plundered the country/plundered his nation, looted copper and diamond mines, pocketed international aid and turned Zaire's National Bank into his own cash drawer.

Appendix: Descriptive Language

Neutral/Ambiguous

- is believed to be on his way to Morocco for a life in permanent exile/ reported headed for exile in Morocco/flew to Morocco
- weakened by prostate cancer
- ailing, long-time dictator is gone

Laurent-Désiré Kabila

Positive

- "We like him—we like him so much"/new leader was praised
- agreed to cooperate with a UN mission to look into the murder [of refugees]
- Richardson and Kabila emerged smiling, calling the talks successful/ he called the meeting with Richardson successful
- gave Richardson his word he will turn the country around
- will respect human rights
- "there is no mass killing in this country"

Negative

- lifelong left-wing revolutionary who now claims to have renounced his Communist past
- long-time Marxist with no governing experience
- declared himself president of the country and changed the name of the country to the Democratic Republic of Congo/named himself head of the state and renamed it the Democratic Republic of the Congo
- proclaimed himself head of a new nation/declared himself president
- he is perhaps a new dictator is disguise/ "We just got rid of a dictator and we hope our new President does not become one too"
- will he be democratic and when will this country hold elections?
- there are questions about the new man in charge/don't know what his ultimate intentions are/"The jury is out on Kabila. If he continues not keeping his promises, he will suffer the same fate as his predecessor: lack of trust, lack of international support, and his own people will turn against him"
- elections played no role in his rise
- elections will be held only when people have been re-educated/he didn't sound democratic when he said people must be re-educated.
- worried that he would block an investigation into atrocities on the part of his troops/refused to cooperate with UN civil rights investigations

Appendix: Descriptive Language

- has a lot to answer for and the killing, we are told, goes on/his troops are still killing refugees
- his soldiers committed atrocities/accused of the murder of refugees/accused of murdering thousands of civilians/accused of ordering the massacre of opponents in 1997 during the civil war/rape, torture, massive killing of civilian refugees—most of it done by Laurent Kabila's forces and their Rwandan Tutsi allies/disturbing confirmation of systematic massacre ... in the Democratic Republic of the Congo/evidence of massive killing the authorities have not managed to conceal
- dictator with an abysmal human rights record
- got the diplomatic cold shoulder from [French president] Jacques Chirac

Neutral/Ambiguous

- rebel leader/long-time rebel leader
- promised a new constitution but did not mention elections
- new leader/leader of the Democratic Republic of Congo/rules the Democratic Republic of Congo/new president/now the president/rules the Democratic Republic of the Congo
- did not admit his government had anything to do with the mass killing of Rwandan refugees/claims he has no responsibility for the killings
- immune from prosecution [by the ICC]
- desperate for American money

United States Policy

Positive

- called upon [Kabila] to plan for elections and to respect human rights
- demanded an independent investigation into charges that rebel forces killed thousands of tribal Rwandans during the civil war
- willing to establish on-going contacts with the new leaders of the Democratic Republic of the Congo
- leading a diplomatic mission to save millions of people still threatened by the aftermath of the civil war in the Congo
- "all of us have the responsibility to stop the killing of innocent civilians"
- not taking their word that the government is taking care of Rwandan refugees

Appendix: Descriptive Language

- Richardson's mission: get assurances from President Kabila that the Democratic Republic of the Congo is willing to get along with the world
- rushing relief supplies to the Democratic Republic of the Congo

Negative

- supported Mobutu for more than three decades/a series of American presidents propped up [Mobutu]
- for the first time there is no NATO participation in a European-led peacekeeping force—read that for no United States participation/is conspicuously absent/looked the other way
- "resisted any pressure to put any form of pressure on governments of the region that have been fuelling the conflict and whose forces are involved in some of the atrocities that have been committed"
- not pushing for a more aggressive UN mandate in the Congo

Neutral/Ambiguous

- viewed Mobutu as a counter-weight to Soviet influence in Africa
- welcomed the relatively peaceful transition [from Mobutu]/welcomed Kabila's call for calm and his plan to form a transitional government soon
- has a military force standing by to help get Americans out of Zaire if needed
- Richardson's mission: to twist the arm of the nation's new president—Laurent Kabila
- officials are wary—they still don't know what [Kabila's] ultimate intentions are/America is listening but watching Kabila very closely
- advised 200 Americans in [Kinshasa] to stay in their homes

The Democratic Republic of the Congo

Positive

- place of incredible beauty/lush hill country/how beautiful it is
- resource rich/vast country with some of the world's richest mineral resources /rich in an extremely valuable metal—[coltan]/has some of the world's richest diamonds/fabulous mineral wealth literally can be scooped out of the ground
- the amazing grace of Congo is that the hardship hasn't hardened everyone

Appendix: Descriptive Language

Negative

- troubled nation/struggling nation
- remains the "heart of darkness"—a place so impenetrable that even experts concede they're only guessing [at the death toll]/war has caused a staggering loss of life
- horrific tragedy
- economy has been destroyed by years of warfare
- in shambles
- has no health care, no infrastructure
- devastated by one disaster after another/no stranger of tragedy/ scene of civil war, famine and tribal warfare/"place as close as you can get to hell on earth"/a war zone/enduring conflict/home of the deadliest conflict since World War II/the poverty and the danger of the place … are unavoidable/has the highest death toll of any conflict since WWII/a new rash of massacres along the Rwandan border/the Rwandan killers [Interahmawe] have regrouped and continue their murderous ways/war ravaged country/living hell on earth/has a bloody history
- childhood is a foreign concept
- a vast war-ravaged wilderness with few roads
- has the highest number of children in armed groups
- an epidemic of rape is raging/rape and lawlessness are still rampant
- government troops accused of looting and rape

Neutral/Ambiguous

- there is no guarantee that it will be democratic/will it be democratic?
- beautiful tragic country/place of terrible beauty—of mountains, great lakes and rolling savanna—as well as human suffering almost beyond description
- has to rebuild itself
- "when [Richard Holbrooke's trip] began the Congo was the most important crisis in Africa, by the time we got here, it had dropped to number three"
- "has not received enough media coverage and that is in relation to the scale of the humanitarian disaster that is taking place"
- neighbours have been meddling in the country for years
- a mountain gorilla preserve is a war zone

Appendix: Descriptive Language

United Nations Peacekeeping Mission

Positive

- "[the UN mission] is a key to regional peace and a key to peace within the Congo ... because the Congolese people have suffered greatly from this and we must stop it"
- people welcomed UN peacekeepers when they first arrived five years ago

Negative

- a UN contingent of 700 Uruguayan troops were supposed to defend the inhabitants but were barely able to defend themselves
- [the French were deployed to] a situation where the UN has failed
- did little to stop the Rwandan genocide in 1994 and now once again the UN is staying on the sidelines when the same group of killers rebuilds its movement
- no indication that any of the countries that make up the UN Security Council, including the United States, is pushing for a more aggressive mandate
- accused of "a massive abuse of trust"/scandal has tainted the UN peacekeeping mission in the Democratic Republic of Congo
- investigating hundreds of allegations of sexual abuse by UN peacekeepers/hundreds of allegation that peacekeepers have sexually exploited the people they came to protect
- UN refuses to give financial or medical help [to victims of sexual abuse]
- Head of UN mission in Congo says he is ashamed
- "there is almost no peacekeeper whose has been held accountable and whose had to face the courts for what they have done"
- they have left a lot of babies behind
- UN staff seen loading prostitutes into UN vehicles ... and driving away
- there are 800 UN peacekeepers [in the region] but people are furious claiming they have done little to protect them

Neutral/Ambiguous

- UN peacekeepers have been here all along ... but authorized to shoot only in self-defence/UN troops are not allowed to go after the [Rwandan killers] "because we don't have the mandate ... from the UN Security Council"

Appendix: Descriptive Language

- presence of 11,000 UN peacekeeping troops has helped to limit the violence, but not stop it
- "a few people have managed to basically cause disgrace for the mission and for the United Nations"
- promised to crack down last year with a zero tolerance policy on UN personnel paying for sex in any way

French-led European Peacekeeping Mission

Positive

- vanguard of an international peacekeeping force trying to end years of bloodshed in the Democratic Republic of Congo/here to stop the [militia]/sent in to stop the fighting
- "This is something politically and militarily very important ... it has a very humanitarian component"
- "We want the French to come to make things back to normal"
- trying to do something new
- insist they will restore order here, unlike the UN
- its mission: protecting civilians

Negative

- will try to enforce a largely meaningless ceasefire in the six-year Congo war that has left 3 million people dead
- humanitarian organizations say the force is not nearly big enough
- a fledgling force that is dangerously undermanned and that is committed to remain here for no more than three months
- have no authority to disarm militias
- 800 French troops to defend one city in a country bigger than Texas and California combined
- has no authority to act outside Bunia and will remain here for only three months—little wonder the young Congolese soldiers don't feel threatened

Neutral/Ambiguous

- sent in to stop the latest round of fighting—it will be very difficult
- authorized to shoot to kill/allowed to use deadly force, if needed/have been authorized to shoot any trouble-makers
- if peacekeeping here means killing children, so be it
- the French peacekeeping force is now coming face to face with the children [child soldiers]

Appendix: Descriptive Language

- it bothers them that they face an army of children
- "It's a pity to see young children with a weapon, but the mandate is clear—every person who threatens the force, we engage them"
- French forces were there to keep an eye on things

Notes

Notes to Chapter 1

1. In his description of Leopold's 1892–93 war against Arab slave traders in eastern Congo, Robert Edgerton, albeit with changes in the names of weapons involved, might well have been describing the Third Congo War that raged some 110 years later: "The Congo conflict was virtually a civil war with large bodies of Africans armed with modern breech-loading rifles, old muskets, as well as spears and arrows, fighting for both sides, sometimes changing their alliances as the fighting wore on" (2002: 98).
2. Carry-overs from past to present can be seen in the role of the Force publique, described by Michela Wrong as "a 15,000–19,000-strong army of West African and Congolese mercenaries ... established to ensure Leopold's word became law. Weapons and ammunition poured into the region. Just as Mobutu was later to give the nod to a system of organized looting by instructing his soldiers to 'live off the land,' Leopold expected the Force Publique to provide for itself, pillaging surrounding villages in search of food" (2000: 43).
   Interviewed for a 2006 British newspaper article, Tina Van Maldren (a Belgian still living in the Congo), described Mobutu as "another Leopold, using the state to rob and murder the Congolese people" (Hari, 2006, May 5). During the Third Congo War the Congolese army was often cited as one of the worst abusers of human rights in the country (see chapters 5 and 6 in this volume) and its "bad behaviour" has remained an issue (see York, 2010, Dec. 3).
3. Because soldiers had to account for every round of ammunition fired, severed hands or ears were used to document to superiors that a bullet

Notes to Chapter 1

had been used effectively. In addition, sometimes, a hand would be cut off to confirm a failed kill or as punishment for a quota not met. A century later, the cutting off of hands became a signature tactic of the civil war that raged in Sierra Leone in the 1990s (see Soderlund et al., 2008: chap. 9).

4 Adam Hochschild also cites a depopulation figure of 10 million in the Congo under Leopold's rule (1998: 233), while Roger Edgerton puts the figure at 14 million, based on a population decline "from something over 20 million people in 1880 to little more than 6 million in 1908" (2002: 156).

5 William Zartman draws our attention to the uniqueness of the Congo's chaotic emergence from colonial rule, describing it as "an isolated exception to the otherwise successful transfer of authority from colonial to independent rule throughout the continent" (1995: 2).

6 Michela Wrong reports that in the war against Kabila's advancing AFDL, "[Mobutu's] soldiers behaved as could only be expected. They emerged from their barracks to prey on their own citizens, building on a tradition firmly established by the Force Publique ... The FAZ [Forces armées zaïroises] gradually disintegrated into a force adept at hijacking cars and stealing beer but utterly unskilled in the business of war" (2000: 252).

7 In the final days of Mobutu's rule, it fell to US envoy Bill Richardson to tell Mobutu that if he didn't leave the capital Kinshasha immediately, he would be in effect "on his own" to deal with Kabila's advancing forces and that this encounter would not be pleasant. Richardson's reported language left little to the imagination: "You'll be dragged though the streets ... and we're not going to stop them" (as quoted in Wrong, 2000: 272). Not surprisingly, Georges Nzongola-Ntalaja reports that Mobutu "became extremely bitter for being publicly shunned by his former mentors, friends and allies between 1990 and 1997, until he was left to die on the run like a wandering dog" (2002a: 143).

8 Shortly after coming to power in 1965 Mobutu renamed the Congo Zaire. Similarly, when he came to power in 1997, Kabila renamed the country the Democratic Republic of the Congo (DRC). In order to avoid unnecessary confusion, we use the term Congo rather than Zaire unless the latter appears in quotations.

9 Filip Reyntjens details the arrival of a number of immigrant groups to eastern Congo prior to and during the period of Belgian colonization. Tensions between the original occupants and the more recent arrivals in the densely populated region led to major outbreaks of violence in the early 1990s. These tensions were compounded first in 1993 by an influx of 200,000 Burundian Hutu refugees, then in 1994 by up to 1.5 million from Rwanda. The net result of this influx reduced the original occupants to minority status (2009: 14–23). The situation was further exacerbated in 1995, when Mobutu's government passed resolutions that demanded "the repatriation, without conditions or delay, of all

Notes to Chapter 1

Rwandan and Burundian refugees and immigrants." The latter was "clearly understood in the Kivus to include the Banyamulenge" (Stearns, 2011: 66-67).

10 It should be pointed out that in the academic literature, the use of language linked to the concept of vertical stratification in Africa (especially in the Great Lakes region) including *communal*, *ethnic*, and *tribal* is a subject of debate. The terms themselves—how they are defined and how they are used—are, very simply, contested territory. In addition, a number of scholars take issue with analyses that view conflict in this part of the world chiefly through the lens of vertical stratification. Rather, they suggest conflict is rooted in issues of class, power, or regional state conflict.

11 Figures on the number of people killed in the Rwandan genocide vary from 800,000 (Carlson, Sung-Joo, and Kupolati, 1999) to 1.1 million (Kuperman, 2001).

12 In addition to removing Mobutu from power, the Rwandan army settled scores with Hutu refugees. In their march from the Rwandan border to Kinshasa, based upon figures offered by the UN High Commissioner for Human Rights, Reyntjens reports "that 246,000 refugees were unaccounted for [and that] 'about 200,000 could well have been massacred,'" thus leading to charges of a new genocide (2009: 93). Stearns claims 60,000 were killed, with the fate of another 180,000 unknown (2011: 136), while Prunier places the figure killed at "around 300,000" (2009: 148). Whatever the precise figure, these human rights abuses were both systematic and significant enough to lead to problems for President Kabila, who in his first year in office had to deal with a UN investigation into what was, at the very least, highly suspect behaviour on the part of his Rwandan sponsors (see *New York Times* reporting reviewed in chapter 5, this volume).

Johan Pottier has credited the Rwandan government with a sophisticated media strategy aimed at downplaying the motivation of revenge against Hutu refugees in their military operations to unseat Mobutu, referring to it as a campaign planned and covered up by "a synchronized production of knowledge ... by which 'instant' journalists, diplomats, aid workers and academics accepted, formulated and spread images of Rwanda that chimed well with the RPF-led regime now in power in Kigali" (2002: 4).

While Paul Kagame appeared to have a keen understanding of the role of media in portraying situations in ways that would encourage international intervention and thus worked to keep media away (see chapter 3, note 1, in this volume), our analysis shows that on the issue of refugee killings, Kagame was in fact less than successful. For example with respect to television news, in the scant coverage from 1997 to 2003, Rwandan refugees were never identified as being *génocidaires* and only once as being Hutu—they were simply referred to as Rwandan. The *New York Times* did report the charges of mass killing of "suspected Hutu *génocidaires* ... including women and children, and burning the bodies" by the Rwandan army in a front-page story as early as May 27, 1997. Moreover, the story had legs, as President Kabila's efforts to block a UN investigation into what were termed possible atrocities continued to be a major news story, dogging Kabila throughout his presidency (see chapters 4 and 5 in this volume). On the basis of guilt over the non-response to the 1994 genocide, we agree with Reyntjens and Pottier that Rwanda probably received a free pass with respect to international condemnation of what was a clear case of cross-border aggression. However, the mass killing of Rwandan Hutu refugees by the Rwandan army was a major story in *New York Times* reporting of the Congo wars, and in the coverage of this story the alleged Rwandan Tutsi perpetrators were by no means excused for their actions.

13 Jason Stearns maintains that "politically and socially ... the RCD was a disaster. Outside of Hutu and Tutsi population of North Kivu, the movement was never able to convince the population that it wasn't a Rwandan proxy. Spontaneously, local militias—focused on ethnic self-defense—were formed, claiming to be protecting Congolese from foreign aggression" (2011: 211). However, with respect to Jean-Pierre Bemba's Mouvement de libération du Congo, Stearns claims that although a Ugandan proxy, "by early 1999 the Congolese were largely masters of their own rebellion" (225).

14 Because Mobutu had provided sanctuary to UNITA's Jonas Savimbi, Angola had entered the First Congo War on the side of Rwanda and Uganda in order to depose him. However, Angola entered the Second Congo War on the side of President Kabila, seemingly alarmed by an air-transported Rwandan military operation aimed at capturing Kinshasa from the west. Because this offensive placed Rwandan troops near the oil-rich Angolan territory of Cabinda, the Angolan president "made up his mind that it was better to have the devil you know ruling Kinshasa than a political unknown" (Stearns, 2011: 192, 197).

15 The Tutsi-dominated government in Rwanda has re-established the conditions which prevailed prior to the 1959 "social revolution" that transferred power to the majority Hutu population at the time of independence a few years later—namely a Tutsi minority, led by Paul Kagame, ruling over a Hutu majority (see Reyntjens, 2004). Needless to say, the situation at home could not be seen as welcoming to Hutu refugees across the border in the Congo and contributed to problems with their repatriation.

16 To cite one example, according to the UN the use of rape or sexual violence in the Congo wars was considered to be the "worst in the world" (Gettleman, 2010, Oct. 3). In a much-documented case in July 2010, armed men raped hundreds of women in the village of Luvungi, a stone's throw from UN peacekeepers, who did not intervene. This all-too-familiar story has been repeated time and time again. The inability

Notes to Chapter 2

to protect civilians, in particular women, from brutal attack led the head of one advocacy group that works with Congelese women to say that the "Congo is the U.N.'s crowning failure" (Gettleman, 2010, Oct. 3).

Notes to Chapter 2

1 This marked the beginning of the virulent Soviet Union–conducted campaign to have Hammarskjöld removed from office and the Secretary-Generalship converted into a three-man (troika) system in which the West, the East, and the non-aligned would be represented.
2 Filip Reyntjens confirms the non-voluntary nature of the repatriation of the refugees: "They were fired upon and the only safe passage open to them led to Rwanda" (2009: 83).
3 Canada put the best face it could on the episode. The Minister of Defence, Douglas Young, commented that "we've had a remarkable success here. Two weeks ago when we really moved into high gear in trying to marshal some support for humanitarian aid to the folks in Zaire, I don't think anyone would have dreamt that we would have over 500,000 people back in Rwanda without having to deploy or fire a shot" (as quoted in Massey, 2000: 9). In a sense there was at least a grain of truth in that. Almost certainly the timing, if not the occurrence, of the AFDL offensive on the refugee camps can be attributed to the threat that an international intervention might actually occur (see Appathurai and Lysyshyn, 1998: 96).

   Based on testimony on the part of an officer involved in planning Operation Assurance, Filip Reyntjens contends that "as a matter of fact, despite appearances, the international force was never seriously considered ... 'It was clear from Day One in mission planning ... that when One Stars [Brigadier-Generals] came in there was an acceptance that the mission would never happen'" (2009: 87). Whatever the case, from the Canadian perspective, the "home run with the bases loaded" in reality became a foul squib into the catcher's mitt. More importantly, the fuel for the conflagration to come remained in place, piled high, and awaiting only a wayward spark.
4 It should be noted that the OAU was disbanded in July 2002 and succeeded by the African Union (AU). The AU has also played little of an independent role in the ongoing Congo crisis, for many of the same reasons that limited its predecessor. The organization spoke in 2005 of plans to create a 6,000–7,000-man force to assist in the international operation in the Congo, but there has yet to be confirmation that this has occurred. The AU's participation in peacekeeping efforts in the DRC, in fact, have been so minimal that the organization is not mentioned at all by some major Congo experts (Reyntjens and Stearns) and only in passing by others (Prunier and Autesserre).

Notes to Chapter 3

5   The SADC is made up of Angola, Botswana, DRC, Lesotho, Madagascar, Malawi, Mauritius, Mozambique, Namibia, Seyshelles, South Africa, Swaziland, Tanzania, Zambia, and Zimbabwe.
6   Autesserre's description of UN behaviour follows closely the "organizational process model" advanced by Graham Allison and Philip Zelikow (1999) as an alternative to the "rational actor model" to describe decision making during the Cuban missile crisis.
7   The LRA specialize in routinely targeting remote Congolese villages to kidnap children for their activities, in the process killing, raping, and mutilating any others they encounter. In 2008, the US tacitly approved Ugandan pursuit of the LRA on Congolese soil by providing military advisers and supplies to the Ugandan military in an unsuccessful effort to eradicate them. President Obama announced an expanded effort of the same kind in November 2010 (York, 2010, Dec. 21), and in October 2011 declared that 100 US military advisers would be sent to coordinate efforts against the LRA. Given the extreme ease with which even large groups can melt into the mountains and forests of the region, success is likely to be elusive.
8   This quotation reveals the importance of images of the Congo as "the Heart of Darkness" (see Dunn 2003; Keim, 1999; and discussion in chapter 6 of this volume).

Notes to Chapter 3

1   The impact of a "CNN effect" apparently was not lost on Rwanda's Paul Kagame. In the run-up to the 1996 invasion of the Congo, Filip Reyntjens notes that the "management of information" was "an essential element of his strategy" and that this was done with a good deal of skill. "In order to avoid the 'CNN Effect' ('there is no humanitarian disaster and, therefore, no reason to intervene if there are no images'), the area surrounding Goma was closed off to both humanitarian organizations and impatient but powerless journalists" (2009: 83). The effectiveness of the strategy was noted by Refugees International Chairman Leonard Rosenblatt, who pointed to "a reverse form" of the CNN effect: "as the humanitarian disaster in eastern Zaire is not shown on television, many people do not believe it is taking place (or feel they can afford to ignore it politically)" (as quoted in Reyntjens, 2009: 86–87).

   Over and above covering up atrocities committed by his forces, Kagame had good reason to discourage media coverage: in 1945 the UN had been created expressly to deal with inter-state aggression, which, although disguised, was clearly taking place.
2   Gamson and Modigliani suggest that five framing devices are used: metaphors, exemplars, catch-phrases, depictions, and visual images (1989: 3). We believe that our detailed examination of visuals and language picked up the impact of all of these framing devices.

Notes to Chapter 3

3. Scholars looking at the same set of news stories can come to opposite conclusions regarding their meaning; this points to a key limitation of content analysis. As Elihu Katz and his colleagues told us long ago, "meaning" is not embedded in content, rather it is dependent on how information is perceived in the eyes of the receiver (1973-74; see also Burgess, Harrison, and Marteny, 1995).
4. It was precisely at the time the Cold War ended that the challenge of the internet led to changes in audience viewing and reading habits and reduced advertising revenues. This began a series of job cuts at virtually all major media organizations, leading one media policy maker to observe that the twentieth century may well have marked the golden age of journalism (Soderlund et al., 2012: 88).
5. It is difficult to verify the number of deaths in humanitarian crises such as the Congo because much of the fighting occurs in hard-to-reach areas and is carried out by unorganized forces. As well, a majority of deaths in most Third World humanitarian crises are in fact indirect, as the very young and very old are especially vulnerable to malnourishment and disease (see Lacey, 2005, Mar. 20). In addition, there is a tendency for NGOs to inflate casualty numbers to aid in their fundraising campaigns (see Hilsum, 2007).
6. As cited by Snow and Barouski major companies active in the Congo include Anglo-Ashanti Gold, Matlor, Anglo-American Plc., Adastra Mining, Lazare Kaplan International Inc., Catalyst Co., and Barrick Gold (2006, Mar. 1).
7. For a comprehensive analysis of television coverage of the Darfur crisis that follows a research strategy similar to that employed in this study, see Abdel Salam Sidahmed, Walter C. Soderlund, and E. Donald Briggs, *The Responsibility to Protect in Darfur: The Role of Mass Media* (2010). In chapter 7 we will compare aspects of Darfur and Congo media coverage.
8. While the 9 percent foreign news content cited for network news corresponds to a Pew Center study (2010), the 13 percent foreign news content for newspapers appears overly generous. For example, using data from the Newspaper Advertising Bureau, Michael Parks cites a figure of "2 percent or less" foreign content in "the average daily newspaper's newshole" (2002: 56).
9. The role of the Rwandan genocide in influencing media coverage of the Congo is worthy of special comment. Anne Chaon, who reported from Rwanda early on during the genocide, points to the problems that reporters, who were not experts on the subject of genocide, had in identifying it. She explains that "we failed to understand that the killing was something totally new, that this was not a continuation of what had happened before" (2007: 62). Thus it was not until some weeks into the killing that "genocide" emerged as the dominant explanatory frame for the humanitarian crisis in Rwanda, replacing the "tribal warfare" frame that had characterized early coverage.

Notes to Chapter 3

Since then the meaning of the "Rwanda frame" appears to have shifted. In her work on the Darfur crisis, Amanda Grzyb explains the transition: "A little over a decade after the Rwandan genocide, the sign 'Rwanda' assumes a new semiotic distinction. The word that once meant "tribal warfare" is now synonymous with the *Western failure to intervene in genocide,* a legacy that directly influences the Western representation of Darfur" (2009b: 66; italics added).

Gérard Prunier refers as well to the ongoing importance of Rwanda in media framing of the Congo crisis. Prunier claims that "the Congolese ... had to fight a permanent uphill battle to remind the media that it was not *they* who had killed 800,000 Tutsi in 1994, and that they had to pay the price for that abomination was fundamentally unfair" (2009: 353). However, while the legacy of the Rwandan genocide fuelled the conflict, it was not until the spring/summer of 2003 that the possibility of a "Rwanda-style genocide" erupting between Lema and Hema peoples in Ituri province prompted the explicit use of the "Western failure to intervene in genocide" frame in media coverage (see chapter 5 of this volume).

10 Allan Thompson agrees. Citing the Red Cross's *World Disasters Report 2005*, he makes the point that "long-drawn-out crises (difficult to describe, let alone film)" tend not to be seen as newsworthy. "By that score, the estimated 3.8 million deaths in the Democratic Republic of Congo since 1998 from war, disease and malnutrition have generated scant media attention. But the dramatic eruption of the Nyiragongo volcano near Goma in early 2002 sparked an influx of journalists, even though it killed fewer than 100 people" (2007b: 439).

11 Television stories, as provided in recorded video format by the Vanderbilt Television News Archive, were coded by Soderlund and Roberts. Inter-coder reliability for quantitative elements of television content was calculated at 83 percent. It should be noted that none of the interpretations offered with respect to television news coverage are in any way the responsibility of the Vanderbilt Archive. Stories appearing in the *New York Times* were coded by Soderlund and Briggs. Inter-coder reliability for quantitative elements of newspaper content was calculated at 88 percent (Holsti, 1969: 140).

There were a number of reasons why CNN was not included in the study. First, we had a limited research budget to acquire stories from the Vanderbilt Archive; second, between 2001 and 2005, less that 70 percent of US households were wired for cable (Journalism.org, 2006), and not all companies include CNN in their basic package; and third, we wanted to have data that were directly comparable to Darfur coverage over the period 2003 to 2007.

12 Both ABC and NBC had reporters on the ground in Goma covering the eruption (Martin Seemungal and Rehema Ellis, respectively), while CBS covered the story from London with visuals from the region.

13 Columbite-tantalium (known in the region as "coltan") is an important

Notes to Chapter 4

component in the manufacture of cellphones and other high-end electronics.

14 In an essay on media coverage of Rwanda, Lindsey Hilsum points to a trend in which "wars in what used to be called the Third World [were] increasingly reported with an emphasis on the humanitarian over the political or military" (2007: 170) The coverage of humanitarian crises through the eyes of NGO spokespersons was a noticeable characteristic of television coverage of Darfur (see Sidahmed et al., 2010: chap. 4).

15 The critical role of language in media framing is explained by Farrel Corcoran: "The key concept here is the power to define, not merely reproduce reality through their narrative devices which actively make things mean ... Reality ... is the result of a particular way of constructing, through preferred meanings, a 'reality' which would have credibility, legitimacy and a taken-for-grantedness" (1984: 49-50).

It is our position that in a news story of perhaps a minute and a half to two minutes in length, any descriptive language that appears is not accidental. Moreover, it is not crucial whether that descriptive language is spoken by a source, a reporter, or an anchor: along with visuals, such language helps to establish a particular frame for a story.

16 Compared with Haiti, in terms of positive descriptors, the Congo actually fared reasonably well (see Soderlund, 2006).

17 Other exceptions are the Rwandan airlift of troops from eastern Congo to capture the Kitona airbase in western Congo at the beginning of the Second Congo War, and the battle between Rwandan and Zimbabwean troops at Mutoto Moya in October 2002 (see Stearns, 2011: 188-90, 273-76).

18 To illustrate how intense this competition for media attention was, Matt Guardino and Danny Hayes (2008) found that between August 1, 2002, and March 19, 2003 (the time when the Second Congo War was winding down and the Third starting to heat up), CBS news ran 497 stories on the run-up to the Iraq War, while ABC news ran 411. During the same time period, the above two networks ran not even one story on the Congo conflict.

Notes to Chapter 4

1 Some thirty years earlier Che Guevara had formed an equally negative assessment of Laurent Kabila's leadership abilities. Interestingly, Kabila's association with the famed Guevara was not mentioned in 1997 assessments of his ability to lead the Congo.

2 Some months later, French amended his assessment: France had moved from a policy of "calling the shots" to one of "carefully picking one's shots" (1997, Oct. 18: A7).

3 Ms. Wrong's widely acclaimed book, *In the Footsteps of Mr. Kurtz: Living on the Brink of Disaster in Mobutu's Congo*, was published in 2000 by Fourth Estate.

Notes to Chapter 5

4 Rumours circulating that Joseph Kabila's mother was a Tutsi (characterized as untrue) were also seen as contributing to his slight chance of success (Onishi and Fisher, 2001, Jan. 21: A10). Jason Stearns explains the basis of the rumour (Joseph was born to his father's Tutsi mistress) but does not verify its truthfulness (2011: 319–20). The younger Kabila certainly proved his detractors wrong: he won presidential elections in 2006 and was re-elected in 2011.

Notes to Chapter 5

1 *King Leopold's Ghost* was published in 1988 and is essential reading for anyone interested in understanding how colonialism contributed to the problems of the Congo (see chapter 1 of this volume).
2 The doctrine of "Responsibility to Protect" (R2P), first put forward in 2001, did not require that genocide be in progress in order to trigger an international response, only that large numbers of people were being killed. It is interesting that in the Congo, just as in Darfur, the question of whether genocide was in progress was still considered an important criterion for intervention to take place.
3 "Privatization of security" is not a new concept for post-colonial Africa. Governments in Sierra Leone and Angola employed the South African mercenary group Executive Options and the British group Sandline International to provide security against insurgent forces during conflicts in the 1990s (see Soderlund et al., 2008, chaps. 9 and 10). In light of the growing use of "military contractors" (the new name for mercenaries), this option should not be dismissed as improbable.
4 *New York Times* reporter Somini Sengupta was named the winner of the 2003 George W. Polk Award for foreign reporting. She was cited for "her articles from Congo, Liberia and other war-torn areas of West Africa." Her articles were described by the selection committee as providing readers with "a political and human dimension to horrific conflicts [often at] great personal risk" (as quoted in McFadden, 2004, Feb. 17: B7).
5 The Lord's Resistance Army (LRA), long active in northern Uganda, was founded by religious mystic Alice Lakwena in 1987 and in 2006 was led by Joseph Kony. In addition to Uganda, the LRA has been involved in armed conflicts in both Sudan and the Democratic Republic of the Congo. An arrest warrant for Kony was issued by the ICC in 2006. In the fall of 2011, the US sent troops trained in counter-insurgency to the region to deal with the LRA.
6 While not without problems, the election went reasonably well. Following one postponement, a first election at the end of July, sporadic violence, and an election run-off at the end of October, in late December the Congolese Supreme Court declared the interim president, Joseph Kabila, the winner against long-time military and political adversary

Notes to Chapter 6

   Jean-Pierre Bemba. Numerous international observer groups deemed the election as having reflected the will of the Congolese people.
7. Beginning in 2004, Kristof was a leading advocate for a strong international response to stop the killings in Darfur (see Sidahmed, Soderlund, and Briggs, 2010, chap. 5).
8. While we generally agree with the argument, it must be pointed out that the British intervention into Sierra Leone came near the end of conflict, not at its beginning. ECOWAS, in fact, was the first international organization to respond (see Soderlund et al., 2008, chap. 9).
9. Lisa Jackson directed the compelling documentary film *The Greatest Silence: Rape in the Congo*. The film won the 2008 Sundance Special Jury Prize in Documentary Film.
10. Cohen's advice to the incoming Obama administration was to press for "an economic common market encompassing Congo, Rwanda, Burundi, Kenya, Tanzania and Uganda." Such a market, he argued, "would give Rwandan businessmen continued access to Congolese minerals and forests" at the same time as it would ensure "the payment of royalties and taxes to the Congolese government." It was argued that "if undertaken with enough will and persistence, an American-led mediation to create a common market in East Africa could end the war and transform the region" (Cohen, 2008, Dec, 16: A37).

Notes to Chapter 6

1. Not all media content has an equal impact in terms of either "alerting" the population to the existence of a crisis or in "framing" its origins, meaning, and impact. Especially problematic in terms of assessing media effects are 20-30-second anchor-read stories, which account for about 45 percent of total television coverage, and one-paragraph "World News Briefings," which account for about a third of total newspaper coverage.
2. In that a UN peacekeeping force was first authorized for the Congo in 1999, relatively early in the conflict, it is important to point out that we did not code items primarily in terms of *advocacy* or *rejection* of intervention in the Congo. Rather, what was evaluated was use of specific language, and/or an overall presentation, that was either *supportive* or *discouraging* with respect to international intervention. In 2007, however, a number of Nicholas Kristof's op-ed articles as well as letters to the editor did call for greater levels of international intervention, and these were coded as supportive. In addition, because the balance between supportive and discouraging content varied so greatly by year, it was felt that calculating total percentages for the table would be misleading.
3. For an insightful comparison of *Washington Post* coverage of Sudan and Somalia over the period 1983 to 1994, see Livingston (1996).

Notes to Chapter 6

4. For an explanation of the construction of the Darfur sample, see Sidahmed et al. (2010: 56).
5. Although we have not come across a systematic study that deals with the question of why Darfur eclipsed Congo in terms of media coverage, the issue has been raised in various contexts by both journalists and scholars: for example, Roger Howard (2006); Rob Crilly (2010) (and his blog and interactions with other bloggers covering the story); Charles Beckett (Polis and his blog); Ethan Zukerman (blog); independent journalists (who appear on the website Frontline); as well as activists and academics who provide informative blogs (Jim Moore and Ingrid Jones). All these blogs are listed at the end of the References. The think tank Polis, which is a joint initiative of the London School of Economics' Department of Media and Communication and the London College of Communication, launched a research project in 2008 to address this very question. We have not, however, seen any of the results.
6. The long-running civil war in southern Sudan, which did not end until 2005, did have a religious component: the Sudanese government was Islamic, while the opposing rebel groups practised indigenous religions or Christianity (see Soderlund et al., 2008: chap. 4). There was also Osama bin Laden's prior connections to Sudan as well as his 2006 call to view any Western intervention in Darfur as being aimed against Islam (see Sidahmed et al., 2010: 86).
7. With respect to images, Jason Stearns points out an interesting irony. Acknowledging that the international news media showed "little interest in a deeper understanding of the conflict," he argues that the alternative—images of shocking atrocities such as gang rape, disembowelment, and cannibalism—would "reinforce the impression that the Congo is filled with wanton savages, crazed by power and greed" (2011: 327–28). Images such as those described by Stearns would hardly be likely to inspire the international community to become involved and in fact would have provided additional reasons for them to avoid it.
8. The most notable of these was the Senate proposal to establish a "no-fly zone" in Darfur.
9. Given the difficulty faced by the US in resourcing its extensive military operations in Afghanistan and Iraq, there is a real question regarding how much it could actually have been able to commit to a peacekeeping force in the Congo.
10. After some initial speculation about taking over leadership of a new Congo peacekeeping mission in 2011, Canada opted out as well (see Thompson, 2008, June 2; Granatstein, 2010, Apr. 7; Granatstein, 2010, June 7; Clark, 2010, Oct. 25).
11. The outlook for the future of foreign news coverage may not be as bleak as the above numbers indicate. Data from The Project for Excellence in Journalism show that between 1996 and 2009, the percentage of news stories with foreign datelines fluctuated between 10 and 15 percent (all networks were clustered at 10 percent in 2009), with the wars in Iraq

Notes to Chapter 7

(in 2003) and Afghanistan (in 2009) getting the lion's share of attention (Pew Center, 2010).

12 While it is true that many foreign bureaus have closed, Steven Livingston and Gregory Asmalov note that the *New York Times*, the *Wall Street Journal*, the BBC, and Al Jazeera continue to maintain bureaus around the world, and new players such as Globalpost and World Focus have stepped into the void (2010: 747). John Hamilton argues as well that while the "single elite model" that dominated foreign reporting for the past century is obsolete, it is being replaced by a network of NGOs, private funders, and indigenous bloggers, with tweeting, text messaging, and YouTube becoming the new tools of the modern journalism trade (Hamilton, 2010: 5). Even the International Reporting Project (IRP) at Johns Hopkins University has shifted over the past decade from granting fellowships predominantly to mid-career, mainstream journalists to mostly freelancers (Schidlovsky, 2010).

13 Research in both the United States and Canada points to international news occupying a low priority in terms of coverage (see Emery, 1989; Riffe et al., 1994; Utley, 1997; Wu, 1998; Halton 2001; Parks, 2002; Sutcliffe et al., 2009).

14 As of October 2011, the US has had advisers in the fight to curb the nefarious Lord's Resistance Army. It is interesting to speculate whether any widely recognized celebrity will take up the cause of calling attention to LRA atrocities, thus adding pressure for stronger efforts to deal with them.

Notes to Chapter 7

1 In this context James Mayall has argued that "the genocide in Rwanda was precipitated by an international peace process that was stronger on conflict management theory than on local knowledge" (2005: 56).

2 Among the most contentious issues still to be resolved is the status of the oil-rich Abyei region, lying between the north and south (see Johnson, 2007). By the terms of the 2005 Comprehensive Peace Agreement, a referendum was to be held in Abyei at the same time as the referendum in the south, but it was postponed at the last minute due to disagreements about who was eligible to vote.

While the independence of the Republic of South Sudan was achieved without major violence, it faces a myriad of internal problems, not the least of which is pervasive poverty. Some expressed fears that South Sudan might turn our to be *a failed state at birth*. For example, *New York Times* East Africa bureau chief Jeffrey Gettleman reports that "a majority of its people live on less than a dollar a day [and] the world's newest state and Africa's 54th state, will take its place at the bottom of the developing world" (2011, July 8: A1).

3 Séverine Autesserre pointed out that the absence of security and consequent lack of economic development in eastern Congo "means that

Notes to Chapter 7

belonging to an armed group is one of the few profitable occupations" (2008: 101).

4 It is worth noting in this connection that of the $1.26 billion budget for MONUSCO for July 2010 to June 2011, just over 80 percent is assessed to just ten states: the US (27.14 percent), Japan (12.53 percent), the UK (8.15 percent), Germany (8.02 percent), France (7.55 percent), Italy (5.0 percent), China (3.93 percent), Canada (3.21 percent), Spain (3.18 percent), and Korea (2.26 percent) (see UN, n.d.).

5 While we do not subscribe to the view that a media-aroused citizenry can seize control of and drive foreign policy, we do believe that it is equally imprudent to maintain that mass media (held to be widely influential in virtually all other areas of political decision making) has no influence on foreign policy (see discussion in the Conclusion of this volume). Specifically, over thirty years of research has demonstrated consistent "agenda-setting" effects, while a more recent stream of research has also confirmed "framing effects," with the latter most likely to occur in cases of "advocacy framing" (see Aday, 2006) of the type seen in *New York Times* coverage of Darfur.

6 A noted scholar in the area of peace building, John Paul Lederach claims that the kinds of social change necessary to establish a lasting peace following disruptive societal conflict needs to be measured "in terms of decades and generations" (as quoted in Ali and Matthews, 2004: 396).

7 This is the subject of another study. Based on an examination of both Darfur and the Congo, we believe that far more attention needs to be given to *building a capacity* on the part of the international community to deal with the kind of "bottom-up tensions" that arise out of conflicting ethnic (and perhaps religious) identities and which Séverine Autesserre brought to our attention (see also our review in chapter 2 of this volume). This is by no means an easy task, as language, culture, and religion will differ from crisis to crisis to the extent that any uniform approach is unlikely to be effective. Yet this should not serve as an excuse to do nothing. As a start, we would encourage the development of graduate courses (perhaps a program) that would integrate students with area specializations and those interested in conflict resolution, leading to cadre of skilled personnel to deal with the issues underlying "protracted social conflict."

8 As was the case with ONUC in the early 1960s, MONUC/MONUSCO at the very least did manage to preserve the official boundaries of the DRC, if not its "territorial integrity."

Notes to Conclusion

1 In an attempt to explain why international interventions occurred in some cases and not in others, a total of five independent variables were examined. In addition to "volume of media coverage," these

were "crisis severity," perceived "risks" involved in an intervention for possible intervening powers, perceived "national interest" on the part of possible intervening powers, and whether the intervention was "supported" or "discouraged" in whatever media coverage was found. The strength of the media "alert" provided the only reasonably strong correlation.
2. For Rwanda, Allan Thompson makes the case explicitly: "Through their absence and a failure to adequately observe and record events, journalists contributed to the behaviour of the perpetrators of the genocide—who were encouraged by the world's apathy and acted with impunity" (2007a: 3). On Darfur, while noting that "coverage came far too late, almost a year after the violence against civilians commenced," Amanda Grzyb concludes that news reports were "fairly accurate," and that "several major newspapers provided excellent coverage [including] far more editorial responses than were printed during the Rwandan genocide, as print-media outlets assumed a greater sense of responsibility for alerting the public to urgent humanitarian crises" (2009b: 78–79).
3. In July 1994, when the Hutu government had been defeated and refugees (including some who had participated in the genocide) started streaming across the border into the Congo, media coverage of the Rwandan crisis increased dramatically. Our conclusion is that although initial reports of what was later termed "genocide" (which began with the downing of President Habyarimana's plane in April) were confusing, the mass killings in Rwanda between mid-April and late July did, in fact, attract a significant amount of media coverage. Although the French intervention, Operation Turquoise, has been criticized severely as to both its motivation and accomplishments, it nevertheless had been authorized by the UN Security Council to respond to the violence.
4. Amada Gryzb explores the role of media in the process of "advocacy and activism" in her analysis of media coverage of Darfur: "While the media played a role in keeping Darfur in the public discourse, it is the NGOs and Darfur activist organizations that have truly kept up the pressure for international intervention" (2009b: 83). Her analysis pointed to the leading role played by citizen advocacy groups in the process: "*the news media themselves became a core target of Darfur advocates in 2005.*" She references the "Be a Witness" campaign, which consisted "of a television advertisement and a companion website revealing the lack of Darfur coverage on network TV news, and comparing this omission to the proliferation of entertainment and celebrity gossip" (2009b: 83–84, italics added).

Notes to Postscript

1. It has been suggested to us that the arrest of General Nkunda had more to do with his development as a potential rival to Paul Kagame than to

his political ambitions in the Congo. Whatever the motivation, following his arrest in Rwanda, General Nkunda was no longer a player in eastern Congo's troubles. As for Ntagana, Andrew Willis reported that he "now serves as a general in the Congolese armed forces, despite being wanted by the International Criminal Court for his use of child soldiers" (2011, Sept. 19).

2   Prendergast points to the "Conflict Minerals Trade Act" and the "Congo Minerals Act" under consideration in the US Congress as perhaps providing a step in developing "a global arrangement to certify conflict-free minerals," which he sees as "a catalyst for a solution to more than a century of resource-driven death and destruction in the heart of Africa" (Prendergast, 2010, Feb. 26).

3   General Ntagana was not the only alleged war criminal on the run in the Congo to remain in the public eye. Commander Ntabo Ntaberi Sheka, a Mai-Mai militia commander who had been indicted by the Congolese government for his involvement in the 2010 gang rape of "at least 387 women, men, girls and boys" in Walikale area of eastern Congo, was running for a seat to represent the very same region in Parliament (Kron, 2011, Nov. 10: A9).

4   The situation in Ivory Coast offers a worrying example of how a contested democratic election can fail to bring about positive political change or stability. The outcome of the autumn 2010 election between the incumbent Laurent Gbagbo and challenger Alassane Quattara led to a virtual civil war after Gbagbo refused to concede defeat in the UN-monitored election. Both men set up competing governments, and violence between their supporters led to the deaths of approximately 3,000 people and the displacement of an additional 500,000 in the four months following the election. Gbagbo was ultimately captured by Quattara's forces with the assistance of international forces. In late November 2011, the International Criminal Court issued an arrest warrant for Gbagbo for crimes committed during the four-month period of post-election violence. He is the first head of state to be taken into custody by the ICC, and there are concerns that the ICC action will further inflame tensions in the divided society (see Burke, 2011, Nov. 29; Smith, 2011, Nov. 29).

References

4International Media & Newspapers (2011). "2011 Newspaper Rankings: Top 200 Newspapers in the World." Retrieved Nov. 9, 2001, from http://www.4imn.com/top200/.

ABC (2000, May 12). *World News.*

——— (2001, Apr. 30). *World News.*

——— (2001, May 7). *World News.*

——— (2002, Jan. 21). *World News.*

——— (2003, June 13). *World News.*

——— (2005, Feb. 10). *World News.*

——— (2005, Feb. 11). *World News.*

Abi-Saab, Georges (1978). *The United Nations Operation in the Congo 1960–1964*. Oxford, England: Oxford University Press.

Adams, Russel and Shira Ovide (2009, January 15). "Newspapers Move to Outsource Foreign Coverage." *Wall Street Journal.* Retrieved Dec. 6, 2010, from http://online.wsj.com/article/SB1123197973917183829.html.

Aday, Sean (2006). "The Framesetting Effects of News: An Experimental Test of Advocacy versus Objectivist Frames." *Journalism and Mass Communication Quarterly* 83 (4): 767–84.

(AFP) Agence France-Presse (2002, Jan. 26). "Rwanda's Not Ready to Leave Congo." *New York Times*: A6.

——— (2004, Jan. 27). "Congo: Punishment Vowed for Rapists." *New York Times*: A11.

——— (2004, June 21). "New Waves of Refugees Flee Congo." *New York Times*: A3.

References

——— (2008, Jan. 7). "Congo Opens Talks on Ending Fighting in Eastern Region." *New York Times*: A10.

Albright, Madeleine and William Cohen (2008). *Preventing Genocide: A Blueprint for U.S. Policymakers*. Report of the Genocide Prevention Task Force. Washington, DC: US Holocaust Memorial Museum, American Academy of Diplomacy, and US Institute of Peace.

Ali, Taisier and Robert Matthews (2004). *Durable Peace: Challenges for Peacebuilding in Africa*. Toronto: University of Toronto Press.

Alleyne, Mark (2005). "The United Nations' Celebrity Diplomacy." *SAIS Review* 25 (1): 175–85.

Allison, Graham and Philip Zelikow (1999). *Essence of Decision: Explaining the Cuban Missile Crisis*. 2nd ed. Reading, MA: Longman.

Andrews, Edwin (2007, June 28). "An African Tragedy, Ignored by the World." *New York Times*: A20. (letter)

Anstey, Roger (1966). *King Leopold's Legacy: The Congo under Belgian Rule, 1908–1960*. London: Oxford University Press.

(AP) Associated Press (1999, Dec. 10). "As Congo's Peace Effort Falters, Holbrooke Issues a Warning." *New York Times*: A9.

——— (2003, Jan. 16). "U.N. Says Congo Rebels Carried Out Cannibalism and Rapes." *New York Times*: A5.

——— (2003, Apr. 7). "966 Congolese Killed in Attacks on Villages." *New York Times*: A6.

——— (2003, May 17). "With Congo Truce in Doubt, U.N. Takes Steps to Send Troops." *New York Times*: A2.

——— (2003, July 10). "U.S. Is Said to Back an Increase In U.N. Peacekeepers for Congo." *New York Times*: A10.

——— (2003, Nov. 6). "Congo: Aid Workers Report Thousands of Rapes." *New York Times*: A6.

——— (2004, June 3). "Congo: Renegade Commanders Capture City." *New York Times*: A6.

——— (2004, Aug. 15). "At Least 180 Killed in Attack of a Refugee Camp in Burundi." *New York Times*: I10.

——— (2004, Oct. 2). "5,900 More Troops for Congo." *New York Times*: A4.

——— (2004, Dec. 20). "100,000 Flee Fighting in Congo, U.N. Says." *New York Times*: A11.

——— (2005, Mar. 3). "U.N. Troops Kill 50 Militiamen in Gun Battle." *New York Times*: A11.

——— (2006, Jan. 7). "Severe Medical Crisis Reported in Congo." *New York Times*: A3.

——— (2006, Jan. 24). "Congo: Ugandan Rebels Kill 8 U.N. Peacekeepers." *New York Times*: A8.

References

——— (2008, Jan. 6). "U.N. Faults Congo Army for Violence." *New York Times*: A6.

——— (2008, Nov. 27). "3,000 Flee Congo Clash." *New York Times*: A11.

——— (2011, Nov. 9). "UN: Repression Ahead of This Month's Presidential Vote in Congo Could Lead to Violence." *Washington Post*. Retrieved Nov. 24, 2011, from http://www.washingtonpost.com/world/africa/ .../glQA87RfM_print.html.

Appathurai, James and Ralph Lysyshyn (1998). "Lessons Learned from the Zaire Mission." *Canadian Foreign Policy* 5 (2): 93-105.

Apter, Andrew (1997, May 23). "U.S. Pressed Congo Too Soon on Elections." *New York Times*: A30. (letter)

Austin, Jay (2009, May 11). "Celebrity Diplomacy: A Negative Force for Development." Retrieved Apr. 5, 2010, from http://jayaustin.info/celebritydiplomacy.pdf.

Autesserre, Séverine (2008). "The Trouble with Congo: How Local Disputes Fuel Regional Conflict." *Foreign Affairs* 87 (3): 94-110.

——— (2010). *The Trouble with the Congo: Local Violence and the Failure of International Peacebuilding*. New York: Cambridge University Press.

Azar, Edward (1990). *The Management of Protracted Social Conflict*. Aldershot, UK: Dartmouth Publishing.

Bacon, Kenneth (2004, Sept./Oct.). "Hiding Death in Darfur." *Columbia Journalism Review* 43 (3): 9-10.

Barratt, Bethany (2005). "Speaking with a Louder Voice: International Human Rights and Celebrity Activism." Paper presented at the Meeting International Studies Association.

Barringer, Felicity (2003, May 13). "U.N. Council May Request Foreign Force For Congo." *New York Times*: A8.

——— (2003, May 14). "France Says It Is Ready to Send Troops to Quell Congo Fighting." *New York Times*: A7.

——— (2003, May 31). "Security Council Votes to Dispatch Peacekeepers to the Congo." *New York Times*: A3.

——— (2003, July 16). "U.S. and Britain, at U.N., Back French Congo Plan." *New York Times*: A6.

——— (2003, July 20). "The World; Peacekeeping Is Back, with New Faces and Rules." *New York Times*: IV4.

Basanisi, Matthias (2008, May 23). "Who Will Watch the Peacekeepers?" *New York Times*: A25.

BBC (2010, Nov. 11). *Country Profiles Zimbabwe*. Retrieved Feb. 9, 2011, from http://www. news,bbc.co.uk/2/ni/africa-country-profiles/1064589.stm.

References

———(2011, Sept. 2). "Blue Nile: Sudan Declares State of Emergency." Retrieved Sept. 4, 2011, from http://www.bbc.co.uk/news/world-africa-1470824.

———(2012, Jan. 10). "Democratic Republic of Congo profile." Retrieved Feb. 24, 2012, from http://www.bbc.co.uk.news/world-africa-13283212.

Bell, Peter (2003, May 29). "Africa's Plight: It's Time to Help." *New York Times*: A24. (letter)

Bellafante, Ginia, (2008, Apr. 8). "Television Review: Congo's Horror, as Seen through a Personal Filter." [Review of "The Greatest Silence: Rape in the Congo."] *New York Times*. Retrieved Aug. 1, 2010, from http:www.query.nytimes.com/gst.fullpage.html?res=9C07ESDC143BF93BA35757C0A96E9C8B63&scp=3&sq=congo&st=nyt.

Belloni, Roberto (2007). "The Trouble with Humanitarianism." *Review of International Studies* 33 (3): 451–74.

Bennett W. Lance (1990). "Toward a Theory of Press-State Relations in the United States." *Journal of Communication* 40 (2): 103–25.

Bennett, W. Lance, Regina Lawrence and Steven Livingston (2007). *When the Press Fails: Political Power and the News Media from Iraq to Katrina*. Chicago: University of Chicago Press.

Berkeley, Bill (2001, Aug. 2). "Editorial Observer; The Rise and Violent Fall of Patrice Lumumba." *New York Times*: A20.

Betts, Richard (1994). "The Delusion of Impartial Intervention." *Foreign Affairs*, 73 (6): 20–33.

Bloomfield, Lincoln (1963). "Headquarters-Field Relations: Some Notes on the Beginning and End of ONCU." *International Organization* 17 (2): 377–89.

Bonner, Raymond (1997, June 6). "For Hutu Refugees, Safety and Heartbreak." *New York Times*: A1.

———(1997, June 8). "New Congo Leader Meets U.S. Envoy on Refugee Issue." *New York Times*: A1.

———(1997, June 22). "Too Little? Too Late? The Foreign Aid Gamble in Africa." *New York Times*: IV5.

Bonner, Raymond and Howard French (1997, May 19). "Rebel Army Captured Zaire in T-Shirts and Tennis Shoes." *New York Times*: A1.

Boulden, Jane (1999). *The United Nations and Mandate Enforcement: Congo, Somalia, and Bosnia*. Kingston, ON: Queen's University Centre for International Relations.

Bowman, Edward and James Fanning (1963). "The Logistics of a UN Military Force," *International Organization* 17 (2): 355–76.

Brennan, Richard (2004, Dec. 21). "Need for Leadership on Sudan and Congo." *New York Times*: A28. (letter)

References

Burgess, Jacquelin, Carolyn Harrison, and Paul Marteny (1995). Contested Meanings: The Consumption of News about Nature Conservation." *Media, Culture & Society*, 13 (4): 499–519.

Burke, Laura (2011, Nov. 29). "ICC Issues Arrest Warrant for Ivory Coast's Gbagbo." *Globe and Mail*. Retrieved Nov. 29, 2001, from http://www.theglobeandmail.com/news/world/icc-issues-arrest-warrant-for-ivory-coasts-gbagbo/article2253674/.

Burns, Arthue Lee, and Nina Heathcote (1963). *Peacekeeping by U.N. Forces*. London: Pall Mall Press.

Bustin, Edouard (1975). *Lunda under Belgian Rule*. Cambridge, MA: Harvard University Press.

Caplan, Gerald (2009). "What Darfur Teaches Us about the Lessons Learned from Rwanda." In A. Gryb (ed.), *The World and Darfur: International Response to Crimes against Humanity in Western Sudan*. Montreal and Kingston: McGill-Queen's University Press, 29–40.

Carey, James (1967). "Harold Adams Innis and Marshall McLuhan." *Antioch Review* 27 (1): 5–39.

Carlson, Ingvar, Han Sung-Joo, and Rufus Kupolati (1999). *Report of the Independent Inquiry into the Actions of the United Nations during the Genocide in Rwanda*. New York: United Nations.

Carson, Lesley (1998, Apr. 8). "Human Rights in Congo." *New York Times*: A18. (letter)

CBS (2001, June 13). *Evening News*.

—— (2001, Aug. 1). *Evening News*.

—— (2003, June 7). *Evening News*.

Chaffee, Steven and John Hochheimer (1985). "The Beginnings of Political Communication in the United States: Origins of the 'Limited Effects' Model." In E. Rogers and F. Balle (eds.), *The Media Revolution in America and Western Europe*. Norwood, NJ: Ablex, 267–96.

Chalk, Frank, Roméo Dallaire, Kyle Matthews, Carla Barquerio, and Simon Doyle (2010). *Mobilizing the Will to Intervene: Leadership and Action to Prevent Mass Atrocities*. Montreal: Montreal Institute for Genocide and Human Rights Studies. Retrieved Nov. 4, 2011, from http://www4.carleton.ca/cfp/app/serve.php/1244.pdf.

Chaon, Anne (2007). "Who Failed in Rwanda, Journalists or the Media?" In A. Thompson (ed.), *Media and the Rwanda Genocide*. Ottawa: International Development Research Centre, 160–66.

Charbonneau, Louis (2011, June 28). "UN Council Renews Congo Peacekeepers' Mandate." Reuters. Retrieved July 12, 2011, from http://www.reuters.com/article/2011/06/28/us-congo-democratic-un-idUSTRE75R51U20110628.

Cheeseboro, Anthony (1998, Aug. 30). "Mandela's Cease-Fire Could Be Bad for Congo." *New York Times*: IV4. (letter)

References

Chopra, Jarat (2000). "The UN's Kingdom of East Timor." *Survival* 42 (3): 27–40.

Chouliaraki, Lillie (2011). "'Improper Distance': Towards a Critical Account of Solidarity as Irony." *International Journal of Cultural Studies* 14 (4): 363–81.

Clark, Campbell (2010, Oct. 25). "For Canadians Peacekeeping a Priority over Combat Roles." *Globe and Mail*: A1.

Clark, Jeffrey (1993). "Debacle in Somalia." *Foreign Affairs* 72: 109–23.

Clark, John (2004). "Suffering and Death on the Periphery of World Politics: The 'Invisibility' of the Congo War as an Example of Hegemony in International Relations." Paper presented to the International Studies Association, Montreal, Quebec. Retrieved Nov. 23, 2008, from http:www.allacademic.com//meta/p_mla_apa_research_citation/0/7/4/3/7/ p74372_index.html.

Cohen, Bernard (1963). *The Press and Foreign Policy*. Princeton, NJ: Princeton University Press.

Cohen, Herman (2001, Apr. 21). "Pressure in Congo." *New York Times*: A14. (letter)

——— (2008, Dec. 16). "Can Africa Trade Its Way to Peace?" *New York Times*: A37.

Cone, Jason (2003, June 8). "Don't Ignore Congo War." *New York Times*: IV12. (letter)

Congo News Agency (2012, Feb. 22). "Kabila Is Open to Dialogue with Tshisekedi, Government Spokesman Says." Retrieved Feb. 24, 2012, from http://congonewsagency.com/.

Constable, Pamela (2007, Feb. 18). "Demise of the Foreign Correspondent." *Washington Post*. Retrieved Dec. 18, 2010, from http://www.washingtonpost.com/wp-dyn/content/article/2007/0216/AR2007021601713_pf.html.

Cooper, Andrew (2005). "Adding 3Ns to the 3Ds: Lessons from the 1996 Zaire Mission for Humanitarian Interventions." Working Paper, Centre for International Governance Innovation, University of Waterloo. Retrieved October 29, 2010, from http://www.irpp.org/events/archive/jun05NGO/cooper.pdf.

——— (2008). *Celebrity Diplomacy*. Boulder, CO: Paradigm Publishers.

Corcoran, Farrel (1984). "Consciousness: A Missing Link in the Coupling of Technology and Communication." *Canadian Journal of Communication* 10 (4): 41–73.

Cowell, Alan (2000, Oct. 8). "OFF THE SHELF; Extravagant Evil and the I.M.F." *New York Times*: III7.

Crilly, Rob (2010). *Saving Darfur: Everyone's Favourite African War*. London: Reportage Books.

References

Crossette, Barbara (1998, Apr.16). "U.N. Investigators of Congo Killings to Be Withdrawn." *New York Times*: A1.

——— (1999: Dec. 12). "Congo Leader Promises Cooperation with Mediator in Civil War." *New York Times*: I13.

——— (2000, Jan. 31). "U.N. Faces Big Challenge in Congo Peacekeeping Mission." *New York Times*: A6.

——— (2000, June 9). "Death Toll in Congo's 2-Year War Is at Least 1.7 Million, Study Says." *New York Times*: A1.

——— (2000, Dec. 15). "U.N. Peacekeeping Mission to Congo Is Revived." *New York Times*: A7.

——— (2001, Feb. 13). "U.N. Plans Fewer Troops for Congo." *New York Times*: A9.

——— (2001, May 16). "U.N. Delegation, Off to Africa, Sees Glimmer of Hope for Congo." *New York Times*: A5.

Daley, Suzanne (1998, Aug. 24). "South Africa's Role." *New York Times*: A4.

Dallaire, Roméo (2003). *Shake Hands with the Devil: The Failure of Humanity in Rwanda*. Toronto, ON: Random House Canada.

Deutsch, Karl and Richard Merritt (1965). "Effects of Events on National and International Images." In H. Kelman (ed.), *International Behavior: A Social-Psychological Analysis*. New York: Holt, Rinehart and Winston, 132–87.

de Waal, Alex (2007). "Darfur and the Failure of the Responsibility to Protect." *International Affairs*, 83 (6): 1039–54.

Diehl, Paul (2008). *Peace Operations*. Cambridge: Polity.

Dobbins, James, Seth Jones, Keith Crane, Andrew Rathnell, Brett Steele, Richard Teltschik, Anga Timilsina (2005). *The UN's Role in Nation-Building: From the Congo to Iraq*. Santa Monica, CA: Rand Corporation.

D'Onofrio, Alyoscia (2007, Oct. 14). "Rape and War: An African Tragedy." *New York Times*: IV11. (letter #4)

Dos Santos Franca, Antonio (1998, Sept. 1). "American Hubris Won't Help Africa." *New York Times*: A24. (letter)

Dunn, Kevin (2003). *Imagining the Congo: The International Relations of Identity*. New York: Palgrave Macmillan.

Durch, William and Tobias Berkman (2006). "Restoring and Maintaining Peace: What We Know So Far." In W. Durch (ed.), *Twenty-First Century Peace Operations*. Washington, DC: United States Institute of Peace, 1–48.

Ebo, Bosah (1992). "American Media and African Culture." In B. Hawk (ed.), *Africa's Media Image*. New York: Praeger, 15–25.

Edgerton, Robert. (2002). *The Troubled Heart of Africa: A History of the Congo*. New York: St. Martin's Press.

References

Emery, Michael (1989). "An Endangered Species: The International Newshole." *Gannett Center Journal* 3 (4): 151-64,

Entman, Robert (1993). "Framing: Toward Clarification of a Fractured Paradigm." *Journal of Communication* 43 (4): 51-58.

——— (2004). *Projections of Power: Framing News, Public Opinion, and U.S. Foreign Policy*. Chicago: University of Chicago Press.

Evans, Gareth and Mohamed Sahnoun (2002). "The Responsibility to Protect." *Foreign Affairs* 81 (6): 99-110.

Fair, Jo Ellen and Lisa Parks (2001). "Africa on Camera: Television News Coverage and Aerial Imaging of Rwandan Refugees." *Africa Today* 48 (2): 35-57. Retrieved Nov. 25, 2008, from http://muse.jhu.edu/journals/africa_today/v048/48.2fair.html.

Fein, Helen (1997, May 30). "Hold Congo to Account." *New York Times*: A28. (letter)

Findlay, Trevor (1999). *The Blue Helmets' First War: Use of Force by the UN in the Congo 1960-64*. Cornwallis Park, Clementsport, NS: Canadian Peacekeeping Press.

Fisher, Ian (1998, Dec. 25). "Kisangani Journal: Where War Is Forever, the Diamonds Are Cheap." *New York Times*: A4.

——— (1999, Aug. 4). "Brutal Bands of Rwandans Bar Way to Peace in Congo." *New York Times*: A1.

——— (2000, Jan. 2). "Ideas and Trends: If Only the Problem Were as Easy as Old Hatreds." *New York Times*: IV10.

——— (2000, Sept. 18). "Congo's War Triumphs over Peace Accord." *New York Times*: A1.

Fisher, Ian and Norimitsu Onishi (1999, Jan. 12). "Congo's Struggle May Unleash Broad Strife to Redraw Africa." *New York Times*: A1.

——— (2000, Feb. 6). "Chaos in Congo: A Primer. Many Armies Ravage Rich Land in the 'First World War' of Africa." *New York Times*: I1.

Fisher, Ian and Rachel Swarns (2001, Jan. 18). "Congo Says Leader Is Alive but Insists His Son in Top Role." *New York Times*: A1.

Ford, Glen (2007, July 18). "A Tale of Two Genocides, Congo and Darfur: The Blatantly Inconsistent U.S. Position." *blackagendareport.com*. Retrieved Jan. 6, 2009, from http://www.blackagendareport.com/index.php?Itemid=37&id=284+option=com_content &task=view.

Forero, Juan (2004, Feb. 5). "Colombia: Millions Caught in Refugee Crisis." *New York Times*: A6.

Franck, Thomas and John Carey (1963). *The Legal Aspects of the United Nations Action in the Congo*. Dobbs Ferry, NY: Oceana Publications.

French, Howard (1997, May 18). "With Mobutu Out, Zaire Rebel Chief Claims Presidency." *New York Times*: A1.

——— (1997, May 19). "Kabila Tightens Grip over Zaire's Capital." *New York Times*: A1.

References

——— (1997, May 20). "Reporter's Notebook: Old Regime Meets the New, and Hatchets Are Buried." *New York Times*: A11.

——— (1997, June 27). "Congolese Troops Detain Top Opposition Leader." *New York Times*: A1.

——— (1997, Sept. 15). "Congo Aid at Risk in Defiance of U.N. over War Refugees." *New York Times*: A1.

——— (1997, Sept. 28). "Hope for Congo's Revolution Dissolves over Old Tensions." *New York Times*: A1.

——— (1997, Oct. 18). "Africa Finds Old Borders Are Eroding." *New York Times*: A1.

——— (1998, May 21). "Congo Leader Losing Luster." *New York Times*: A1.

——— (1998, Aug. 4). "New Congo Leader Facing Rebellion by Former Allies." *New York Times*: A1.

——— (1998, Aug. 9). "The World: Congo Catches Rwanda's Disease." *New York Times*: IV3.

——— (1998, Aug. 14). "Rebels Closing In on Blacked-Out Congo Capital." *New York Times*: A1.

——— (1998, Aug. 19). "Top Fear in Congo Conflict: Wider Regional Violence." *New York Times*: A3.

——— (2001, Jan. 21). "In Congo, a Lesson in Where Easy Paths Lead." *New York Times*: IV3.

Fuller, Kathryn (2000, Feb. 13). "In Central Africa, Signs of Hope and Fear." *New York Times*: IV4. (letter)

Fuller, Thomas (2003, June 5). "European Peacekeepers to Go to Congo on Non-NATO Mission." *New York Times*: A5.

Funai, Go and Catherine Morris (2008, December). *Disaster in the DRC: Responding to the Humanitarian Disaster in North Kivu.* Washington, DC: United States Institute of Peace.

Gamson, William and Andre Modigliani (1989). "Media Discourse and Public Opinion on Nuclear Power: A Constructionist Approach." *American Journal of Sociology* 95 (1): 1–37.

Gettleman, Jeffrey (2007, Mar. 28). "After Congo Vote, Neglect and Scandal Still Reign." *New York Times*: A1.

——— (2007, Oct. 7). "Rape Epidemic Raises Trauma of Congo War." *New York Times*: 11.

——— (2007, Oct. 25). "Congo's Army Clashing with Militias." *New York Times*: A3.

——— (2008, Oct. 18). "Rape Victim's Words Help Jolt Congo into Change." *New York Times*: A1.

——— (2008, Oct. 31). "Tenuous Truce Holds in Besieged Congo City." *New York Times*: A12.

——— (2008, Nov. 3). "News Analysis: In Congo, a Little Fighting Brings a Lot of Fear." *New York Times*: A6.

References

———— (2008, Nov. 8). "U.N. Chief and African Leaders Seek Congo Peace." *New York Times*: A11.

———— (2008, Nov. 19). "As Fighting Ebbs, Confusion and Desperation Reign on Congo's Front Line." *New York Times*: A6.

———— (2008, Nov. 20). "Rebels Used Boots, Not Suits, Seek to Govern Congo." *New York Times*: A16.

———— (2008, Nov. 21). "Mai Mai Fighters Third Piece in Congo's Violent Puzzle." *New York Times*: A14.

———— (2008, Dec. 4). "Rwanda Stirs Deadly Brew of Troubles in Congo." *New York Times*: A6.

———— (2008, Dec, 30). "Rebels Kill Nearly 200 in Congo, U.N. Says." *New York Times*: A13.

———— (2009, Jan. 21). "Congo: Joint Offensive against a Militia." *New York Times*: A12.

———— (2009, Jan. 24). "A Congolese Leader Who Once Seemed Untouchable Is Caught." *New York Times*: A6.

———— (2010, October 3). "Mass Rapes in Congo Reveals U.N. Weakness." *New York Times*. Retrieved November 10, 2010, from http://www.nytimes.com/2010/10/04/world/africa/04congo.html.

———— (2011, July 4). "Sudanese Struggle to Survive Endless Bombings Aimed to Quell Rebels." *New York Times*: A4.

———— (2011, July 8). "Newest Nation Is Full of Holes and Problems." *New York Times*: A1.

Gettleman, Jeffrey and Neil MacFarquhar (2008, Oct. 28). "Congo Rebels Advance: Protesters Hurl Rocks at U.N. Compound." *New York Times*: A6.

———— (2008, Oct. 29). "U.N. Blocked from Pulling Workers Out of Congo." *New York Times*: A8.

Gettleman, Jeffrey, Graham Bowley and Stephen Castle (2008, Nov. 1). "With Tense Calm in Congo, Time to Assess the Damage." *New York Times*: A9.

Ghanem, Salma (1997). "Filing in the Tapestry: The Second Level of Agenda Setting." In M. McCombs, D. Shaw, and D. Weaver (eds.), *Communication and Democracy: Exploring the Intellectual Frontiers in Agenda-Setting Theory*. Mahwah, NJ: Lawrence Erlbaum Associates, 3–14.

Gibbs, David (1991). *The Political Economy of Third World Intervention: Mines, Money, and U.S. Policy in the Congo Crisis*. Chicago: University of Chicago Press.

———— (2000). "The United Nations, International Peacekeeping and the Question of 'Impartiality': Revisiting the Congo Operation of 1960." *Journal of Modern African Studies* 38 (3): 359–82.

References

Gitlin, Todd (1980). *The Whole World Is Watching: Mass Media in the Making and Unmaking of the New Left*. Berkeley, CA: University of California Press.

Globe and Mail (2011, Nov. 11). "Democratic Republic of Congo: Violence in the Air." *Globe and Mail*: A18.

Goffman, Erving (1974). *Frame Analysis*. Cambridge, MA: Harvard University Press.

Gordon, J. King (1967). *The United Nations in the Congo: A Quest for Peace*. Baltimore, MD: Johns Hopkins University Press.

Gormley, William (1976). *The Effects of Newspaper-Television Cross-Ownership on News Hegemony*. Chapel Hill, NC: Institute for Research in Social Science.

Gorney, Cynthia (2002). *The Business of News: A Challenge for Journalism's Next Generation*. New York: Carnegie Corporation for New York Forum on the Public Interest and the Business News.

Graber, Doris (2005). *Mass Media and American Politics*. 7th ed. Washington, DC: Congressional Quarterly Press.

Granatstein, J.L. (2010, Apr. 7). "Defining Canada's Role in Congo." *Globe and Mail*: A17.

—— (2010, June 7). "Canada as a Peacekeeper Again?" *Windsor Star*: A7.

Grignon, François and Daniela Kroslak (2008). "The Problem with Peacekeeping." *Current History* 107 (708): 186–87.

Gross, Kimberly (2008). "Framing Persuasive Appeals: Episodic and Thematic Framing, Emotional Responses, and Policy Options." *Political Psychology* 29 (2): 169–92.

Grzyb, Amanda (2009a). "Introduction: The International Response to Darfur." In A. Grzyb (ed.), *The World and Darfur: International Response to Crimes against Humanity in Western Sudan*. Montreal and Kingston: McGill-Queen's University Press, 2–25.

—— (2009b). "Media Coverage, Activism, and Creating Public Will." In A. Grzyb (ed.), *The World and Darfur: International Response to Crimes against Humanity in Western Sudan*. Montreal and Kingston: McGill-Queen's University Press, 61–91.

Guardian (2011, Feb. 3). "Pro-Mugabe Militias Blamed as Zimbabwe Violence Erupts." *Guardian-World News*. Retrieved Feb. 9, 2011, from http://www.guardian.co.uk/world/2011/feb03/pro-mugabe-militas-zimbabwe-violence.

Guardino, Matt and Danny Hayes (2008). "Whose Views Made the News? Media Coverage and the March to War in Iraq." Paper presented at the Annual Meeting of the Midwest Political Science Association, Chicago.

Guéhenno, Jean-Marie (2005, Oct. 29). "Abuse by Peacekeepers." *New York Times*: A18. (letter)

References

Hachten, William (2004). "Reporting Africa's Problems." In C. Okigbo and F. Eribo (eds.), *Development and Communication in Africa*. Lanham, MD: Rowman and Littlefield, 79–87.

Hall Jamieson, Kathleen and Peter Waldman (2003). *The Press Effect: Politicians, Journalists, and Stories That Shape the Political News*. New York: Oxford University Press.

Halton, Dan (2001). "International News in the North American Media." *International Journal* 56 (3): 499–515.

Hamilton, John (2010). "Reporting from Faraway Places: Who Does It and How." *Nieman Reports* 63 (3): 4–5.

Hamilton, John and Eric Jenner (2004). "Redefining Foreign Correspondence." *Journalism* 5 (3): 301–21.

Harden, Blaine (2000, Apr. 6). "Diamond Wars. Africa's Gems: Warfare's Best Friend." *New York Times*: A1.

Hari, Johann (2006, May 5). "Congo's Tragedy: The War the World Forgot." *The Independent*. Retrieved Dec. 14, 2010, from http://independent.co.uk/news/world/africa/congos-tragedy-the-world-forgot-476929.html.

Harris, Bob (2007, Nov. 26). "Violence against Women in the D.R. Congo: The Most Horrible Thing You Will Read Today—And, Unfortunately, Perhaps, The Last You'll Hear of It for Weeks." *This Modern World*. Retrieved Nov. 26, 2008, from http://www.thismodernworld.com.4077.

Hartley, Aidan (2006, July 28) "Congo's Election, the U.N.'s Massacre." *New York Times*: A29.

Hartung, William (2000, Feb. 10). "U.S. Role in Congo War." *New York Times*: A30. (letter)

Hawk, Beverley (1992). "Introduction: Metaphors of African Coverage." In B. Hawk (ed.), *Africa's Media Image*. New York: Praeger, 3–14.

Hennessy, Michael (2001). "'Operation 'Assurance': Planning a Multi-National Force for Rwanda/Zaire." *Canadian Military Journal* (Spring): 11–20. Retrieved October 29, 2010, from http://www.journal.forces.gc.ca/vo2/no1/doc/11-20-eng.pdf.

Herbst, Jeffrey and Greg Mills (2003). *The Future of Africa: A New Order in Sight?* Adelphi Paper 361. New York: Oxford University Press.

Heritage Foundation (2011). *Index of Economic Freedom Zimbabwe*. Retrieved Feb. 9, 2011, from http://www.heritage.org/index/country/zimbabwe.

Hill, David (2003, May 16). "Mass Graves, Pointed Question." *New York Times*: A26. (letter)

Hilsum, Lindsey (2007). "Reporting Rwanda: The Media and Aid Agencies." In A. Thompson (ed.), *Media and the Rwanda Genocide*. Ottawa: International Development Research Centre, 167–87.

References

Hochschild, Adam (1998). *King Leopold's Ghost: A Story of Greed, Terror and Heroism in Colonial Africa.* New York: Houghton Mifflin.

——— (2003, Apr. 20). "The World: Chaos in Congo Suits Many Parties Just Fine." *New York Times:* IV3.

Hoge, Warren (2004, Nov. 20). "Congo: Anan Says Peacekeepers Abused Women and Children." *New York Times:* A6.

——— (2005, Jan. 8). "Congo: Sex Abuse by Peacekeepers Said to Persist." *New York Times:* A7.

——— (2005, Feb. 28). "U.N. Is Transforming Itself, but into What Is Unclear." *New York Times:* A3.

——— (2005, Mar. 25). "Report Calls for Punishing Peacekeepers in Sex Abuse." *New York Times:* A8.

——— (2005, Oct. 19). "Report Finds U.N. Isn't Moving to End Sex Abuse by Peacekeepers." *New York Times:* A5.

——— (2005, Dec. 20). "Aid Effort in Africa Undermined by New Violence." *New York Times:* A5.

Holmes, Steven (2003, Nov. 7). "On Visit, Congo President Faults U.S. Farm Subsidies." *New York Times:* W7.

Holsti, Ole (1969). *Content Analysis for the Social Sciences and Humanities.* Reading, MA: Addison-Wesley.

Howard, Lise Morjé (2008). *UN Peacekeeping in Civil Wars.* New York: Cambridge University Press.

Howard, Roger (2006). *What's Wrong with Liberal Interventionism: The Dangers and Delusions of Interventionist Doctrine.* London: Social Affairs Unit.

——— (2007, May 16). "Where Anti-Arab Prejudice and Oil Make the Difference" *The Guardian.* Retrieved Jan. 23, 2011, from http://www.guardian.co.uk/commentisfree/2007/may/16/comment.sudan.

(ICISS) International Commission on Intervention and State Sovereignty (2001). *The Responsibility to Protect: Report of the International Commission on Intervention and State Sovereignty.* Ottawa: International Development Research Council.

Iltis, Tony (2008, Nov. 7). "Congo: Western Intervention behind Bloodbath." *International News, Green Left Weekly* 774. Retrieved Nov. 11, 2008, from http://www.greenleft.org.au/2008774/39908.

International Crisis Group (2010, Mar. 3). "Zimbabwe: Political and Security Challenges to the Transition." Retrieved Feb. 8, 2011, from http://www.crisisgroup.org/en/publications-type/media-release/2010/Africa/Zimbabwe-political-and-security-challenges-to-the transition-aspx.

I Want Media (2006). "Media Layoffs." Retrieved Sept. 8, 2010, from http://www.iwantmedia.com/layoffs.html#first.

Iyengar, Shanto (1991). *Is Anyone Responsible? How Television Frames Political Issues.* Chicago: University of Chicago Press.

References

Jackson, Lisa (2007, Oct. 14). "Rape and War: An African Tragedy." *New York Times*: IV11. (letter #3)

Jakobsen, Peter (1996). "National Interest, Humanitarianism or CNN: What Triggers UN Peace Enforcement after the Cold War." *Journal of Peace Research* 33 (2): 205–15.

Janssen, Dieter (2008). "Humanitarian Intervention and the Prevention of Genocide." *Journal of Genocide Research* 10 (2): 289–306. Retrieved Sept. 1, 2010, from http://www.informaworld.com.smpp.section?content=a794143515&fulltext-713240928.

Johnson, Douglas (2007). "Why Abyei Matters: The Breaking Point of Sudan's Comprehensive Peace Agreement." *African Affairs* 107 (462): 1–19.

Jones, Brian (2001). *Peacemaking in Rwanda: The Dynamics of Failure*. Boulder, CO: Lynn Rienner.

Jones, Brian and Michael O'Hanlon (2009, Apr. 29). "Democratic Republic of Congo: World's Deadliest Spot." *Washington Times*. Retrieved Apr. 8, 2010, from http://www.brookings.edu/opinions/2009/0429_congo_jones.aspx.

Journalism.org (2006). "Cable TV Audience." Retrieved Nov. 9, 2001, from http://journalism.org/node.509.

Kagwanja, Peter and Alba Lamberti (2005, Apr. 21). "Let's Turn the Screw on Robert Mugabe." International Crisis Group. Retrieved Feb. 9, 2011, from http://www.crisisgroup.org/en/regions/africa/southern-africa/zimbabwe/lets-turn-the-screws-on-robert-mugabe.aspx.

Kampf, David (2007, Mar. 1). "The Democratic Republic of Congo: Beyond the Elections." *African Security Review* 16 (2). Retrieved Nov. 26, 2008, from http://www.iss.co.za/static/templates.tmpl_html.php?node_id=2605&slink_id=4947& slink_type=12&link_ID=29.

Kaplan, Robert (2000). *The Coming Anarchy: Shattering the Dream of the Post Cold War*. New York: Random House.

Katz, Elihu and Paul Lazarsfeld (1955). *Personal Influence: The Part Played by People in the Flow of Mass Communication*. New York: The Free Press.

Katz, Elihu, Jay Blumler, and Michael Gurevitch (1973–74). "Uses and Gratifications Research." *Political Opinion Quarterly* 37 (4): 509–23.

Kavanagh, Michael. (2010, November 29). "Congo's Army Is Pillaging Country's Natural Resources, United Nations Says." *Bloomberg*. Retrieved Dec. 4, 2010, from http://www.bloomberg.com/news/print/2010-11-29/congo-s-army-is-pillagin-country.

Keim, Curtis (1999). *Making Africa: Curiosities and Invention of the American Mind*. Boulder, CO: Westview Press.

Keller, Edmond J. (2002). "Culture, Politics and the Transnationalization of Ethnic Conflict in Africa: New Research Imperatives." *Polis/RCSP/*

References

CPSR, vol. 9, Numéro Spécial. Retrieved March 24, 2012, from http://www.polis.sciencespobordeaux.fr/vol10ns/keller.pdf.

Kenzen, Martin (1999, Jan. 15). "Africa's Borders at Risk." *New York Times*: A22. (letter)

Khadr, Salah (2008, July 21). "Arab Media Blind to Darfur." *Al Jazeera*. Retrieved Jan. 26, 2011, from http://english.aljazeera.net/programmes/listeningpost/2008/07/200871114233!

Kim, Janet (2006, Oct. 19). "Children as Soldiers." *New York Times*: A26. (letter)

Kipling, Ty (2007, Oct. 14). "Rape and War: An African Tragedy." *New York Times*: IV11. (letter #1)

Klapper, Joseph (1960). *The Effects of Mass Media*. New York: The Free Press.

Klugman, Jeni (1999). *Social and Economic Policies to Prevent Complex Humanitarian Emergencies: Lessons from Experience*. United Nations University World Institute for Development Economics Research. Retrieved Mar. 9, 2011, from http://www.reliefweb.int/library/complex.pdf.

Knudsen, Tonny (2006) "The English School: Sovereignty and International Law." In J. Sterling-Folker (ed.), *Making Sense of International Theory*. Boulder, CO: Lynne Rienner, 311–17.

Koch, George (1996). "Operation Political Assurance: How Jean Chretien's African Crusade Descended into a Farce." *Alberta Report* 23 (52): 13–14. Retrieved Oct. 15, 2010, from http://find.galegroup.com/gtx/retrieve.do?ContentSet=IAC Document Number A 30300039.

Kosicki, Gerald (1993). "Problems and Opportunities in Agenda Setting Research." *Journal of Communication* 43 (2): 100–27.

Kristof, Nicholas (1997, May 20). "In Congo, a New Era with Old Burdens." *New York Times*: A1.

――― (1997, May 25). "Why Africa Can Thrive Like Asia." *New York Times*: IV1.

――― (2003, May 27). "What Did You Do during the African Holocaust?" *New York Times*: A25.

――― (2006, May 16). "Dithering through Death." *New York Times*: A25.

――― (2007, June 14). "Africa's World War." *New York Times*: A31.

――― (2007, June 18). "Dinner with a Warlord." *New York Times*: A19.

――― (2007, June 21). "Op-Ed Columnist: A Student, a Teacher and a Glimpse of War." *New York Times*: A23.

――― (2007, June 25). "Op-Ed Columnist: A 'Painful Way to Die.'" *New York Times*: A19.

――― (2008, June 15). "The Weapon of Rape." *New York Times*: IV14.

Kron, Josh (2011, Nov. 10). "An Unruly Election Campaign Mirrors Congo's Lingering Political Instability." *New York Times*: A9.

References

Kuperman, Alan (2001). *The Limits of Humanitarian Intervention: Genocide in Rwanda.* Washington, DC: Brookings Institution.

——— (2006). "Suicidal Rebellions and the Moral Hazard of Humanitarian Intervention." In Timothy Crawford and A. Kuperman (eds.), *Gambling on Humanitarian Intervention: Moral Hazard, Rebellion and Civil War.* New York: Routledge, 1–25.

Lacey, Marc (2002, Jan. 19). "Tens of Thousands Flee a Devastating Volcano in Congo." *New York Times*: A3.

——— (2002, Jan. 27). "The World: Hell on Earth: An Inferno to Make Dante Shudder." *New York Times*: IV14.

——— (2002, Aug. 20). "Combatants in African Nations May Soon Give Peace a Chance." *New York Times*: A1.

——— (2002, Nov. 21). "War Is Still a Way of Life for Congo Rebels." *New York Times*: A1.

——— (2003, Apr. 9). "Letter from Africa: With All Little Wars, Big Peace Is Elusive." *New York Times*: A4.

——— (2003, Aug. 12). "New Activism by African Nations: Joining Forces to Referee Their Own Disputes." *New York Times*: A8.

——— (2003, Oct. 21). "Hope Glimmering as War Retreats From Congo." *New York Times*: A1.

——— (2004, June 4). "2 Die in Congo Demonstrations as Protestors Storm U.N. Sites." *New York Times*: A8.

——— (2004, Dec. 18). "In Congo War, Even Peacekeepers Add to Horror." *New York Times*: A1.

——— (2004, Dec. 19). "Strife in Congo Town Sows Fear of Return to All-Out War." *New York Times*: I3.

——— (2005, Feb. 26). "Militia Fighters Kill 9 Peacekeepers in Congo as Instability Continues." *New York Times*: A6.

——— (2005, Mar. 6). "Congo Tribal Killings Create a New Wave of Refugees." *New York Times*: I3.

——— (2005, Mar. 20). "Beyond the Bullets and Blades." *New York Times*: IV1.

——— (2006, Mar. 26). "Congo, with Iraq in Mind, Faces Voting and Threats." *New York Times*: I10.

——— (2005, May 23). "U.N. Forces Using Tougher Tactics to Secure Peace." *New York Times*: A1.

Laderman, Scott (1997, May 23). "Whose Democracy?" *New York Times*: A30. (letter)

Lasswell, Harold (1938). *Propaganda Technique in the World War.* New York: P. Smith.

——— (1948). "The Structure and Function of Communication in Society." In L. Bryson (ed.), *The Communication of Ideas: A Series of Addresses.* New York: Institute for Religious and Social Studies, 37–51.

References

Lefever, Ernest (1965). *Crisis in the Congo: A United Nations Force in Action.* Washington, DC: Brookings Institution.

Lemarchand, René (2009a). *The Dynamics of Violence in Central Africa.* Philadelphia: University of Pennsylvania Press.

——— (2009b). "Reflections on the Congo Crisis in Eastern Congo." *Brown Journal of World Affairs* 16 (1): 119–32.

Leslie, Winsome (1993). *Zaire: Continuity and Political Change in an Oppressive State.* Boulder, CO: Westview Press.

Levitt, Rachel (2008, Nov. 11). "Global Perspectives on the Congolese Conflict." *UTNE.* Retrieved Nov. 28, 2009, from http://www.utne.com/blogs;blog.aspx?blogid+34&tag=Congo.

Levitz, Stephanie (2012, Jan. 3). "Tension Remains after Election Violence, Senior Canadian Soldier in Congo Says." Retrieved Feb. 24, 2012, from http://www.ipolitics.ca/2012/01/03/tension-remains-after-election-violence-senior-canadian-soldier-in-congo-says/.

Lippmann, Walter (1922). *Public Opinion.* New York: Macmillan.

Livingston, Steven (1996). "Suffering in Silence: Media Coverage of War and Famine in the Sudan." In R. Rotberg and T. Weiss (eds.), *The Media, Public Policy and Humanitarian Crises.* Washington, DC: Brookings Institution, 68–88.

——— (1997). *Clarifying the CNN Effect: An Examination of Media Effects According to Type of Military Intervention.* Research Paper R-18. Cambridge, MA: Joan Shorenstein Center, John F. Kennedy School of Government, Harvard University.

Livingston, Steven and Todd Eachus (1995). "Humanitarian Crises and U.S. Foreign Policy: Somalia and the CNN Effect Reconsidered." *Political Communication* 12 (4): 413–29.

——— (1999). "Rwanda: U.S. Policy and Television Coverage." In H. Adelman and A. Suhrke (eds.), *The Path of a Genocide: The Rwanda Crisis from Uganda to Zaire.* New Brunswick, NJ: Transaction Publishers, 209–28.

Livingston, Steven and Gregory Asmalov (2010). "Networks and the Future of Foreign Affairs Reporting." *Journalism Studies* 11 (5): 745–60.

MacArthur, Julie (2008) "A Responsibility to Rethink?" *International Journal* 30 (4): 422–43.

MacFarquhar, Neil (2008, Nov. 4). "Congo: U.N. Secretary General Ready to Broker Cease-Fire." *New York Times*: A13.

MacKenzie, Lewis. (1993). *Peacekeeper: The Road to Sarajevo.* Vancouver: Douglas and McIntyre.

Mahoney, Richard (1983). *JFK: Ordeal in Africa.* New York: Oxford University Press.

Mansson, Katrina (2005). "Use of Force and Civilian Protection: Peace Operations in the Congo." *International Peacekeeping* 12 (4): 503–19.

References

Marlow, Iain and El Akkad (2010, Dec. 7). "Momentum Building to Tackle Coltan Mining." *Globe and Mail:* B3.

——— (2010, Dec. 8). "Industry Begins to Move of 'Blood Minerals.'" *Globe and Mail:* B10.

Martin, Guy (2000). "France's African Policy in Transition: Disengagement and Redeployment." Paper delivered at the African Studies Intersdsiciplinary Seminar, Center for African Studies, University of Illinois at Urbana-Champaign. Retrieved Apr. 11, 2010, from http://www.afrst.illinois.edu/events/archive/objects/pdfs/sem-martin-2000-pdf.

Massey, Simon (1998, Feb. 15). "Operation Assurance: The Greatest Intervention That Never Happened." *The Journal of Humanitarian Assistance.* Retrieved April 11, 2010, from http://sites.tufts.edu/jha/archives/123.

Mayall, James (2005). "The Legacy of Colonialism." In S. Chesterman, M. Ignatieff, and R. Thakur (eds.), *Making States Work: State Failure and the Crisis of Governance.* New York: United Nations University, 36–58.

Mazrui, Ali (1995). "The African State as a Political Refugee." In D. Smock and C. Crocker (eds.), *African Conflict Resolution: The U.S. Role in Peacemaking.* Washington, DC: United States Institute of Peace Press, 9–25.

——— (1997). "Crisis in Somalia: From Tyranny to Anarchy." In H. Adam and R. Ford (eds.), *Mending Rips in the Sky: Options for Somali Communities in the 21st Century.* Laurenceville, NJ: Red Sea Press Inc., 5–11.

——— (1998). "The Failed State and Political Collapse in Africa." In O. Otunnu and M. Doyle (eds.), *Peacemaking and Peacekeeping for the New Century.* Lanham, MD: Rowman and Littlefield.

Mbuga, Martin (1997, May 23). "Disastrous Benchmarks." *New York Times:* A30. (letter)

McCombs, Maxwell and Amy Reynolds (2002). "News Influence on Our Pictures of the World." In J. Bryant and D. Zilman (eds.), *Media Effects: Advances in Theory and Research.* 2nd ed. Mahwah, NJ: Lawrence Erlbaum Associates, 1–18.

McCombs, Maxwell and Donald Shaw (1972). "The Agenda-Setting Function of Mass Media." *Public Opinion Quarterly* 36 (3): 176–87.

——— (1993). "The Evolution of Agenda-Setting Research: Twenty-Five Years in the Marketplace of Ideas." *Journal of Communication* 43 (2): 58–67.

McCombs, Maxwell, Donald Shaw, and David Weaver (1997). *Communication and Democracy: Exploring the Intellectual Frontiers in Agenda-Setting Theory.* Mahwah, NJ: Lawrence Erlbaum Associates.

McFadden, Robert (2004, Feb. 17). "Journalists Who Braved Iraq and African Wars Are Among 14 Polk Award Winners." *New York Times:* B7.

References

McKinley, James (1997, May 18). "Zairian Rebel and His Plan Puzzle West." *New York Times*: A1.

——— (1997, May 22). "Congo's Neighbors Played Crucial Role in Civil War." *New York Times*: A1.

——— (1997, May 30). "Taking Office, Congo's Ruler Promises Vote." *New York Times*: A1.

——— (1997, Oct. 13). "Fighting Outlasts Defeat of Mobutu." *New York Times*: A1.

McLuhan, H. Marshall (1964). *Understanding Media: The Extension of Man*. Toronto: McGraw-Hill.

McNeil, Donald (1997, May 27). "Reports Point to Mass Killing of Refugees in Congo." *New York Times*: A1.

——— (1997, June 1). "The World: In Congo Forbidding Terrain Hides a Calamity." *New York Times*: IV4.

——— (1998, Dec. 6). "The World: A War Turned Free-for-All Tears at Africa's Center." *New York Times*: IV5.

——— (1999, June 30). "Congo Cease-Fire Talks: Little Incentive to Proceed." *New York Times*: A3.

——— (1999, July 11). "Congo Rivals Sign Cease-Fire without 2 Rebel Groups." *New York Times*: A9.

——— (1999, July 12). "Not Quite a Triumph in Congo." *New York Times*: A9.

McVeigh, Tracy (2011, Oct. 29). "Congo's Militias Mobilizing Again, Leading Peace Activist Warns." Retrieved Nov. 24, 2011, from http://www.guardian.co.uk/world/2011/oct/29/congo-militias-mobilizing-again/print.

Mermin, Jonathan (1997). "Television News and American Intervention in Somalia: The Myth of a Media-Driven Foreign Policy." *Political Science Quarterly* 112 (3): 385–403.

Minear, Larry, Colin Scott, and Thomas Weiss (1996). *The News Media, Civil War, and Humanitarian Action*. Boulder, CO: Lynne Rienner.

Misra, Amalendu (2008). *Politics of Civil Wars: Conflict, Intervention and Resolution*. London and New York: Routledge.

Mobekk, Eirin (2009). "Security Sector Reform and the UN Mission to the Democratic Republic of Congo: Protecting Civilians in the East." *International Peacekeeping*, 16 (2): 273–86.

Moeller, Susan (1999). *Compassion Fatigue: How the Media Sell Disease, Famine, War and Death*. New York: Routledge.

MONUC (2010, July 1). "Helping Bring Peace and Stability in the DRC." Retrieved Dec. 20, 2010, from http://www.un.org/en/peacekeeping/missions/monuc/.

Mutua, Makau (2002, Aug. 2). "Struggling to End Africa's World War." *New York Times*: A21.

References

Natsiois, Andrew (1996a). "Illusions of Influence: The CNN Effect in Complex Emergencies." In R. Rotberg and T. Weiss (eds.), *From Massacres to Genocide: The Media, Public Policy and Humanitarian Crises*. Washington, DC: Brookings Institution, 149–68.

——— (1996b). "Commanders' Guidance: A Challenge of Complex Humanitarian Emergencies." *Parameters* (Summer): 50–66. Retrieved Mar. 9, 2011, from http://www.carlisle..army.mil.USAWC/PARAMETERS/articles/96summer/natsios.

NBC (2000, June 11). *Nightly News*.

——— (2002, Jan 25). *Nightly News*.

——— (2008, Feb. 13). *Nightly News*.

——— (2008, Feb. 14). *Nightly News*.

Neack, Laura (1995). "UN Peace-Keeping: In the Interest of Community or Self?" *Journal of Peace Research* 32 (2): 181–96.

NYT (1997, June 12). "Congo under Laurent Kabila." *New York Times*: A28. (editorial)

——— (1997, June 26). "Decisive Days for Congo." *New York Times*: A26. (editorial)

——— (1997, Sept. 2). "Stonewall in Congo." *New York Times*: A20. (editorial)

——— (1997, Dec. 17). "Ms. Albright's Awkward African Tour." *New York Times*: A30. (editorial)

——— (1998, May 4). "New Congo, Old Politics" *New York Times*: A18. (editorial)

——— (1998, Aug. 5). "Reversal of Future in Congo." *New York Times*: A22. (editorial)

——— (1998, Aug. 26). "Africa's Widening War." *New York Times*: A20. (editorial)

——— (1999, Aug. 3). "An Elusive Peace in Congo." *New York Times*: A14. (editorial)

——— (2000, Jan. 31). "A Peace Strategy for Congo." *New York Times*: A24. (editorial)

——— (2000, Feb. 29). "Risks and Realities in Congo." *New York Times*: A20. (editorial)

——— (2001, Jan. 18). "Turmoil in Congo." *New York Times*: A22. (editorial)

——— (2001, Jan. 26). "The Conflict in Congo." *New York Times*: A18. (editorial)

——— (2001, Feb. 2). "General Powell Engages Africa." *New York Times*: A18. (editorial)

——— (2001, Mar. 5). "Glimmerings of a Congo Peace." *New York Times*: A16. (editorial)

References

——— (2001, May 29). "The Looting of Congo." *New York Times*: A14. (editorial)

——— (2002, Aug. 1). "Bringing Congo's Great War to an End." *New York Times*: A24. (editorial)

——— (2003, May 31). "Stopping the Genocide in Congo." *New York Times*: A14. (editorial)

——— (2003, June 25). "Doing It Right in Congo." *New York Times*: A24. (editorial)

——— (2005, Oct. 24). "The Worse U.N. Scandal." *New York Times*: A20. (editorial)

——— (2006, Oct. 12). "Armies of Children." *New York Times*: A28. (editorial)

——— (2007, June 12). "Still Dying in Congo." *New York Times*: A22. (editorial)

——— (2008, Nov. 13). "Rwanda's Shadow." *New York Times*: A36. (editorial)

——— (2008, Nov. 18). "France Moves to Add Troops." *New York Times*: A11.

——— (2008, Dec. 16). "A Policy for Preventing Genocide." *New York Times*: A36. (editorial)

——— (2011, Nov. 22). Times Topics: "Congo." *New York Times*. Retrieved Nov. 24, 2011, from http://topics.nytimes.com/top/news/international/.../index/html.

Nzongola-Ntalaja, Georges (2002a). *The Congo from Leopold to Kabila: A People's History*. London and New York: Zed Books.

——— (2002b). "Civil War, Peacekeeping and the Great Lakes Region." In R. Laremont (ed.), *The Causes of War and Consequences of Peacekeeping in Africa*. Portsmouth, NH: Heinemann, 91–115.

O'Brien, Connor Cruise (1962). *To Katanga and Back: A U.N. Case History*. New York: Simon and Schuster.

O'Neill, John Terrence and Nicholas Rees (2005). *United Nations Peacekeeping in the Post-Cold War Era*. London: Routledge.

Onishi, Norimitsu (1998, Aug. 24). "Congo Recaptures a Strategic Base." *New York Times*: A1.

——— (1999, July 9). "The Guns of Africa." *New York Times*: A8.

——— (2000, May 5). "A Shadow on Africa." *New York Times*: A1.

——— (2001, Jan. 17). "Congo Leader Reportedly Dead after Being Shot by Bodyguard." *New York Times*: A1.

——— (2001, Apr. 15). "Who Runs Congo? The People, New Leader Says." *New York Times*: I3.

Onishi, Norimitsu and Ian Fisher (2001, Jan. 21). "Doubts on Whether Kabila's Son Can Lead Congo." *New York Times*: I8.

References

Onyango-Obbo, Charles (2003, July 12). "Poor in Money, but Even Poorer in Democracy." *New York Times*: A11.

Opala, Joseph (2000, Apr. 24). "Clinton's Africa Policy: A Thousand Triumphs, a Million Dead." *World History Archives: U.S. Foreign Policy: Africa as a Whole*." Retrieved Apr. 8, 2010, from http://www.hartford-hwp.com/archives/45/index-sae.html.

Oxfam (2007 February). *A Fragile Future: Why Scaling Down MONUC Too Soon Could Spell Disaster for the Congo*. Oxfam Briefing Paper No. 97.

Parks, Michael (2002). "Beyond Afghanistan: Foreign News: What's Next?" *Columbia Journalism Review* 40 (5): 53–57.

(PBS) Public Broadcasting System (2007, Nov. 20). "On Our Watch." *Frontline*. Retrieved June 19, 2008, from http://www.pbs.org/wghh/pages/frontline/darfur/etc/script.html.

Perry, Alex (2009, Feb. 9). "Congo Needs Protection." *Time*: 34–37.

Perse, Elizabeth (2001). *Media Effects and Society*. Mahwah, NJ: Lawrence Erlbaum Associates.

Pew Project for Excellence in Journalism (2010). "The State of the News Media 2010." Retrieved Dec. 13, 2010, from http://www.stateofthemedia.org/2010/.

Pflanz, Mike (2011, Dec. 11). "Democratic Republic of Congo Elections 'Lack Credibility.'" *Telegraph*. Retrieved Feb. 24, 2012, from http://www.telegraph.co.uk/news/worldnews/Democratic-of-Congo-elections-lack-credibility.htm.

Polgreen, Lydia (2006, June 23). "In Congo, Hunger and Disease Erode Democracy." *New York Times*: A1.

——— (2006, July 1). "Congo Nears Historic Election, Praying for Peace." *New York Times*: A1.

——— (2006, July 23). "Rwanda's Shadow, from Darfur to Congo." *New York Times*: IV3.

——— (2007, Dec. 13). "After Clashes, Fear of War on Congo's Edge." *New York Times*: A1.

——— (2007, Dec. 16). "Frustration with Charities and U.N. in Congo." *New York Times*: I35.

——— (2007, Dec. 19). "Resolving Crisis in Congo Hinges of Foreign Troops." *New York Times*: A14.

——— (2008, Jan. 10). "Fighting in Congo Rekindles Ethnic Hatreds." *New York Times*: A1.

——— (2008, Jan. 22). "Congo Agrees to Peace Deal with Rebels." *New York Times*: A3.

——— (2008, Jan. 23). "Congo Death Rate Unchanged since War Ended." *New York Times*: A8.

——— (2008, Apr. 3). "Congo: Investigators Check Allegations That Peacekeepers Engaged in Torture." *New York Times*: A10.

References

——— (2008, Dec. 11). "A Massacre Unfurls in Congo, Despite Nearby Support." *New York Times*: A11.

——— (2008, Dec. 13). "Report to U.N. Shows Evidence of Proxy War in Militias Ties to Rwanda and Congo." *New York Times*: A5.

——— (2008, Dec. 20). "Congo Warlord, Linked to Abuses, Seeks Bigger Stage." *New York Times*: A1.

——— (2009, Jan. 12). "Rebel Force in Congo Shows Signs of Division." *New York Times*: A5.

Pottier, Johan (2002). *Re-Imagining Rwanda: Conflict, Survival and Disinformation in the Late Twentieth Century*. Cambridge, UK: Cambridge University Press.

Power, Samantha (2003). *"A Problem from Hell": America and the Age of Genocide*. New York: Perennial.

Prendergast, John (2010, Feb. 26). "A Light at the End of the Tunnel in Congo." *Foreign Policy*. Retrieved Apr. 3, 2010, from http://www.foreignpolicy.com/articles/2010/02/26/a_light_at_the_end_of_the_tunnel_in_congo.

Prunier, Gérard (2009). *Africa's World War: Congo, the Rwandan Genocide, and Making of a Continental Catastrophe*. New York: Oxford University Press.

Quist-Adade, Charles (2001). *In the Shadows of the Kremlin and the White House: Africa's Media Image from Communism to Post-Communism*. Lanham, MD: University Press of America.

Ramsbotham, Oliver, Tom Woodhouse, and Hugh Miall (2009). *Contemporary Conflict Resolution*. 2nd ed. Cambridge: Polity Press.

Reich, Ken (2006, June 2). "Third World Newspaper Coverage Remains Spotty." *Take Back the Times*. Retrieved Nov. 26, 2008, from http://takebackthetimes.blogspot.com/2006/06/third-world-newspaper-coverage-remains.html.

reliefweb (2011, June 28). "Democratic Republic of the Congo." Retrieved Aug. 29, 2011, from http://refliefweb.int/node/422791.

Reuters (2002, Dec. 5). "U.N. Approves More Congo Peacekeepers." *New York Times*: A21.

——— (2003, Jan. 25). "U.N. Extends Inquiry into Looting of Congo." *New York Times*: A5.

——— (2003, Apr. 10). "African Leaders Hold Rwanda and Uganda to Peace Agreement." *New York Times*: A7.

——— (2003, Oct. 7). "Congo: New Massacre Reported." *New York Times*: A9.

——— (2003, Oct. 11). "Congo: U.N. Finds New Massacre." *New York Times*: A8.

——— (2004, Jan. 24). "Congo: Boat Massacres Reported." *New York Times*: A6.

References

———— (2004, Feb. 5). "Convoy Attacked in Congo." *New York Times*: A4.
———— (2004, May 11). "Congo: Inquiry into Reports of Sex Abuse by U.N. Staff." *New York Times*: A6.
———— (2004, Nov. 11). "U.N. Peacekeepers in Joint Patrols in Congo." *New York Times*: A9.
———— (2005, Mar. 17). "Congo: Worst Crisis Now." *New York Times*: A6.
———— (2005, June 1). "U.N. Council Condemns Sex Abuse by Its Troops." *New York Times*: A9.
———— (2006, Feb. 13). "U.N. Pleads for Aid to Save Lives in Congo." *New York Times*: A3.
———— (2006, July 5). "Congo Rebels Take Eastern Town in Setback to U.N." *New York Times*: A4.
———— (2006, Nov. 25). "U.N. Investigators Find Mass Grave in Army Camp in East Congo." *New York Times*: A5.
———— (2007, Jan. 13). "Congo: Soldiers Riot and Loot Over Pay." *New York Times*: A4.
———— (2007, Nov. 12). "Congo and Rwanda Agree to Align Against Rebels." *New York Times*: A9.
———— (2007, Dec. 25). "Youths Again Forced to fight in Congo, Aid Group Says." *New York Times*: A4.
———— (2008, Oct. 15). "Congo: Rebels Clash with Army." *New York Times*: A14.
———— (2008, Nov. 2). "Europe Weighs Sending Congo Troops." *New York Times*: I14.
———— (2008, Dec. 27). "Fleeing Rebels Kill 15." *New York Times*: A8.
———— (2008, Dec. 6). "Congo Peace Talks Planned." *New York Times*: A8.
———— (2008, Dec. 17). "Rwanda: Support for Rebels Denied." *New York Times*: A8.
———— (2008, Dec. 27). "Congo: Fleeing Rebels Kill 15: *New York Times*. A8.
———— (2010, Apr. 4). "Nkunda Case Set for Rwanda Military Court Hearing." *Saturday Nation* (Kenya). Retrieved Jan. 26, 2011, from http://www.nation.co.ke/News/africa/-/1006/892654/-/121cskgz/index.html.
Reyntjens, Filip (2000). *Burundi: Prospects for Peace*. London: Minority Rights Group International.
———— (2004). "Rwanda, Ten Years on: From Genocide to Dictatorship." *African Affairs* 103 (411): 177–210.
———— (2009). *The Great African War: Congo and Regional Geopolitics, 1996–2006*. New York: Cambridge University Press.
Rieff, David (2002). "Humanitarianism in Crisis." *Foreign Affairs* 81 (2): 111–27.
———— (2003). *A Bed for the Night: Humanitarianism in Crisis*. New York: Simon and Schuster.

References

Riffe, Daniel, Chalres Aust, Ted Jones, Barbara Shoemake, and Shyam Sundar (1994). "The Shrinking Foreign Newshole for The New York Times." *Newspaper Research Journal* 15 (3): 74-88.

Robinson, Geoffrey (2003). "If You Leave Us Here, We Will Die." In N. Mills and K. Brunner (eds.), *The New Killing Fields: Massacre and the Politics of Intervention*. New York: Basic Books: 159-83.

Robinson, Piers (2000). "The Policy-Media Interaction Model: Measuring Media Power during Humanitarian Crisis." *Journal of Peace Research* 37 (5): 613-33.

––––––– (2002). *The CNN Effect: The Myth of News, Foreign Policy and Intervention*. New York: Routledge.

Roessler, Philip and John Prendergast (2006). "Democratic Republic of the Congo." In W. Durch (ed.), *Twenty-First Century Peace Operations*. Washington, DC: United States Institute of Peace, 229-318.

Rogers, Everett and James Dearing (1988). "Agenda-Setting Research: Where Has It Been, Where Is It Going?" In J. Anderson (ed.), *Communication Yearbook* 11. Newbury Park, CA, 555-94.

Rotberg, Robert (2002). "The New Nature of State Failure." *Washington Quarterly* 25 (3): 85-96.

Russo, Diana (2010). "Is the Foreign News Bureau Part of the Past." *Global Journalist*. Retrieved Dec. 3, 2010, from http://www.globaljournalist.org/stories/2010/01/30/is-the-foreign-new-bureau-of-the-past/.

Sachs, Jeffrey and Robert Rotberg (1997, May 29). "Help Congo Now." *New York Times*: A21.

Sahnoun, Mohamed (1994). *Somalia: The Missed Opportunities*. Washington, DC: United States Institute of Peace.

Salamon, Julie (2001, Sept. 6). "Critic's Notebook: Telling the Story of Congo's War, amid the Chaos." *New York Times*: E1.

Salwen, Michael (1988). "Effects of Accumulation of Coverage on Issue Salience in Agenda-Setting." *Journalism Quarterly* 65 (2): 100-6, 130.

Schabas, William (2006). *Preventing Genocide and Mass Killing: The Challenge for the United Nations*. London: Minority Rights Group International.

Scheufele, Dietram (1999). "Framing as a Theory of Media Effects." *Journal of Communication* 49 (1): 103-22.

Schidlovsky, John (2010). "It's Not Like It Used to Be." *Nieman Reports*, 64 (3): 47-49.

Schneider, Daniel (2008, Aug. 13). "United Nations Inquiry Finds Evidence of Abuse." *New York Times*: A8.

Sengupta, Somini (2003, May 27). "Congo War Toll Soars as U.N. Pleads for Aid." *New York Times*: A1.

––––––– (2003, June 1). "Into Africa: Pricking the West's Conscience." *New York Times*: IV1.

References

——— (2003, June 4). "Terror Persists as Congolese Await U.N. Force." *New York Times*: A3.

——— (2003, June 7). "French Soldiers Arrive in Congo with a Tough Mission." *New York Times*: A3.

——— (2003, June 11). "Won't Disarm Congo Armies, U.N. Force Declares." *New York Times*: A3.

——— (2004, Feb. 14). "Killing of a UN Observer in Congo Heightens a Mission's Fears." *New York Times*: A7.

——— (2004, Mar. 29). "Attack in Congo Mars Peace Transition." *New York Times*: A4.

——— (2004, Apr. 11). "Warring Militias in Congo Test U.N. Enforcement Role." *New York Times*: A10.

——— (2004, June 7). "2 U.N. Peacekeepers Killed in Eastern Congo." *New York Times*: A3.

Sengupta, Somini, with Marc Lacey (2003, July 6). "Poor and War-Weary, Africa Turns Eyes to Bush for Help." *New York Times*: I1.

Sezibera, Richard (2002, Aug. 9). "An African Accord." *New York Times*: A14. (letter)

Sheridan, Mary Beth (2010, May 13). "Sudan Accord in Peril, U.S. Says." *Washington Post*: A8.

——— (2010, Dec, 30). "U.S. More Hopeful Sudan Will Hold Vote." *Washington Post*: A6.

Sidahmed, Abdel Salam, Walter Soderlund, and E. Donald Briggs (2010). *The Responsibility to Protect in Darfur: The Role of Mass Media*. Lanham, MD: Lexington Books.

Simons, Marlise (2006, Mar. 19). "Congo Warlord Handed to International Court." *New York Times*: I10.

Slackman, Michael (2006, Apr. 24). "Bin Laden Says West Is Waging War against Islam." *New York Times*: A8.

Smith, David (2011, Nov. 29). "Democratic Republic of Congo Voting Extended into Second Day." *Guardian*. Retrieved Nov. 29, 2011, from http://www.guardian.co.uk/world/2011/nov/29/democratic-republic-congo-voting-extended?newsfeed=true.

Smith, David (2011, Dec. 9). "Congo Election Sparks Violent Protests." *Guardian*. Retrieved Feb. 24, 2012, from http://www.guardian.co.uk/world/2011/dec10/congo-election-result-violent-protests.

Snow, Keith and David Barouski (2006, Mar. 1). "Behind the Numbers: Untold Suffering in the Congo." *Third World Traveler*. Retrieved Nov. 3, 2008, from http://www.thirdworldtraveler.com/Africa/Congo_BehindNumbers.html.

Soderlund, Walter (2001). *Media Definitions of Cold War Reality: The Caribbean Basin, 1953–1992*. Toronto, ON: Canadian Scholars' Press.

References

——— (2006). "U.S. Television News Framing of Haitian President, Jean-Bertrand Aristide, February 2004." *Journal of Haitian Studies* 12: 78–111.

Soderlund, Walter, E. Donald Briggs, Kai Hildebrandt, and Abdel Salam Sidahmed (2008). *Humanitarian Crisis and Intervention: Reassessing the Impact of Mass Media*. Sterling, VA: Kumarian Press.

Soderlund, Walter, Colette Brin, Lydia Miljan, and Kai Hildebrandt (2012). *Cross-Media Ownership and Democratic Practice in Canada: Content-Sharing and the Impact of New Media*. Edmonton, AB: University of Alberta Press.

Sozinho, Sozi (1998, May 6). "Human Rights in Congo." *New York Times*: A22. (letter)

Spooner, Kevin (2009). *Canada, the Congo Crisis, and UN Peacekeeping, 1960–64*. Vancouver: UBC Press.

Stearns, Jason (2011). *Dancing in the Glory of Monsters: The Collapse of the Congo and the Great War of Africa*. New York: Public Affairs.

——— (2011, Nov. 8). "Congolese Candidate Tshisekedi Declares Himself President." *Christian Science Monitor*. Retrieved Nov. 11, 2011, from http://www.csmonitor.com/World/Africa/Africa-Monitor/2011/11/08/Congolese-candidate-Tshisekedi-declares-himself-president.

Stewart, Ian (2002). *Ambushed: A War Reporter's Life on the Line*. Chapel Hill, NC: Algonquin Books of Chapel Hill.

Stroehlein, Andrew (2005, June 14). "In Congo, 1,000 Die per Day: Why Isn't It Media Story?" CSMonitor.com. Retrieved Nov. 25, 2008, from http://www.csmonitor.com/2005/0614/p09s02-coop.html.

Sutcliffe, John, Walter Soderlund, Kai Hildebrandt, and Martha Lee (2009). "The Reporting of International News in Canada: Continuity and Change." *American Review of Canadian Studies* 39 (2): 1–16.

Swarns, Rachel (2001, Dec. 23). "Imagine: The Struggle to be Heard." *New York Times*: IV4.

Swarns, Rachel (2002, Dec. 18). "Congo and Its Rebels Sign Accord to End War." *New York Times*: A12.

Swing, William (2006, Aug. 4). "U.N. Forces in Congo." *New York Times*: A16. (letter)

Szalai, Georg (2009, Jan. 7). "Layoffs in U.S. up 59% from 2007." *Hollywood Reporter*. Retrieved Sept. 8, 2010, from http://www.hollywoodreporter.com/hr/content_display/finance/news/e3i4ac0111edbf301ob3a00ea53fd0aeda.

Thakur, Ramesh (2010). "Intervention or Protection: Semantics in This Case Could Make a World of Difference." *Literary Review of Canada* 18 (10): 11–12.

References

Thompson, Allan (2007a). "Introduction." In A. Thompson (ed.), *The Media and the Rwanda Genocide*. Ottawa, ON: International Development Research Centre, 1–11.

——— (2007b). "The Responsibility to Report: a New Journalistic Paradigm." In A. Thompson (ed.), *The Media and the Rwanda Genocide*. Ottawa, ON: International Development Research Centre, 433–45.

——— (2008, June 2). "Canada Spurns UN Plea on Congo." Thestar.com. Retrieved Sept. 14, 2010, from http://www.thestar.com/article/435224--canada-spurns-un-plea-on-congo.

Traub, James (2005, July 3). "The Congo Case." *New York Times Magazine*: VI35–39.

Tull, Denis (2009). "Peacekeeping in the Democratic Republic of Congo: Waging Peace and Fighting War." *International Peacekeeping* 16 (2): 215–30.

Turner, Thomas (2007). *The Congo Wars: Conflict, Myth and Reality*. New York: Zed Books.

UN (n.d.). "Background Note: United Nations Peacekeeping." Retrieved Feb. 19, 2011, from http://www.un.org/en/peacekeeping/documents/backgroundnote.pdf.

——— (1960, July 14). Security Council Resolution S/4387 [renumbered 143].

——— (1960, July 22). Security Council Resolution S/4405 [renumbered 145].

——— (1960, Aug. 9). Security Council Resolution S/4426 [renumbered 146].

——— (1966, Nov. 15). Security Council S/1080.

——— (1998, Aug. 31). (S/PRST/1998/26). "Statement by the President of the Security Council."

——— (1998, Dec. 11). (S/PRST/1998/36). "Statement by the President of the Security Council."

——— (1999, Apr. 9). Security Council Resolution 1234.

——— (1999, July 15). (S/1999/790). "Report of the Secretary-General on the United Nations Preliminary Deployment in the Democratic Rebublic of the Congo."

——— (1999, Aug. 6). Security Council Resolution 1258.

——— (1999, Nov. 5). Security Council Resolution 1273.

——— (1999, Nov. 30). Security Council Resolution 1279.

——— (2000, Feb. 24). Security Council Resolution 1291.

——— (2001, Apr. 17). Seventh Report of the Secretary-General on the United Nations Organization Mission in the Democratic Republic of the Congo.

References

——— (2007, Jan. 4). United Nations Integrated Mission in Timor-Leste. Retrieved Jan. 6, 2007, from http://www.unmiset.org/unmisetwebsite.nsf/6e7440fbabe0154a49256fle002b424/05ccda24553e2c5d4.

——— (2010). *International Human Development Indicators, 2010.* Retrieved Nov. 16, 2010, from http://hdr.undp.org/en/statistics/.

——— (2010, Oct. 8). (S/2010/512), "Report of the Secretary-General on the United Nations Organization Stabilization Mission in the Democratic Republic of the Congo."

Urquhart, Brian (2003, Aug. 7). "A Force behind the U.N." *New York Times*: A23.

Utley, Garrick (1997). "The Shrinking of Foreign News: From Broadcast to Narrowcast." *Foreign Affairs* 76 (2): 2–10.

Vallely, Paul (2009, Jan. 17). "From A-Lister to Aid Worker: Does Celebrity Diplomacy Really Work?" *The Independent*. Retrieved Apr. 5, 2010, from http://www.independent.co.uk/news/people/profiles/from-alister-to-aid-worker-does-celebrity-diplomacy-really-work-1365964.html.

van Nieuwkerk, Anthoni (2001). "Subregional Collaborative Security: Lessons from the OAU and SADC." *South African Journal of International Affairs* 8 (2): 81–94.

Vigon, Larry (2004, Dec. 24). "Cloud Over Peacekeeping." *New York Times*: A18. (letter)

Von Einsiedel, Sebastian (2005). "Policy Responses to State Failure." In S. Chesterman, M. Ignatieff, and R. Thakur (eds.), *Making States Work: State Failure and the Crisis of Governance*. New York: United Nations University Press, 13–35.

Weaver, David (2007). "Thoughts on Agenda Setting, Framing, and Priming." *Journal of Communication* 57 (1): 142–47.

Weiner, Tim (2000, May 20). "Solitary Republican Senator Blocks Peacekeeping Funds." *New York Times*: A1.

Weiss, Herbert (1967). *Political Protest in the Congo: The Parti Solidarie Africain during the Independence Struggle*. Princeton: NJ: Princeton University Press.

——— (1995). "Zaire: Collapsed Society, Surviving State, Future Polity." In I.W. Zartman (ed.), *Collapsed States: The Disintegration of Legitimate Authority*. Boulder, CO: Lynne Rienner: 157–70.

Weiss, Herbert and Tatiana Carayannis (2005). "The Enduring Idea of the Congo." In R. Larémont (ed.), *Borders, Nationalism, and the African State*. Boulder, CO: Lynne Rienner, 135–77.

Werner, Jake (2002, July 18). "Congo's Longtime Plight." *New York Times*: A20. (letter)

References

West, Michael (2001, Jan. 23). "A Chance for Congo." *New York Times*: A20.

Wheeler, Nicholas (2002). *Saving Souls: Humanitarian Intervention in International Society*. Oxford: Oxford University Press.

Wheeler, Mark (2011). "Celebrity Diplomacy: United Nations' Goodwill Ambassadors and Messengers of Peace." *Celebrity Studies* 2 (1): 6-18.

Willame, Jean-Claude (1972). *Patrimonialism and Political Change in the Congo*. Stanford, CA: Stanford University Press.

Williams, Paul (2007). "Thinking about Security in Africa." *International Affairs* 83: 1021-38.

Willis, Andrew (2011, Sept. 19). "World Watches Nervously as Congo's November Poll Nears." *Irish Times*. Retrieved Sept. 21, 2011, from http://www.irishtimes.com/newspaper/world/2011/0919/12224304356188.html.

Windsor Star (2010, Aug. 27). "Mass Rapes Prompt UN Review." *Windsor Star*: C2.

——— (2010, Dec. 6). "Congo's Plight: A Tragedy without End." *Windsor Star*: A6.

——— (2011, Nov. 21). "Congo's Election: Will Ballots End the Misery? *Windsor Star*: A6.

Wines, Michael (2004, Dec. 3). "U.N. Reports a Possible Push into Congo by Rwandans." *New York Times*: A6.

Wolfsfeld, Gadi (1997). *Media and Political Conflict: News from the Middle East*. Cambridge, UK: Cambridge University Press.

——— (2004). *Media and the Path to Peace*. Cambridge, UK: Cambridge University Press.

Wrong, Michela (2000). *In the Footsteps of Mr Kurtz: Living on the Brink of Disaster in the Congo*. London: Fourth Estate.

——— (2001, Jan. 29). "The Congo That Never Was." *New York Times*: A23.

——— (2001, Nov. 11). "Che in Africa." *New York Times*: VII24.

Wu, Haoming (1998). "Investigating the Determinants of International News Flow: A Meta-Analysis." *Gazette* 60 (3): 493-512.

York, Geoffrey (2010, Mar. 27). "The War That Won't End." *Globe and Mail*: F1.

——— (2010, Dec. 3). "Congo Army Awash in Criminality: UN." *Globe and Mail*: A18.

——— (2010, Dec. 21). "Canada Silent as UN Mobilizes against Feared Massacre." *Globe and Mail*: A19.

——— (2011, Oct. 26). "Congo Election Unraveling into Conflict." *Globe and Mail*: A19.

Young, Crawford (1965). *Politics in the Congo*. Princeton, NJ: Princeton University Press.

References

——— (2006). "The Heart of the African Conflict Zone: Democratization, Ethnicity, Civil Conflict, and the Great Lakes Crisis." *Annual Review of Political Science* 9: 301–28. Retrieved Dec. 14, 2010, from http://www.annualreviews.org.

Zartman, I. William (1995). *Collapsed States: The Disintegration and Restoration of Legitimate Authority.* Boulder, CO: Lynne Rienner.

Blogs

Beckett, Charles. http://www.charliebeckett.org/
Crilly, Rob. http://frontlineclub.com/blogs/robcrilly/
Jones, Ingrid. http://meandophelia.blogspot.com/
Moore, Jim. http://blogs.law.harvard.edu.jim/
Zuckerman, Ethan. http://www.ethanzuckerman.com/blog

Index

ABC News, 59, 60, 62, 87, 135, 138, 186n12, 187n18
Abyei, 146, 191n1
advocacy. See under mass media
advocacy framing, 192n5
Advocacy Lab, 107
Afghanistan, 62, 138, 190n9, 191n11
Africa: Islam and, 133–34; lack of knowledge about, 134–35
African Union (AU), 183n4
Africa's World War, 10, 13–16. See also Second Congo War
Agence France-Presse, 100
agenda setting, xvii, 41–44, 121, 162, 192n5. See also alerting function
aggressor-victim frame, 59
al-Bashir, Omar, 146
Albright, Madeleine, 71, 119
alerting function: of mass media, xviii, 41–43, 44, 49–52, 121, 159–60, 189n1, 193n1, 193n2; of television news, 52, 63, 123. See also agenda setting
Alliance des forces démocratiques pour la libération du Congo-Zaïre (AFDL), 13
Amnesty International, 161
anchor-read stories, 189n1
Andrews, Edwin, 110
Angola, 3, 9, 13, 14, 70, 73, 74, 116, 182n14, 188n3
Annan, Kofi, 32, 72, 77, 81, 94, 97, 137
Anstey, Roger, 3, 5

Apter, Andrew, 67
Arab world, 133–34
Arusha Agreement, 145
Asian tsunami, 138
Asmalov, Gregory, 191n12
Associated Press, 104
atrocities, 35–36. See also rampages; rape; sexual violence
attribute framing, 50
Australia, 152
Autesserre, Séverine, 11, 17, 35–38, 191–92n3, 192n7
Axworthy, Lloyd, 28
Azar, Edward, 10–11, 12, 17, 143

Babcock, Glenys, 168
Bandow, Douglas, 69
Banyamulenge, 113
Banyamulenge refugees, 100
Baril, Maurice, 27
Barouski, David, 47–48
Barre, Said, 147, 148
Barringer, Felicity, 97
Bartleman, James, 27
Basanisi, Matthias, 114
"Be a Witness" campaign, 193n4
Belgium, 3, 5–8, 19–22, 68, 147, 148, 180n9
Bell, Peter, 95–96
Bellafante, Ginia, 138
Bemba, Jean-Pierre, 14, 82, 86, 182n13, 189n6
Bennett, Lance, 136

227

Index

Berkeley, Bill, 60
Berlin Conference (1884–85), 4
Berthiaume, Christiane, 98
Berthiaume, J.A., 22
Bilak, Alexandra, 110
bin Arubi, Kikaya, 165
bin Laden, Osama, 134, 190n6
Biroto, Mwenge, 112
Bisimwa, Bertrand, 116
Blair, Dennis, 145, 146
Blue Nile, 146
Bonner, Raymond, 66, 69
Bosnia, 22, 102
Bourque, André, 110
Brennan, Richard, 101, 114
Brodey, Reed, 72
brutal repression frame, 59
Bukavu, 33, 100, 103, 127, 150
Buki, Sylvain, 84
Bunia, 33, 58, 108, 127
Burundi, 44, 78, 100
Bush, George H.W., 135
Bush, George W., 58, 95, 97, 131, 136, 137

Canada: contribution to ONUC, 23; opting out (2011), 190n10; participation in Operation Assurance, 26–27
Canadian Institute for Strategic Studies, 97
CARE, 95
Carson, Lesley, 72
Carter Center, 105, 169
Cato Institute, 69
CBS, 138, 186n12, 187n18
celebrities, 57, 62, 133, 139
Center for Conflict Resolution, 78
Central Organ Mechanism for Conflict Prevention, Management and Resolution, 29
Chalk, Frank, 153, 161
Challenger, Gray and Christmas, 137
Channel 4, 106
Chaon, Anne, 185n9

Cheeseboro, Anthony, 74
child soldiers, 53, 54, 56, 57, 105, 107, 112, 175, 177–78, 184n7, 194n1
Chiluba, Fredrick, 29
China, 146
Chirac, Jacques, 173
Chopra, Jarat, 156
Chrétien, Jean, 26–27
civil society, 161
Clark, Jeffrey, 148
Clark, John F., 46–47
Clinton, Bill, 27, 57, 72, 81, 135–36, 161
Clooney, George, 139
CNN, 186n11
CNN effect, xvii, 42, 45, 130, 159, 162, 184n1
Cohen, Bernard, 42
Cohen, Herman J., 86, 119, 189n10
Cohen, William, 119
Cold War, 8–9, 12, 59, 135
Colombia, 99
coltan, 15, 53, 56, 59, 174, 186–87n13
Conflict Minerals Trade Act, 194n2
conflict resolution, at community level, 37
communal or identity groups, 11
communication problems, 23
communism, 8, 59
compassion fatigue, 60, 69, 131
competing crises, 62
Comprehensive Peace Agreement, 191n2
Cone, Jason, 96
Congo: background, 1–3; under Belgian rule, 5–8; descriptive language about, 174–75; fragmentation fears, 74, 75; lack of knowledge about, 134–35; lack of US interest in, 135–37; under Leopold, 3–5; under Mobutu, 8–9; mortality rate, 17, 113–14; negative images of, 134–35, 190n7; natural resources of, xvi, 1, 3, 15, 34, 75, 88, 92–93, 155, 166, 174, 194n2. *See also* eastern Congo

Index

Congo conflict: assessments of media coverage of, 44–49; celebrities and, 139; compared with Darfur coverage, 128–40, 190n5; complex character/long duration of, 130–32; crises competing with, 138–39; framing, 9–12; lack of media coverage of, 109–10; perceptions of need for intervention in, 132–33; radical Islam and, 133–34; reasons for neglect, 130–39; television coverage of, 51–58, 121–23, 131, 138, 139. *See also* First Congo War; Second Congo War; Third Congo War
Congo Free State, 4, 5
Congolese National Army (FAC), 35, 106–7, 108, 112, 113, 114, 155, 165
Congolese National Commission for Demobilization and Reinsertion (CONADER), 35
Congolese Rally for Democracy, 76, 84, 88, 91
Congo Minerals Act, 194n2
Corcoran, Farrel, 187n15
corporate/national greed frame, 131
corporations, 89, 92–93, 185n6
Council on Foreign Relations, 117
Cowell, Alan, 82
Crossette, Barbara, 72, 79, 86
Curry, Ann, 53–54, 139

Daley, Suzanne, 74
Dallaire, Roméo, 147–48, 153, 161
danger, 62
Darfur, xv, 57, 62, 142, 146, 161, 193n2, 193n4; media coverage of, compared with Congo, 122, 128–40, 190n5
datelines, 125–26, 129, 130, 190–91n11
de Beer, Hannelie, 77, 83
Democratic Forces for the Liberation of Rwanda (FDLR), 167
Democratic Republic of the Congo. *See* Congo
Deng, Frances, 133

descriptive language. *See* language
d'Escury, Jean-François Collot, 102
Des Forges, Alison, 78
Deutsch, Karl, 65
diamonds, 15, 53, 59, 75, 80–81, 99, 171, 174
Díaz de Villegas y Herrería, Vicente, 115
Diemu, Chikez, 112
Dinger, John, 67
diplomatic actions, 163
Disarmament, Demobilization, and Reintegration (DDR), 35
diseases, 17, 105–5
distance framing, 44, 55
Dixon, Barbara, 101
D'Onofrio, Alyoscia, 111
Doss, Alan, 115, 116
drama, 60–61
Dunn, Kevin, 135
Dusaidi, Claude, 28
Dyilo, Thomas Lubanga, 105, 107

eastern Congo, 11, 15, 17, 29, 34, 44, 54, 75, 78, 87, 88, 94, 95, 100, 106, 108, 110, 111, 112, 113, 119, 127, 129, 139, 155, 166, 167, 180n9
East Timor, 152, 156
Ebo, Bosah, 134
Economic Community of West African States (ECOWAS), 98, 150, 189n8
Edgerton, Robert, 2, 179n1, 180n4
editorials, 124, 128
education, 6
Egeland, Jan, 102, 104, 105, 109, 162
elections, 33, 37, 39, 67, 68, 103, 105–6, 140, 167–69, 172, 188n6, 194n4
empathy framing, 44, 45, 54, 55
Entman, Robert, 43
episodic framing, 44
equipment, 23
ethnic cleansing frame, 59
ethnicity, 11
ethnocentrism, 61

Index

European Union, 115
evaluation function, of mass media, xviii, 43–44, 49–50, 54, 123
evaluative descriptors, 57–58. *See also* language
Executive Options, 188n3

failure to report, 160
Fair, Jo Ellen, 44–45
Farrow, Mia, 139
Fawcett, Rick, 169
Fein, Helen, 68
First Congo War, 10, 12–13, 52
Fisher, Ian, 15, 75, 77, 78, 79, 82, 83
force, 163
Force publique, 4, 179n2
Forces armées congolaises, 32
Ford, Glen, 48
foreign bureaus, 138, 191n12
foreign news content, 185n8, 191n13
frames/framing, xvii, xviii, 43–46, 49, 50, 51, 57, 59, 63, 123, 130, 162, 184n2, 189n1, 192n5; advocacy, 192n5; aggressor-victim, 59; attribute, 50; brutal repression, 59; corporate/national greed, 131; distance, 44, 55; empathy, 44, 45, 54, 55; episodic, 44; ethnic cleansing, 59; genocide, 59; good vs. evil, 130; intractable conflict, 58, 59, 60, 130, 135, 162; poor leadership, 131; proxy forces, 131; regional level of analysis, 12, 18; Rwanda, 186n9; Rwandan genocide, 131; thematic, 44, 67, 69, 73, 75, 82; tribal warfare, 92, 131; Western responsibility, 130
France/French peacekeeping, 127, 135, 187n2; descriptive language, 177–78; motives for intervention, 24–25; Third Congo War and, 93–96, 98, 117; waning influence in Africa, 66
French, Howard, 66, 69, 70, 71, 73
front-page stories, 124, 128
Fuller, Kathryn, 80

Gamson, William, 43
genocide, 131, 137; R2P and, 188n2; Third Congo War and, 93–94, 119. *See also* Rwandan genocide
Genocide Convention, 143
genocide frame, 59
Gettleman, Jeffrey, 108, 110, 115, 117, 118, 127, 165, 191n2
Ghagbo, Laurent, 194n4
Gitlin, Todd, 43, 65
Goma, 53, 88, 113, 115, 150, 184n1, 186n10, 186n12
good vs. evil frame, 130
Gormley, William, 122
governments, and media, 160
Graber, Doris, 123
Granatstein, J.L., 150
Gregg, Judd, 81
Grenell, Richard, 94
Gross, Kimberly, 123
Grzyb, Amanda, 131, 193n2, 193n4
Guardino, Matt, 187n18
Guéhenno, Jean-Marie, 104
Guevara, Che, 87, 187n1

Haiti, 138, 156, 187n16
Hamilton, John, 191n12
Hammarskjöld, Dag, 19–22, 183n1
Hara, Fabienne, 92
Harden, Blaine, 81
Harland, David, 103
Harris, Bob, 48
Hartley, Aidan, 106
Hartung, William, 80
Hawk, Beverley, 134
Hayes, Danny, 187n18
Hema-Lendu conflict, 92–94, 98, 102, 115
Hennessy, Michael, 27
Henry, Sean, 26
Herbst, Jeffrey, 136–37, 155
Heritage Foundation, 144
Hill, David, 95
Hilsum, Lindsey, 187n14
Hochschild, Adam, 92–93, 180n4
Hoge, Warren, 101

230

Index

Holbrooke, Richard, 30, 54, 56, 77–79, 81, 83, 175
Holmes, John, 110
Howard, Lise Morje, 151
Howard, Roger, 133
Human Rights Watch, 72, 78, 94, 105
Hussein, Saddam, 95
Hutu Interahamwe militia, 12, 15, 32, 53, 76, 77, 89, 98, 112, 113, 131, 147, 155, 175
Hutu refugees, xvii, xviii, 9, 12–13, 16, 24, 28, 53, 54, 68, 69, 72, 89, 148, 180n9, 181–82n12, 182n15; difficulties posed by intervening, 25–26; satellite images of, 45. *See also* Rwandan genocide
Hutu-Tutsi tribal violence, 100
hypodermic needle theory, 41

Idi, Willy Kingombi, 81
Iltis, Tony, 130
immediacy, 60
impartiality, 22
inaction, 163
independence, 6–7, 21
indexing theory, 136
Index of Economic Freedom, 144
Indian peacekeepers, 114
Indonesia, 156
infrastructure, 6, 7
inside-page news stories, 124
Institute for Strategic Studies, 79
Institute for the Study of Genocide, 68
Interahamwe. *See* Hutu Interahamwe militia
Inter-Congolese Dialogue, 32
Interim Emergency Multinational Force, 33
International Coalition for the Responsibility to Protect, 162
International Commission on Intervention and State Sovereignty (ICISS), xix, 42; Report, 141–57, 162, 163
International Criminal Court (ICC), 105, 107, 126

International Crisis Group (ICG), 85, 89, 92, 106, 113, 114, 145
International Monetary Fund, 82
International Reporting Project, 191n12
International Rescue Committee, 52, 82, 100, 101, 111
intractable conflict frame, 58, 59, 60, 130, 135, 162
Iraq, 62, 95, 105, 134, 138, 187n18, 190n9, 190–91n11
Islam, radical, 133–34
issue salience, 42
ivory, 4
Ivory Coast, 194n4
Ituri, 91, 92, 94, 95, 102
Iyengar, Shanto, 44

Jackson, Lisa, 111, 189n9
Jamieson, Kathleen Hall, 43
Janjaweed militias, 131
Jones, Bruce, 137

Kabila, Joseph, 16, 32, 33, 39, 56, 103, 116, 119, 156, 166, 167–69, 188n4, 188n6; initial framing of, 84–86
Kabila, Laurent-Désiré, 9, 10, 13–14, 15, 16, 27, 31, 32, 34, 52, 53, 56, 57, 60, 65–72, 73, 82, 84, 116, 124, 129, 172–73, 174, 187n1; death of, 16, 52, 83–85, 86, 124; one-year assessment of, 72–73
Kagame, Paul, 9, 12, 15, 26, 28, 45, 85, 88, 89, 116, 181n12, 182n15, 184n1, 193n1
Kahandja, Biyoya Makutu, 70
Kampf, David, 48
Kaplan, Robert, xv, 132
Kasavubu, Joseph, 19
Katanga, 2, 7, 20–23, 33
Katz, Elihu, and colleagues, 185n3
Kazana, 106–7
Keim, Curtis, 134
Kenya, 138–39
Kenzen, Martin, 76
Kim, Janet, 107

Index

Ki-moon, Ban, 114, 116, 169
Kingdom of the Kongo, 2
Kinshasa, 167
Kipling, Ty, 111
Kisangani, 82, 100
Kivu, 87, 119
Kiwanja, 118
Knudsen, Tonny Brems, 149
Kony, Joseph, 119, 188n5
Koppel, Ted, 60, 62, 87
Kosovo, 149, 156
Kristof, Nicholas, xv, 67, 94, 109–10, 114, 127, 137, 162, 189n7, 189n2
Kron, Josh, 166
Kuperman, Alan, 149

Lacey, Marc, 88, 89, 92, 98, 99, 101, 102, 105
Ladyi, Henri, 167
Lancet, 104
land disputes, 37
language, descriptive, xviii, 44, 50, 57–58, 171–78, 187n15
Lasswell, Harold, 41
Lederach, John Paul, 192n6
Lemarchand, René, 166
Leopold II, King, 3–5, 7, 179n1, 180n4
Leslie, Winsome, 3
letters to the editor, 128, 130
Levitt, Rachel, 49
Levitte, Jean-David, 82–83, 86
Liberia, 150
limited effects theory, 41
Lippmann, Walter, 42
Livingston, Steven, 191n12
Lord's Resistance Army (LRA), 34, 103, 105, 114, 119, 155, 184n7, 188n5, 191n14
Lumumba, Patrice, 7, 8, 19, 21, 22
Lunda people, 2, 3
Lusaka Agreement, 16, 29, 30, 31, 32, 35, 76–77, 78, 79, 82, 86
Lusaka Conference, 29, 30

Mackenzie, Lewis, 22, 23
Mai-Mai militias, 33, 34, 89–90, 111, 112, 117, 167
Mamdani, Mahmood, 134
Mandela, Nelson, 74
massacres, 98–99, 103, 107, 118
Massey, Simon, 135
mass media: advocacy and, 54, 108–12, 122, 128, 130, 161, 162, 189n2, 192n5, 193n4; alerting function of, 41–43, 123; budget cutbacks in, 137–38, 185n4; evaluation function of, xviii, 43–44, 49–50, 54, 123; impact on "will to intervene," 159–64; influence on foreign policy, 192n5; and lack of knowledge about Africa, 134–35; literature on Congo coverage and, 44–49; public attitudes and, 153; theories of, 41–44. *See also New York Times;* television
Mayall, James, 191n1
Mazrui, Ali, xvii, 11, 135
Mbuga, Martin, 67
McCombs, Maxwell, 43
McKay, John, 168
McKinley, James, 66, 71
McLuhan, Marshall, 122
McNeil, Donald, 68, 75, 76
Medair, 96
media. *See* mass media
media-sexiness, 60
Merritt, Richard, 65
Mills, Greg, 136–37, 155
Misra, Amalendu, 149, 155
Mobutu, Joseph-Désiré (Mobutu Sese Seko), xviii, 8–13, 15, 16, 18, 24–26, 47, 49, 52, 54, 56–58, 65, 66–74, 80, 82, 84, 88, 124, 129, 143, 149, 168, 171–72, 174, 179n2, 180nn6–9, 181n12, 182n14
Modigliani, Andre, 43
Moeller, Susan, xvii, 60, 69, 131
Montreal Institute for Genocide and Human Rights, 161

Index

MONUC (UN Mission to the Democratic Republic of the Congo), xvii, 30–38, 126–27, 132, 150, 155, 157, 192n8. *See also* UN peacekeeping
MONUSCO (UN Organization Stabilization Mission in the Congo), 38–39, 155, 157, 192n4, 192n8. *See also* UN peacekeeping
moral clarity, 61
moral dilemma, 149
morality tale, 94
Moreno-Ocampo, Luis, 105
Morjane, Kamel, 99
mortality rate, 17, 113–14
Mounoubai, Manodje, 91
Mountain, Ross, 103, 105
Mouvement de libération du Congo (MLC), 14, 76, 86, 182n13
Mova, Henri, 105
Movement for Democratic Change, 145
Mt. Nyiragongo volcano, 52, 53, 54, 56, 57, 88, 186n10
Mugabe, Robert, 144–45
Mursal, Hussein, 112
Murthy, Jaya, 115
Mutua, Makau, 89
Mwamba, Alexis Thambe, 119

National Congress for the Defense of the People, 34
NBC, 138, 186n12
Neack, Laura, 147
neutrality, 22
newspapers, cutbacks in, 138
New York Times: compared with television, 121–23, 131; coverage of Darfur, compared with Congo, 128–40; coverage of Second Congo War (table), 125; coverage of Third Congo War (table), 125; framing of Second Congo War, 65–90; framing of Third Congo War, 91–120; quantitative indicators of Congo coverage, 123–28; as source of print media coverage, 50; as supporting or discouraging intervention, 127–28, 189n2

New York Times Index, 50, 60
Ngoga, Pascal, 88
NGOs. *See* non-governmental humanitarian aid groups
Nightline, 60, 62, 87
Nkunda, Laurent, 17, 33, 34, 48, 100, 106, 108–9, 111–19, 165–66, 167, 193–94n1
non-governmental humanitarian aid groups (NGOs), 56, 139, 161, 185n5, 187n14, 191n12, 193n4
Ntaganda, Jean Bosco, 165, 167, 194n1, 194n3
Nuba peoples, 146
Nzongola-Ntalaja, Georges, 8, 154, 180n7

Obama, Barack, 137, 189n10
O'Hanlon, Michael, 137
Onishi, Norimitsu, 15, 75, 76, 79, 81, 83, 84, 86
ONUC (Opération des Nations Unies au Congo), xvii, 19–24, 80, 117, 147, 148, 192n8
Opala, Joseph, 136
op-ed articles, 124, 128, 130
Operation Artemis, 33, 55, 95, 126, 132, 152
Operation Assurance, xvii, 24–28, 45, 135, 146, 183n3; CNN effect and, 45
Operation Grandslam, 22
Operation Turquoise, 193n3
Organization of African Unity (OAU), 29, 183n4
organizational learning, 151
Oxfam, 88, 161

Pakistani peacekeepers, 114
Parks, Lisa, 44–45
Parmlee, Jennifer, 62
patrimonialism, 143
peacekeeping: communications problems, 23; equipment for, 23; lack of unity of command, 24; privatizing, 97–98. *See also* UN peacekeeping

233

Index

Pearson, Nigel, 96
Pendergast, Kiernan, 152
Perse, Elizabeth, 42, 121, 122
Petterson, Donald, 139
Pew Center, 138
Polgreen, Lydia, 48, 61, 106, 111, 112, 118, 119, 165
policy consensus, 137
Polis, 190n5
poor-leadership frame, 131
Portugal, 2-3
Potgeiter, Jakkie, 79
Pottier, Johan, 45-46, 181n12
Powell, Colin, 85, 131
Prendergast, John, 89, 116, 166
Pretoria Peace Agreement, 32
prevention, 143-47
priests and nuns, 7
privatization: of peacekeeping, 97-98; of security, 188n3
Project Enough, 116, 166
Project for Excellence in Journalism, 138, 190n11
protracted social conflict theory, 11-12, 17, 143
proxy forces frame, 131
Prunier, Gérard, 16, 49, 60, 62, 128, 181n12, 186n9
public opinion, 41

Quattara, Alassane, 194n4
Quist-Adade, Charles, 134

racial segregation, 6
rampages, 35-36
Ramsbotham, Oliver, 12
rape, 35-36, 39, 54, 96, 98, 99, 107, 110, 111, 114, 115, 127, 139, 155, 173, 175, 182n16, 190n7, 194n3. See also sexual violence/abuse
Rassemblement congolais pour la démocratie (RCD), 14, 32, 56, 76
Red Cross, 186n10
Refugees International, 104, 184n1
regional level of analysis framework, 12, 18

Reich, Ken, 48
reporters: danger to, 62; job cuts and, 137-38, 185n4; human-impact stories and, 139
research methods, 49-51
Resolution 1080, 27
Resolution 1234, 30
Resolution 1291, 30-31
responsibility to prevent, 142, 143-47
responsibility to protect (R2P), xvi, xix, 142-57; genocide and, 188n2
responsibility to react, 142, 147-54
responsibility to rebuild, 142, 154-57
Reuters, 100, 106, 107, 108, 112, 114, 116
Reynolds, Amy, 43
Reyntjens, Filip, 1, 12, 73, 89, 144, 154, 180n9, 181n12, 182n16, 183n2, 183n3, 184n1
Rice, Susan, 133
Richardson, Bill, 56, 69, 70, 172, 174, 180n7
Rieff, David, 160
Rikhye, Indar, 23
Robinson, Piers, 44
Rosenblatt, Leonard, 184
Ross, Brian, 53
Rotberg, Robert, 68, 136
rubber, 4
Rubin, James P., 72
Rudd, David, 97
Rwanda, 12, 17, 44, 66, 68, 73, 74, 85, 86-87, 94, 100, 111, 118, 155; civil war, 12; First Congo War and, 12-13; and rapprochement with Congo, 165-66; Second Congo War and, 13-16; Western inaccuracies about, 134. See also Hutu refugees
Rwanda frame, 186n9
Rwandan armed forces (FAR), 26, 34
Rwandan genocide, 9, 12, 18, 27, 46, 49, 52-53, 76, 88, 93, 94, 109, 112, 113, 118, 131, 145, 147-48, 160-61, 167, 173, 176, 181n11, 181-82n12, 185n9, 186n9, 193n3
Rwandan genocide frame, 131

Index

Rwandan Patriotic Army, 45
Rwandan Patriotic Front, 12, 146

Sachs, Jeffrey, 68
Saiki, Kemal, 107
Salamon, Julie, 61, 62, 87
Sandline International, 188n3
Save the Children, 107, 112
Savimbi, Jonas, 9, 182n14
Second Congo War, 10, 13–16, 46, 53, 54, 56, 57–58, 106, 132; media coverage of, 123, 124; *New York Times* coverage of (table), 125; *New York Times* framing of, 65–90; start of, 72–75
self-interest, as factor driving Congo conflict, 75
Sengupta, Somini, 93–94, 96, 99, 188n4
September 11, 2001 (9/11), 42, 62, 87, 133, 134, 136, 142
sex scandals, 53, 55, 56, 58, 100, 101–2, 104, 127, 176, 177. *See also* rape; sexual violence
sexual violence/abuse, 17, 110–11, 114
Sezibera, Richard, 89
Shariff, Ahmed, 108
Shattuck, John, 69
Sheka, Ntabo Ntaberi, 194n3
Sidahmed, Abdel Salam, and colleagues, 122
Sierra Leone, xv, 62, 81, 109, 132, 180n3, 188n3, 189n8
Signals Squadron, 23
simplicity, and television news, 61
Singer, P.W., 98
slavery, 2
Snow, Keith Harmon, 47–48
Soderlund, Walter, and colleagues, 159
Solana, Javier, 95
Somalia, 25, 28, 60, 79, 135–36, 147, 148, 161
Somalia effect, 81
Southern African Development Community (SADC), 16, 29

Southern Kordofan, 146
South Sudan, 119, 131, 145–46, 152, 190n6. *See also* Sudan
Soviet Union, 9, 22, 171, 174, 183n1
Sozinho, Sozi, 72
Spearman Rank Order Correlation, 159
Stearns, Jason, xvii, 2, 17, 18, 49, 59–60, 61, 118, 167, 183n12, 188n4, 190n7
Stewart, Colin, 105
Stewart, Ian, 62
Stroehlein, Andrew, 47
Sudan, 99, 129, 133, 145–46, 190n6, 191n1. *See also* South Sudan
Suez Crisis, 20
Sun City, 88
Swarns, Rachel, 83, 87, 90
Swing, William, 56, 99, 107

Taylor, Charles, 98
Tchei, 106
television news coverage: advocacy and, 122; compared with newspaper coverage, 121–23; of Congo conflict, 51–58, 131, 138, 139; of Darfur, 128; simplicity and, 61
Thakur, Ramesh, 142, 144, 153
Thant, U, 21, 23
thematic framing, 44, 67, 69, 73, 75, 82
Third Congo War, 10, 16–18, 53–54, 56, 57, 106; ceasefire in, 115, 116, 117; media coverage of, 124; *New York Times* coverage of (table), 125; *New York Times* framing of, 91–120
Thompson, Allan, 186n10, 193n2
Thonier, Jean Paul, 96
Tomé, Patricia, 91
torture, 114
Touré, Hamadoun, 100
Traore, Modibo, 102
Traub, James, 103, 155
tribalism, 75
tribal rivalries, 11

Index

tribal warfare thematic frame, 92, 131
Tshisekedi, Étienne, 69, 168–69
Tshombe, Moise, 7, 20–23
Tutsis, 9, 12–13, 14, 15, 28, 46, 54, 61, 66, 69, 71, 73, 76, 78, 89, 100, 108, 111, 113, 115, 118, 119, 134, 145, 148, 173, 182n12, 182n15, 186n9, 188n4

Uganda, 12, 13, 14, 15, 31, 34, 53, 60, 73, 74, 75, 82, 86–88, 91, 103, 105, 119, 155, 182n14, 184n7, 188n5
UNEF, 20
UN Human Development Index, 2
UNICEF, 102, 107, 115
United States: datelines originating in, 129; image of, 57; lack of government interest in Congo, 135–37, 190n9; Mobutu and, 68; Operation Assurance and, 28; policies, 173–74; responsibility of, 70; Third Congo War and, 94, 97
Universal Declaration of Human Rights, 143
UN-MIK (UN Interim Administration Mission in Kosovo), 156
UNMIS (UN Mission in Sudan), 152
UN Mission to the Democratic Republic of the Congo. *See* MONUC
UNMIT (UN Integrated Mission in East Timor), 156
UN Organization Stabilization Mission in the Congo. *See* MONUSCO
UN peacekeeping/peacekeepers: criticism of, 18, 94, 101–4, 106, 108, 114, 115, 116, 118, 162; descriptive language, 176–77; differing perceptions of need for, 132–33; early, 20; impartiality and, 150; killing of, 99, 102, 105; failures, 28, 79, 135–36, 147; negative evaluations of, 58; and responsibility to protect (R2P), xvi, xix, 142–57; sex abuse scandal, 53, 55, 56, 58, 100, 101–2, 104, 127, 176; size of forces, 90, 97, 100, 102, 117, 127; voluntary participation and, 147. *See also* MONUC, MONUSCO, ONUC
UN peace monitoring, 132
UN Security Council: criticism of, 116–17; trip to Africa, 86
UNTAET (UN Transition Mission in East Timor), 156
Urquhart, Brian, 98

van den Wildenberg, Sylvie, 111
Vanderbilt Television News Archive, 52, 186n11
van Eck, Jan, 78
Van Maldren, Tina, 179n2
Van Woudenberg, Anneke, 94, 112, 118
vertical stratification, 181n10
Vigon, Larry, 101
Vlassenroot, Koen, 116
Vollot, Daniel, 96
von Einsidel, Sebastian, 144
von Horne, Carl, 22

Waldman, Peter, 43
Wambia dia Wamba, Ernest, 14
Wedenig, Johannes, 102
Werner, Jake, 88
West, Michael, 84
Western responsibility frame, 130
Wilkenson, Rob, 88
Willame, Jean-Claude, 7, 143
Williamson, Richard S., 93
will to intervene, 159–64
Wolfsfeld, Gadi, 59–61
Wooten, Jim, 52
World Bank, 82, 87
World Food Program, 98, 99
World News Briefings, 124, 189n1
World Policy Institute, 80
World Trade Organization, 82
World Wild Life Fund, 80
Wrong, Michela, 5–9, 46, 82, 85, 87, 124, 179n2, 180n6

Index

York, Geoffrey, 155, 168
Young, Crawford, 14
Young, Douglas, 183n3

Zaire, 171, 174, 180n8
Zartman, William, 11, 180n5
Zimbabwe, 83, 144–45
Zink, Richard, 168